RED ARMY
HANDBOOK

1939–1945

STEVEN J. ZALOGA AND LELAND S. NESS

SUTTON PUBLISHING

First published in 1998 by
Sutton Publishing Limited · Phoenix Mill
Thrupp · Stroud · Gloucestershire · GL5 2BU

This new paperback edition first published in 2003

British Library Cataloguing in Publication Data
A catalogue record for this book is available from the British Library.

ISBN 0-7509-3209-0

Typeset in 10/13 pt Sabon.
Typesetting and origination by
Sutton Publishing Limited.
Printed and bound in England
by J.H.Haynes & Co., Sparkford.

CONTENTS

Introduction   v

1. Red Army Infantry   1

2. Red Army Armoured Force   61

3. Red Army Cavalry   101

4. Red Army Artillery   119

5. Red Army Airborne and Special Units   143

6. Weapons of the Red Army: Armoured Vehicles   157

7. Weapons of the Red Army: Infantry Weapons   189

8. Weapons of the Red Army: Artillery   199

Bibliography   223

Index   227

INTRODUCTION

On the eve of war in 1941, the Soviet armed forces were the largest in the world, and they consisted of two main branches: the Army and the Navy. The Red Army was officially known at the time as the Red Army of Workers and Peasants (*RKKA: Rabochiy Krestyanskaya Krasnaya Armiya*). Under the Army were the Ground Forces, Air Force, National Air Defence Force and Armed Forces Support. The Ground Forces were the largest single element, making up 79.3 per cent of the armed forces, while the Air Force was 11.5 per cent and the Navy only 5.8 per cent. The primary focus of this book is the Ground Forces.

By the start of 1939 the Red Army consisted of 84 rifle divisions, 14 mountain rifle divisions, 5 rifle brigades, about 25 cavalry divisions, 4 tank corps, 24 separate light tank brigades and 4 heavy tank brigades. With war evidently approaching the Army began activating new rifle divisions in August 1939 and on 17 September reservists were mobilized. Following the conclusion of the campaign in Poland in September 1939 in October the tank corps were abolished and further rifle divisions activated.

The Red Army had been in the forefront of European military innovation in the mid-1930s, being pioneers in large mechanized formations and in other revolutionary combat arms including paratroops, glider assault troops and self-propelled artillery. However, much of the progressive leadership of the Army was destroyed in the senseless purges that Stalin inflicted on the armed forces in 1936–7. Not only were many senior leaders shot or imprisoned, but the atmosphere of menace and betrayal stifled honest evaluations of the progress of the armed forces; senior leadership was taken over by inept cronies of Stalin from the days of the Russian Civil War of 1918–20 who were ill-prepared to manage a modern army and many of the innovations of the mid-1930s were squandered, with the large tank formations being broken up and the horse cavalry being returned to prominence.

In a matter of months the Red Army had gone from one of the most progressive in the world – with exceptional, if largely untested, deep-strike capability – to one that, strangely enough, almost mirrored the doomed French Army. The bulk of its strength was now to be found in ponderous infantry divisions reinforced by scattered tank units in the infantry support role and large holdings of General Headquarters (GHQ) artillery. Operational level manoeuvre was now entrusted to cavalry and cavalry/mechanized formations.

On 9 May 1940, the day before the German tide broke over France, the Soviet General Staff defined the Army's force structure as being built around 161 rifle divisions (including 10 mountain rifle divisions and 7 motorized rifle divisions), 24 cavalry divisions (including 5 mountain cavalry divisions) and 38 tank brigades (comprising 18 with T-26 light tanks, 16 with BT fast tanks, 3 with T-28 medium tanks and 1 with a T-35 heavy tank). These were supported by sixty-one corps artillery regiments and forty-five GHQ artillery regiments.

The Red Army's incredibly poor performance against the tiny Finnish Army in

1939–40 and the stunning defeat of France in 1940 forced Stalin to reconsider his appalling handling of Army affairs. Although he did not remove all of his toadies from the senior ranks, a return to professional standards was begun and many junior officers were released from prison and rehabilitated. The fall of the highly respected French Army was shocking, especially the role played by the German panzer forces. On 6 July 1940 the Red Army began forming eight mechanized corps (each of two tank and one motorized divisions) plus two separate tank divisions; in December a ninth mechanized corps was added, and in February 1941 orders went out to create no fewer than twenty more. Even without the baleful effects of the Stalinist purges such an expansion would have strained the pool of available leadership well beyond any reasonable expectations of success. Filling out these new formations with the appropriate equipment and support (including logistics structure and spare parts) proved no less daunting.

The turmoil in army policy in 1938–41 left the Red Army in a state of permanent crisis. To further complicate matters, the Soviet government embarked on a major rearmament programme in 1939–40, beginning the production of a new generation of tanks, aircraft and other weapons. The situation became even more chaotic with the mass induction of conscripts in 1940, followed by the gradual call-up of reservists. The propaganda image of the Red Army was of an enormous military machine equipped with modern weapons, led by officers trained in sophisticated tactics and guided by modern military doctrine; in reality, the Red Army of 1941 was hopelessly ill-prepared for modern war.

No matter how many shining new tanks and advanced artillery pieces were paraded through Red Square, the Red Army was still, at its heart, a vast peasant army drawn from a poor society where electrification and indoor plumbing were still rare, and where familiarity with modern technology was very limited. The officers were drawn from the ranks of the collectivized peasants, or from peasant families who had recently migrated to the new industrial cities that sprang up in the 1930s. They were not well educated and their personal experiences left them ill prepared to handle modern military equipment or contemporary military tactics. The Russian Civil War had destroyed Russia's traditional military caste, and the Communist Party's distrust of the potential of Bonapartist ambitions among successful military commanders did not encourage its rebirth. The leadership situation was further exacerbated by the lack of a strong non-commissioned officer (NCO) tradition in the Red Army, a fatal shortcoming in a conscript army attempting to absorb new technology. To add insult to injury, the Communist Party insisted on a dual-command authority, with political commissars in the army second-guessing the commander. Mistrust and betrayal beget martinets, not combat leaders. The lack of well-trained officers forced the Red Army to employ cookbook tactics, following rigid and unimaginative templates under a tightly centralized command.

The rank and file of the troops in 1941 were recent conscripts with little military training, or reservists called up from their civilian jobs. These troops were perfectly capable of quickly being taught the rudiments of the simple military arts common to soldiers since Napoleonic times. But the Red Army had an impossible time finding well-prepared young men with existing skills to learn demanding military tasks quickly as tankers, artillerymen, radio operators or combat engineers. An additional problem, not yet adequately confronted in Russian histories of the war, was the widespread disaffection in the lower ranks in 1941. The brutal collectivization campaign against the peasantry, which in Ukraine reached an almost genocidal fury, had a corrosive effect on morale no matter how strident the political propaganda.

The result of these deficits was an army ill prepared to conduct modern war. Red infantry formations attacked in massed waves not through a lack of textbook examples of modern infantry tactics; they did so because their commanders were unprepared to lead large formations, and their troops were unprepared to execute anything more sophisticated than a simple massed charge. Tank platoons were so ill trained that most tanks were lost due to mechanical breakdowns, and not to enemy action. Thousands of tanks with the simplest of mechanical problems were abandoned in 1941. A tanker's training was poor and the lack of radios, except in platoon and company command tanks, made it nearly impossible to coordinate tank formations. A standard tactic was for the platoon commander to instruct his other tanks to follow his example – an approach their more experienced German adversary labelled 'a hen with her chicks'. The consequences on the battlefield were tragic and the Soviet tank force lost six tanks for every German tank – a ratio which lasted well into the middle of the war.

The Red Army that faced the German onslaught in 1941 was built around a mix of large, complex and awkward rifle divisions and untrained and poorly supported mechanized units. The destruction of this Army in the vast encirclement battles of 1941 forced the leadership to adopt completely different approaches to force structure.

After the débâcle of the German invasion in the summer of 1941, the Red Army was painfully rebuilt, retrained and re-equipped. Rifle divisions were reduced in size and heavy weapons centralized to simplify commanders' jobs at all levels. This speeded up the activation process and fifty-five additional rifle divisions were formed from reservists in June and July, followed by 117 more from August to December. A further ninety-three rifle divisions were formed from militia units, *NKVD* (*Narodniy Kumissariat Vnutrennikh del*: People's Commissariat for Internal Affairs, i.e. state police) elements and by conversion. The mechanized corps were disbanded and replaced by much smaller tank brigades and separate battalions, operating largely in the role of infantry support – a less demanding environment for leadership. As losses (including precious experienced leadership) continued to mount, even more extreme measures were adopted. The activation of rifle divisions was replaced in large part by the formation of rifle brigades, essentially little more than independent rifle regiments. Although no fewer than 159 such brigades were raised between September and November 1941, most had rather short lives, being bereft of heavy weapons and lacking logistics support.

The Red Army of 1942 was a fundamentally new Army from the tragic set-up of 1941. The lessons of war were learned from costly battlefield experience. Consolidation began in the armoured troops in early 1942, with the creation of tank corps. Although not immediately successful, strengthening of the corps structure during the winter of 1942–3 yielded powerful formations capable of deep penetration and sustained combat. Their inability to hold terrain led to the creation of mechanized corps in late 1942 and these two complementary forces were consolidated into powerful tank armies. Employment of these massed forces was invariably accompanied by heavy losses, due in part to a continued Soviet inability to deploy mobile, responsive artillery, but, together with increasing competence and confidence on the part of their commanders, they were sufficient to steamroller the opposing German forces.

The rifle troops also began their laborious organizational rebuilding in 1942. As the commanders gained experience, heavy weapons were returned at all levels and service support was modestly increased. In 1943 the process of consolidating the rifle brigades into divisions was begun so that by the end of the year two-thirds of these inefficient formations had been removed from the order of battle. The final standard rifle division organization table was issued in December 1944. Although slightly weaker in artillery than its foreign contemporaries, it was a well-balanced formation supported by generous allocations of GHQ artillery as needed.

Nevertheless, not even the massive manpower of the Soviet Union and the ruthless mobilization process of its Stalinist government could maintain a force of over 500 rifle divisions and the equivalent of thirty-six mechanized divisions in the field against heavy losses. The mechanized units appear to have been kept close to full strength during 1944–5 but the story was not the same for the rifle troops. Only three rifle divisions were formed during 1943–5 and many of those in existence fell dramatically below their authorized levels. Authority to draft reduced-strength organization tables was delegated to the front commands, and these generated a variety of schemes for systematically redistributing losses to keep formations as balanced as possible.

In four years of war the Red Army completely reinvented itself. The rifle divisions were smaller and leaner but with a higher ratio of close-support weaponry. Their weakness in artillery reflected not a lack of faith in that arm, but rather a decision to centralize these assets on a scale never seen before, including the creation of entire artillery corps for the support of selected operations. The mechanized forces were well-balanced units, with heavy assault guns providing at least some of the high-explosive firepower normally the responsibility of artillery.

Although the structure of the Red Army in 1945 did not conform to Western conventional wisdom, it did suit the needs of the Soviet Union. A strong emphasis on strictly following orders suited the political system, reducing the training requirements of the officer corps and the signals and liaison demands within the tactical framework. Deliberate planning also reduced the strain on the inexperienced junior officers created during the massive expansion of forces and permitted centralization of many assets, including fire support and logistics. In the end, the Soviet Army was organized appropriately for its environment, which is, after all, the standard by which it must be judged. By the end of the war in May 1945, the Red Army was the largest and arguably the most powerful Army the world had ever seen. This is the subject of this handbook.

This book, then, is not a conventional account of the development of the Red Army in the war years. Rather, it is an attempt to provide military historians with a unique reference work to fill the gap in existing English language accounts of the Red Army during the Second World War (the Great Patriotic War, as it is known to the Russians). Over the past two decades, there has been a resurgence in interest in the Eastern Front among military historians. Spearheaded by the ground-breaking work of Professor John Erickson in the United Kingdom and by David Glantz in the United States, the Red Army has finally been receiving much overdue attention by Western military scholars. Nevertheless, there remain some significant gaps in coverage. Much of the recent scholarship has focused on the strategic and operational level of Eastern Front fighting; the tactical level of war from the Russian perspective has not been the subject of as much attention. For readers interested in the Eastern Front in the Second World War, there has been a glaring lack of information on the organization and equipment of the Red Army. Furthermore, much of the published material is based on inaccurate German wartime accounts.

This handbook attempts to redress this problem and has been based heavily on new Russian material made available since the collapse of the Soviet Union in 1991. The main problem facing the authors of this book was to define the scope of the material to be presented here within the space available. Due to the size limits of this series, the authors decided against a general depiction of the Red Army, since such an approach would result in a book with insufficient detail and one little different from available publications. Instead, the authors chose to focus on areas ill served by existing publications, especially organization and equipment. In order to provide sufficient detail, the authors elected to emphasize coverage of the combat arms.

In any book of this type, the contributions of many individuals must be noted. The authors would like to give their thanks to many friends and colleagues who helped with this publication including Colonel David Glantz (US Army, Ret'd), Lieutenant-Colonel James Loop (US Army, Ret'd), and Janusz Magnuski. Thanks also to Janne Kemppi for the invaluable Finnish documents. The photographs in this book, unless otherwise noted, were all taken by official Red Army combat photographers. The largest fraction of these come from photographs provided by the USSR to the US Office of War Information (OWI) during the Second World War. These photographs are quite scattered now and were located in various US archives, including the US National Archives' record groups of the OWI and US Army Military Intelligence Division, and other government collections. Other photographs came from official Soviet and Russian sources, as well as private collections, and the authors would like to thank Janusz Magnuski, Andrey Aksenov, Aleksandr Koshchetsev, Rustem Ismagilov, Slava Shpakovskiy, Mikhail Baryatinskiy and Just Probst for their help in providing these.

Thanks also to Janne Kemppi for the invaluable Finnish documents, and to Alex Kiyan for his sharp eye and research.

		9 May 1940	22 Jun 1941	1 Jan 1942	1 Jul 1942	1 Jan 1943	1 Jul 1943	1 Jan 1944	1 Jul 1944	1 Jan 1945	1 May 1945
Headquarters	Fronts	0	4	12	14	15	18	17	18	18	16
	Armies	0	27	58	76	67	81	75	73	72	72
	Rifle Corps	52	62	6	19	34	82	161	167	174	174
	Cavalry Corps	5	4	7	12	10	9	8	8	8	8
	Tank Corps	0	0	0	22	20	24	24	24	24	24
	Mechanized Corps	0	29	0	0	8	13	13	13	14	14
Infantry	Rifle Divisions (inc mountain & motorized)	161	198	389	425	407	462	489	502	517	517
	Rifle Brigades	3	5	159	144	177	98	57	35	15	17
	Ski Brigades	0	0	1	2	48	3	3	4	2	0
	Tank Destroyer Brigades	0	0	0	17	11	6	0	0	0	0
	Separate Rifle Regiments	0	1	13	8	7	6	10	10	8	5
	Fortified Regions	?	57	19	53	45	45	48	47	47	47
	Ski Battalions	0	0	85	25	0	0	0	0	0	0
Cav	Cavalry Divisions	24	13	82	46	31	27	26	26	26	26
	Cavalry Brigades	2	0	0	0	0	0	0	0	0	0
	Separate Cavalry Regiments	0	0	7	5	5	0	0	0	1	1
Armor	Tank Divisions	0	61	7	2	2	2	2	2	2	2
	Motorized Divisions	0	31	0	0	0	0	0	0	0	0
	Armored Car Brigade	3	1	1	1	1	1	0	0	0	0
	Tank Brigades	38	0	76	192	176	182	166	150	145	147
	Assault Gun Brigades	0	0	0	0	0	0	0	0	9	12
	Mechanized Brigades	0	0	1	0	26	42	43	44	47	47
	Motor Rifle Brigades	0	0	2	29	27	21	26	25	24	25
	Motorcycle Brigades	0	0	0	1	0	0	0	0	0	0
	Separate Tank Regiments	6	0	1	0	83	118	122	110	75	78
	Separate Assault Gun Regiments	0	0	0	0	0	57	109	207	212	235
	Motorcycle Regiments	0	29	7	5	5	8	8	11	11	11
	Separate Tank Battalions	0	1	100	80	71	45	26	6	0	0
	Separate Aerosan Battalions	0	0	18	0	54	57	57	0	0	0
	Special Motorized Battalions	0	0	0	0	0	0	0	10	11	11
	Armored Train Battalions	?	8	40	64	62	66	61	61	61	59
	Separate Armored Car & Motorcycle Battalions	3	0	2	22	40	44	44	47	46	43
A/B	Airborne Divisions	0	0	0	0	10	10	16	14	9	9
	Airborne Brigades	6	16	36	30	1	21	3	1	3	3
Artillery	Artillery Divisions	0	0	0	0	25	25	26	26	37	37
	Rocket Divisions	0	0	0	0	4	7	7	7	7	7
	Anti-Aircraft Divisions	0	0	0	0	27	63	78	80	80	80
	Separate Artillery Brigades	0	0	0	0	0	17	22	73	66	69
	Separate Anti-Aircraft Brigades	0	0	1	0	1	3	8	0	0	0
	Separate Mortar Brigades	0	0	1	0	7	11	11	13	8	8
	Separate Rocket Brigades	0	0	0	0	11	10	13	12	15	11
	Anti-Tank Brigades	0	10	0	0	0	27	50	56	56	66
	Separate Artillery Regiments	106	169	158	323	273	235	229	135	144	136
	Separate Mortar Regiments	0	0	0	75	102	171	170	163	150	142
	Separate Anti-Tank Regiments	0	0	57	151	176	199	172	147	111	98
	Separate Rocket Regiments	0	0	8	70	91	113	108	107	107	107
	Separate Anti-Aircraft Regiments	0	2	2	35	123	212	221	225	214	210
	Separate Artillery Battalions	12	12	28	24	25	41	28	25	24	24
	Separate Anti-Aircraft Battalions	?	45	108	126	109	112	114	104	97	97
	Separate Rocket Battalions	0	0	73	52	59	37	42	48	44	46
	Separate Anti-Tank Battalions	0	0	0	0	2	44	48	28	10	9
	Separate Mortar Battalions	0	8	15	1	12	5	1	1	1	1
PVO Stranyi	PVO Stranyi Corps HQ	?	3	2	0	0	0	0	12	14	15
	PVO Stranyi Division HQs	?	2	3	2	0	0	0	12	11	18
	PVO Stranyi Brigade HQs	?	9	2	2	0	0	8	0	0	3
	PVO Stranyi Corps Region HQs	?	0	1	2	2	5	7	0	0	0
	PVO Stranyi Division Region HQs	?	0	14	13	15	13	14	0	0	0
	PVO Stranyi Brigade Region HQs	?	40	14	14	11	11	11	11	10	0
	Standard Anti-Aircraft Divisions	0	0	0	0	0	0	15	17	17	18
	Standard Anti-Aircraft Machine Gun Divisions	0	0	0	0	0	0	0	2	2	1
	Standard Anti-aircraft Brigades	0	0	0	0	0	0	0	11	21	21
	Searchlight Divisions	0	0	0	0	0	0	4	4	4	4
	Anti-Aircraft Regiments	?	?	29	56	76	106	115	126	137	131
	Anti-Aircraft Machine Gun Regiments	?	?	3	5	8	14	27	25	26	27
	Searchlight Regiments	?	?	2	9	9	4	7	4	4	7
	Anti-Aircraft Battalions	?	?	154	118	158	168	214	212	193	204
	Anti-Aircraft Machine Gun Battalions	?	?	0	0	7	21	27	20	26	24
	Searchlight Battalions	?	?	0	0	1	13	18	16	20	23

Table 1 Soviet ground forces – structure and evolution, 1940–45.

CHAPTER 1

RED ARMY INFANTRY

The basic structure of the Soviet infantry prior to the huge losses in the opening phases of Barbarossa had been established by the massive reorganization embodied in the December 1935 rifle division TO&Es (table of organization and equipment). Where previously a rifle platoon had consisted of three rifle squads and a grenadier squad, the new platoon was divided into three (four in war) identical rifle squads. The new rifle squad now consisted of a squad leader, an observer/scout, a 2-man light-machine gun team, a 2-man grenadier team and six riflemen. The main effect was to give each wartime rifle platoon four light-machine guns instead of three, while retaining the four rifle grenade launchers. As before, the rifle company was built around three rifle platoons and a machine gun platoon. The latter provided two squads each of seven men with a water-cooled Maxim M1910 machine gun carried on a one-horse cart. Divisions based in rough terrain were authorized to replace each cart with two pack horses and one additional horse handler.

As before, the infantry battalion of three rifle companies was supported by a machine gun company with three 4-gun platoons. Each platoon was divided into two sections, each of which had a section leader, an assistant section leader, a driver with a 2-horse wagon and two 4-man gun squads with M1910s. The infantry regiment consisted of three such battalions, an anti-tank (AT) battery and a regimental gun battery.

At the division level the 1935 TO&E added a tank battalion (three companies each of fifteen tanks), a reconnaissance battalion and an anti-aircraft (AA) battalion to each division, and expanded the engineer company to a 2-company battalion and the signal company to battalion strength. The new TO&Es also provided a nine-fold increase in mortar allocation but the weapons themselves were still in development so implementation of this aspect had to wait. Another improvement called for in the 1934–8 five-year plan was the provision of tactical radios down to the company level. This, however, was delayed even longer due to equipment shortages, and, indeed, was not finally implemented until after the war.

THE SEPTEMBER 1939 TO&E (NO. 04/20–38)

The first divisional structure to see combat was that mandated in the September 1939 TO&Es. This new organization introduced a number of modern features and made the division, on paper at least, one of the most powerful in the world.

Infantry armament had been strengthened through the introduction of new weapons. The new family of mortars introduced in the late 1930s – the 50mm PM-38/39, the 82mm PM-36/37 and the 120mm HM-38 – were all effective designs, and the new TO&Es made full use of them.[1] Being the first nation to introduce a 120mm mortar gave the Red

1

A Red Army infantry company marches to the front in the summer of 1941. The infantry force in 1941 was made up of new conscripts led by inexperienced young officers. Their performance in 1941 was often heroic but seldom successful. Few would survive the 1941 campaign: either killed during the German invasion or taken prisoner and dying from malnutrition and disease in the German camps. It is said that more than 90 per cent of the age cohorts conscripted in 1941 died during the war.

	Men	Main Weapons
Regiment HQ	67	
Signal Company	104	
Mounted Scout Platoon	41	
Scout Platoon	62	
Three Battalions, each		
Battalion HQ	4	
Signal Platoon	44	
Scout Platoon	62	
Three Rifle Companies, each	234	
Company HQ	13	
Three Rifle Platoons, each	62	4 light MGs
Light Mortar Section	11	3 50mm mortars
Machine Gun Platoon	22	2 medium MGs, 2 AT rifles
Machine Gun Company	94	12 medium MGs
Mortar Company	18	4 82mm mortars
Anti-Tank Platoon	18	2 45mm AT guns
Pioneer Squad	7	
Trains	43	
Anti-Tank Battery	66	6 45mm AT guns
Infantry Gun Battalion	159	6 76mm infantry guns
Mortar Battery	41	4 120mm mortars
Anti-Aircraft Company	52	3 quad MGs & 6 heavy MGs
Pioneer Platoon	48	
Chemical Platoon	37	

Table 1.0 Infantry Regiment (TO 04/21), from September 1939.

	Officers	Warrant & Political Officers	NCOs	Other Ranks	Light Machine Guns	Medium Machine Guns	Heavy Machine Guns	Quad AA MGs	Anti-Tank Rifles	50mm Mortars	82mm Mortars	120mm Mortars	Anti-Tank Guns	Anti-Aircraft Guns	Infantry Guns	Artillery Pieces	Motorcycles	Field Cars	Trucks	Tractors	Horses	Wagons	Carts
Division Headquarters	35	47	27	78	3	0	0	0	0	0	0	0	0	0	0	0	1	9	13	0	31	0	0
Signal Battalion	19	15	63	215	0	0	0	0	0	0	0	0	0	0	0	0	5	1	27	0	40	2	20
Reconnaissance Battalion	21	20	73	214	49	0	0	0	6	0	0	0	0	0	0	0	52	5	28	0	97	1	5
Three Infantry Regiments, each	123	100	458	3,354	142	54	3	6	18	27	12	4	12	0	6	0	10	1	33	0	1,050	328	94
Artillery Headquarters	2	1	12	40	0	0	0	0	0	0	0	0	0	0	0	0	0	0	1	0	31	0	8
Light Artillery Regiment	73	64	255	1,506	26	0	0	3	0	0	0	0	0	0	0	36	0	1	11	0	1,470	266	98
Medium Artillery Regiment	35	53	217	998	18	0	0	3	0	0	0	0	0	0	0	24	9	6	39	39	658	186	46
Anti-Aircraft Battalion	18	15	78	241	0	0	0	0	0	0	0	0	0	12	0	0	3	1	54	5	0	5	0
Anti-Tank Battalion	15	16	47	204	0	0	0	0	0	0	0	0	18	0	0	0	32	1	22	27	0	9	0
Pioneer Battalion	22	21	83	474	36	0	0	0	0	0	0	0	0	0	0	0	6	1	56	10	54	54	3
Supply Company	7	8	31	148	5	0	0	0	0	0	0	0	0	0	0	0	3	0	148	0	0	0	0
Maintenance Company	1	15	19	55	2	0	0	0	0	0	0	0	0	0	0	0	0	0	15	0	0	0	0
Bakery	0	10	18	168	2	0	0	0	0	0	0	0	0	0	0	0	0	1	25	1	0	0	0
Medical Battalion	1	42	35	182	1	0	0	0	0	0	0	0	0	0	0	0	1	0	34	0	123	20	42
Field Hospital	0	26	19	59	2	0	0	0	0	0	0	0	0	0	0	0	1	0	26	0	0	0	0
Veterinary Hospital	0	10	6	48	1	0	0	0	0	0	0	0	0	0	0	0	0	0	6	0	22	7	0
Artillery Supply Column	12	20	67	377	7	0	0	0	0	0	0	0	0	0	0	0	2	1	91	10	524	250	5
Postal & Payroll	0	6	3	6	0	0	0	0	0	0	0	0	0	0	0	0	0	0	0	0	8	4	0

Table 1.1 Rifle division summary (TO 04/20-38), from September 1939.

Army a considerable advantage, as the weapon quickly proved very useful.

The rifle company of the 1939 division was configured into a headquarters (HQ) platoon (with signal and trains squads), three rifle platoons (each of four rifle squads), a light mortar section and a machine gun platoon. A rifle squad was armed with a light-machine gun and fourteen rifles. The machine gun platoon consisted of two squads each with a Maxim machine gun carried on a cart. The MG platoon was also to include two Rukavishnikov M1939 AT rifles, but in fact these were never produced. The battalion machine gun company was made up of a HQ platoon and three machine gun platoons each with four weapons. Also supporting the battalion was an anti-tank (AT) platoon and a mortar platoon.

The most noticeable change to the division was the addition of a second artillery regiment with one battalion of 122mm M1910/30 or M1938 howitzers and one of 152mm M1909/30 howitzers. This complemented the existing field artillery regiment which used a mix of 76mm M02/30 or M1936 field guns and 122mm M1910/30 or M1938 howitzers. Nominally, the field artillery regiment held three batteries of 76mm guns and six of 122mm howitzers in its three battalions, but this ratio was often reversed or otherwise changed as dictated by the stock of available weapons (see Table 1.1).

The provision for twelve 76mm guns, thirty-six 122mm howitzers and twelve 152mm howitzers was in advance of every other divisional establishment in the world. Several factors, however, served to limit the effectiveness of this massive firepower. Most importantly, not enough attention had been paid to communications and the shortage of signal assets usually limited the artillery to pre-planned fire. Second, the bulk of the pieces actually in service were rather elderly designs with short range, none in excess of 10,000 m. A third factor was that all the battalions except the 152mm were horse drawn – although this was true of most Western European armies as well, the vast size of the Soviet theatre of operations tended to highlight this shortcoming.

With the decision to create large-scale mechanized formations in the late 1930s most of the infantry division tank battalions were withdrawn and concentrated under new armoured formations. The standard division under the September 1939 organization, thus, did not include a tank battalion. A few top-line divisions, however, did retain their armoured component. Such a battalion consisted of a headquarters and three companies. The HQ command element consisted of two T-26 infantry tanks and a field car, and it was supported by a signal platoon (three radio trucks, including one for air-to-ground communications), a motorcycle platoon (seven solo and two sidecar motorcycles) and a trains group. Two of the companies were equipped with T-26 tanks, each consisting of three 3-tank platoons plus one tank in company HQ. The third company was provided with T-37 amphibious light tanks and consisted of three 5-tank platoons plus one tank in company HQ.

The anti-tank firepower of the division was also substantially increased. An anti-tank battalion with eighteen 45mm guns was added to the divisional structure, along with a 6-gun AT company to each infantry regiment to supplement the two such weapons in each battalion AT platoon, for a division total of fifty-four. The divisional anti-tank capabilities were to be completed by an anti-tank section in each rifle company equipped with two anti-tank rifles. Initial designs, however, proved difficult to produce and the first fifty of the revised 14.5mm *PTRD*-1941 weapons did not come off the production line until late 1940, and even then ammunition could not be produced until late 1941.

The anti-aircraft battalion was small but indicated an appreciation for the potential of

tactical air power. Two of the batteries (western platoons) each manned four 37mm M1939 guns, while the third battery was provided with four 76mm M1931 guns. Supplementing the efforts of these few weapons were the anti-aircraft-machine gun (AAMG) platoons scattered around the division. The most common weapon was a quadruple mounting of the 7.62mm M1910 Maxim machine gun. Each artillery regiment had a platoon with three of these, as did each rifle regiment AA company. The rifle regiment's AA company was filled out with two more platoons, each equipped with three 12.7mm *DShK* heavy machine guns on AA mounts, although it seems unlikely that the TO&Es for these weapons were completely filled, even as late as 1941.

In a striking departure from prior practice, the 1939 TO&E introduced motor vehicles as the primary logistical support for the rifle division. The new division included no fewer than 670 motor vehicles, mostly medium-size trucks, to keep the division supplied. Unfortunately, motor vehicle production had not yet reached the stage where 100 divisions could be supplied with almost 700 trucks apiece, and this plan was never fully implemented.

The massive size and complexity of these divisions at all levels could have yielded a very powerful force had certain prerequisites been met. Such formations require highly competent staff and decisive leadership at all levels and a responsive and flexible communications system. Unfortunately, the Stalinist purges of the late 1930s had stripped the Army of much of its leadership and left the remainder timid and confused, while the technology (and manufacturing) of the day was not quite up to the task of providing these forces with the signal assets they needed. Nevertheless, it was divisions thus organized that formed the basis of the Soviet forces engaged in the Russo-Finnish War (the Winter

Although the Soviet government claimed high levels of literacy, lack of education remained a problem in an increasingly technical military force. Here, a young conscript reads to other troops; the two soldiers to the left are wearing the pre-war Model 1936 helmet while the two to the right wear the new Model 1940 helmet.

War) between 30 November 1939 and 12 March 1940. The divisions proved extremely difficult to control, often being defeated in detail by smaller Finnish units.

REPERCUSSIONS OF THE WINTER WAR (NO. 4/100–118)

Eventual Soviet victory and an understandable disinclination to speak out in that era contributed to an apparent reluctance to draw the appropriate conclusions from the Finland experience. When new TO&Es were issued for the rifle division on 13 June 1940 only detail changes were made. Although the rifle squad size was cut from 15 men to a more manageable 12, two men in each rifle squad were now to be armed with semi-automatic rifles to maintain small-unit firepower. Sub-machine guns had been successfully used by the Finns in the war, albeit in relatively small numbers, and similar weapons were introduced into the Soviet infantry.[2] The success of mortars in the war prompted the *Stavka* to enlarge the battalion mortar company by adding a third mortar to each of the two platoons, although the number of 120mm weapons remained the same. At the same time the little 50mm mortars were decentralized by abolishing the rifle company light mortar section and adding a 4-man mortar squad with one weapon to each rifle platoon. The overall structure and size of the rifle division, however, remained unchanged.

Soviet infantry training ranged from barely adequate to non-existent after the outbreak of the war. During the desperate years of 1941–2, units were hastily formed and committed to combat with little or no training. More fortunate units were given basic training, which seldom included many tactical lessons. Here, a platoon goes through basic bayonet drill using the standard Moisin Nagant rifle. This dependable weapon was essentially unchanged since the First World War.

RECIPE FOR DISASTER (NO. 04/400-417)

The 1940 TO&Es never saw combat, for they were superseded on 5 April 1941 by a new set of documents. The new organization streamlined the division somewhat but the overall structure was little changed.

The infantry manoeuvre elements remained essentially the same. A rifle squad consisted of a squad leader, a 2-man light machine gun team, two men with sub-machine guns and six riflemen. All men except the sub-machine gunners and the light machine gunner were to be armed with semi-automatic rifles.[3] A rifle platoon consisted of four such squads and a 4-man 50mm mortar team. The earlier provision of anti-tank rifles was dropped, in light of their unavailability. Company, battalion and regiment elements remained almost the same as the 1940 TO&E, except that rifle squad size was reduced again, to 11 men, and the former battalion trains elements were now concentrated in a regimental transport company.

Signal facilities in the battalion were good for the time, at least on paper, with a runner assigned to each rifle platoon and company HQ, and wiremen to the machine gun company HQ and the mortar company HQ. The infantry battalion signal platoon had a 7-man radio group (with four *RRU* radios and a *6-PK* radio) and three wire/optical squads totalling twenty-two men and three telephone carts. This would permit the assignment of backpack *RRU* radio to each rifle company but it seems unlikely that they were actually available in significant numbers by the time of the German invasion.

Signal assets at the regimental level were distributed on an inexplicable basis. The regimental gun battery was provided with no fewer than six *RRU* transceivers to permit its three platoons to operate independently but the heavy mortar battery had only a wire team with a cart. The regimental signal company provided one model *5-AK* radio, two *6-PK* radios and two wire/optical platoons, along with a messenger section and a switchboard team. The regimental reconnaissance, anti-tank and anti-aircraft units had no dedicated signal personnel or radios.

While the firepower of the regiment had changed only slightly (more mortars, no AT rifles), a reduction in support elements permitted a 25 per cent reduction in overall personnel strength.

Divisional fire support was provided by the two artillery regiments. The field artillery regiment contained two battalions, each with one 4-gun battery of 122mm howitzers and two 4-gun batteries of 76mm guns. Each type of battery included a large wire signal section and a radio squad with a paper authorization of three transceivers. Both types of batteries were thus fully up to international standards in communications (to the extent radios were actually available) but lacked the integral ammunition columns usually found in such units. This must have reduced their flexibility somewhat. The artillery battalion included three more radios plus three wire

teams in its signal platoon, along with a transport platoon with sixteen 2-horse wagons for ammunition.

The howitzer regiment had three battalions, two of 122mm and one of 152mm weapons. It was structurally similar to the light artillery regiment, including radio allocation, but used trucks and tractors to move the guns and ammunition (the troops still walked). As in most armies of the time, fire command computation was carried out on site by the commanders and forward observers rather than by dedicated fire control personnel.

Scouting for the division was the responsibility of the reconnaissance battalion. The line companies of this battalion were stripped to the basics, each consisting of three platoons and little else. In the motorized rifle company each platoon consisted of a 2-man HQ, three 12-man rifle squads and a 4-man mortar squad, with each platoon sharing three trucks. The light tank and armoured car companies each consisted of one combat vehicle in the company HQ and three platoons (each with three armoured cars in the armoured car company or five T-38 tankettes in the light tank company). The only trains elements of note in the entire battalion was a 5-man maintenance section with a single truck.

The weakness of the reconnaissance elements at all levels of the division was the shortage of radios with which to report the information gathered. Neither platoon of the infantry regiment had any radios, while in the divisional battalion the rifle company and the tank company were also without radios; in this battalion the radios were found in the armoured car company (it is unclear how many of the armoured cars were so equipped), and in the battalion signal platoon with three radio trucks.

The anti-tank and anti-aircraft battalions remained essentially unchanged from the

	Officers	Political Officers	NCOs	Other Ranks	Pistols	Submachine Guns	Rifles & Carbines	Semi-Automatic Rifles	Light Machine Guns	Medium Machine Guns	Quad AA Machine Guns	Heavy Machine Guns	50mm Mortars	82mm Mortars	120mm Mortars	45mm AT Guns	76mm Infantry Guns	Riding Horses	Draft Horses	Carts	Wagons	Trucks
Regiment HQ & Staff	15	3	2	2	16	2	4	0	0	0	0	0	0	0	0	0	0	9	0	0	0	0
Supply Department	7	0	2	6	6	0	6	0	0	0	0	0	0	0	0	0	0	3	0	0	0	0
Headquarters Platoon	1	0	4	23	0	3	11	9	1	0	0	0	0	0	0	0	0	0	8	0	4	0
Mounted Reconnaissance Platoon																						
Platoon Headquarters	1	0	1	0	0	2	0	0	0	0	0	0	0	0	0	0	0	2	0	0	0	0
Three Mounted Squads, each	0	0	1	9	0	4	0	5	1	0	0	0	0	0	0	0	0	10	0	0	0	0
Infantry Reconnaissance Platoon																						
Platoon Headquarters	1	0	1	2	0	2	0	2	0	0	0	0	0	0	0	0	0	0	0	0	0	0
Four Rifle Squads, each	0	0	1	11	0	3	0	7	1	0	0	0	0	0	0	0	0	0	0	0	0	0
Signal Company																						
Company Headquarters	1	1	4	18	2	0	22	0	0	0	0	0	0	0	0	0	0	2	*11	*9	*1	0
Radio Platoon	1	0	3	6	1	0	9	0	0	0	0	0	0	0	0	0	0	1				0
1st Telephone & Optical Platoon	1	0	3	22	1	0	25	0	0	0	0	0	0	0	0	0	0	1				0
2nd Telephone & Optical Platoon	1	0	3	13	1	0	16	0	0	0	0	0	0	0	0	0	0	1				0
Anti-Aircraft Machine Gun Company																						
Company Headquarters	1	1	1	0	2	0	1	0	0	0	0	0	0	0	0	0	0	0	0	0	0	0
Light AAMG Platoon	1	0	6	24	7	0	18	0	0	0	6	0	0	0	0	0	0	0	0	0	0	6
Heavy AAMG Platoon	1	0	3	12	4	0	10	0	0	0	3	0	0	0	0	0	0	0	0	0	0	3
Pioneer Company																						
Company Headquarters	2	1	1	1	2	0	2	0	0	0	0	0	0	0	0	0	0	2	0	0	0	0
Two Pioneer Platoons, each	1	0	6	35	0	5	2	33	0	0	0	0	0	0	0	0	0	0	0	0	0	0
Equipment Squad	0	0	1	3	0	0	0	4	0	0	0	0	0	0	0	0	0	0	0	0	3	0
Chemical Platoon	1	0	3	16	1	0	19	0	0	0	0	0	0	0	0	0	0	0	0	0	4	0
Three Infantry Battalions, each																						
Battalion Headquarters	4	0	0	1	2	1	2	0	0	0	0	0	0	0	0	0	0	3	0	0	0	0
Signal Platoon	1	0	8	24	0	1	32	0	0	0	0	0	0	0	0	0	0	0	3	3	0	0
Three Rifle Companies, each																						
Company Headquarters	1	1	1	4	2	0	5	0	0	0	0	0	0	0	0	0	0	0	1	1	0	0
Medical Section	0	0	1	4	1	0	0	0	0	0	0	0	0	0	0	0	0	0	0	0	0	0
Three Rifle Platoons, each																						
Platoon HQ	1	0	1	1	1	1	1	0	0	0	0	0	0	0	0	0	0	0	0	0	0	0
Four Rifle Squads, each	0	0	1	10	1	2	0	8	1	0	0	0	0	0	0	0	0	0	0	0	0	0
Mortar Squad	0	0	1	3	1	0	3	0	0	0	0	0	1	0	0	0	0	0	0	0	0	0
Machine Gun Platoon																						
Platoon HQ	1	0	0	1	1	0	1	0	0	0	0	0	0	0	0	0	0	0	2	0	1	0
Two MG Squads, each	0	0	1	4	1	0	4	0	0	1	0	0	0	0	0	0	0	0	0	0	0	0
Machine Gun Company																						
Company Headquarters	1	1	2	4	2	0	6	0	0	0	0	0	0	0	0	0	0	1	1	1	0	0
Three MG Platoons, each																						
Platoon HQ	1	0	0	0	1	0	0	0	0	0	0	0	0	0	0	0	0	0	4	0	2	0
Four MG Squads, each	0	0	1	6	2	0	5	0	0	1	0	0	0	0	0	0	0	0	0	0	0	0
Mortar Company																						
Company Headquarters	1	1	1	4	2	0	5	0	0	0	0	0	0	0	0	0	0	0	0	0	0	0
Three Mortar Platoons, each	1	0	2	12	1	1	13	0	0	0	0	0	0	2	0	0	0	0	2	2	0	0
Anti-Tank Platoon	1	0	2	15	3	0	15	0	0	0	0	0	0	0	0	2	0	1	8	0	0	0
Supply Platoon	1	0	3	29	1	0	20	0	0	0	0	0	0	0	0	0	0	0	38	0	19	0
Medical Platoon	1	0	3	4	1	0	2	0	0	0	0	0	0	0	0	0	0	0	4	0	2	0
Regimental Gun Battery																						
Battery Headquarters																						
Command Section	2	1	2	1	*13	*5	*114	0	0	0	0	0	0	0	0	0	0	5	1	1	0	0
Scout Squad	0	0	1	6				0	0	0	0	0	0	0	0	0	0	7	0	0	0	0
Signal Section	0	0	4	12				0	0	0	0	0	0	0	0	0	0	3	6	0	3	0
Three Gun Platoons, each	1	0	2	21				0	0	0	0	0	0	0	0	0	2	4	16	0	0	0
Ammunition Platoon	1	0	3	21				0	0	0	0	0	0	0	0	0	0	1	18	0	9	0
Trains Group	0	0	2	9				0	0	0	0	0	0	0	0	0	0	0	6	0	3	0
Anti-Tank Battery																						
Battery Headquarters	1	1	1	2	2	0	3	0	0	0	0	0	0	0	0	0	0	5	0	0	0	0
Three AT Platoons, each	1	0	2	14	3	0	14	0	0	0	0	0	0	0	0	2	0	1	8	0	1	0
Heavy Mortar Battery																						
Battery Headquarters	1	1	1	8	1	1	9	0	0	0	0	0	0	0	0	0	0	3	1	1	0	0
Two Mortar Platoons, each	1	0	2	18	2	2	15	0	0	0	0	0	0	0	2	0	0	2	12	0	0	0
Transportation Company			**107		5	6	92	0	0	0	0	0	0	0	0	0	0	1	176	0	88	0
Medical Company			**55		4	0	27	0	0	0	0	0	0	0	0	0	0	0	24	4	10	0
Veterinary Hospital			**12		1	0	8	0	0	0	0	0	0	0	0	0	0	0	6	0	3	0
Workshops			**34		3	0	15	0	0	0	0	0	0	0	0	0	0	0	0	0	0	0
Band			**13		5	0	8	0	0	0	0	0	0	0	0	0	0	0	0	0	0	0

*total for all subordinate units
**total personnel strength (rank breakdown unknown)

Table 1.2 Infantry regiment (TO 04/401), from April 1941.

	Officers & Warrant Officers	Political Officers	NCOs	Other Ranks	Submachine Guns	Light Machine Guns	Medium Machine Guns	Quad AA Machine Guns	Heavy Machine Guns	50mm Mortars	82mm Mortars	120mm Mortars	Anti-Aircraft Guns	Anti-Tank Guns	Infantry Guns	Artillery Pieces	Motorcycles	Field Cars	Trucks	Tractors	Horses	Wagons	Carts
Division Headquarters	27	48	14	44	7	2	0	0	0	0	0	0	0	0	0	0	0	6	13	0	12	0	1
Signal Battalion	17	15	53	193	5	0	0	0	0	0	0	0	0	0	0	0	3	1	18	0	29	1	15
Reconnaissance Battalion																							
Battalion HQ & trains elements	14	3	13	14	11	0	0	0	0	0	0	0	0	0	0	0	5	1	16	0	0	0	0
Motorized Rifle Company	4	1	16	103	41	9	0	0	0	3	0	0	0	0	0	0	0	0	9	0	0	0	0
Armored Car Company	5	1	7	29	1	0	0	0	0	0	0	0	0	0	0	0	0	1	0	0	0	0	0
Light Tank Company	5	1	13	17	1	0	0	0	0	0	0	0	0	0	0	0	0	1	0	0	0	0	0
Three Infantry Regiments, each	131	56	435	2,560	315	116	54	6	3	27	18	4	12	0	6	0	0	1	17	0	727	227	54
Artillery Headquarters	3	1	16	49	0	0	0	0	0	0	0	0	0	0	0	0	0	0	7	0	0	0	0
Field Artillery Regiment																							
Regimental HQ & Battery	25	4	22	75	7	0	0	0	2	0	0	0	0	0	0	0	0	0	2	0	76	10	0
Two Field Artillery Battalions, each																							
Battalion HQ & trains elements	9	0	18	99	2	0	0	0	0	0	0	0	0	0	0	0	0	0	0	0	87	26	4
Two Gun Batteries, each	5	1	16	77	6	2	0	0	0	0	0	0	0	0	0	4	0	0	0	0	77	6	0
Howitzer Battery	5	1	16	81	6	2	0	0	0	0	0	0	0	0	0	4	0	0	0	0	81	6	0
regimental trains elements	9	0	15	45	0	0	0	0	0	0	0	0	0	0	0	0	0	0	5	0	44	21	1
Howitzer Regiment																					0		
Regimental HQ & Battery	24	4	26	92	8	0	0	0	3	0	0	0	0	0	0	0	0	1	13	0	0	0	0
Two Light Howitzer Battalions, each																							
Battalion HQ & trains elements	9	0	16	81	0	0	0	0	0	0	0	0	0	0	0	0	0	0	13	6	0	0	0
Three Batteries, each	5	1	12	64	3	2	0	0	0	0	0	0	0	0	0	4	0	0	3	7	0	0	0
Medium Howitzer Battalion																							
Battalion HQ & trains elements	9	0	16	81	0	0	0	0	0	0	0	0	0	0	0	0	0	0	13	6	0	0	0
Three Batteries, each	5	1	12	66	3	2	0	0	0	0	0	0	0	0	0	4	0	0	3	7	0	0	0
regimental trains elements	15	0	46	134																			
Anti-Aircraft Battalion																							
Battalion HQ & trains elements	11	3	17	44	2	0	0	0	0	0	0	0	0	0	0	0	0	1	12	0	0	0	0
Two 37mm Light Batteries, each	4	1	11	43	3	0	0	0	0	0	0	0	4	0	0	0	0	0	5	0	0	0	0
76mm Heavy Battery	3	1	16	73	2	0	0	0	0	0	0	0	4	0	0	0	0	0	11	5	0	0	0
Anti-Tank Battalion																							
Battalion HQ & trains elements	8	3	19	22	2	0	0	0	0	0	0	0	0	0	0	0	0	1	9	0	0	0	0
Three AT Batteries, each	4	1	7	47	3	0	0	0	0	0	0	0	0	6	0	0	0	0	4	7	0	0	0
Pioneer Battalion	32	4	87	398	0	0	4	0	0	0	0	0	0	0	0	0	0	1	47	0	60	21	8
Chemical Company	3	1	11	43	3	1	0	0	0	0	0	0	0	0	0	0	0	6	12	0	0	0	0
Motor Transport Battalion	28	4	37	190	14	0	0	0	0	0	0	0	0	0	0	0	4	1	140	0	0	0	0
Artillery Workshop	6	0	21	18	0	0	0	0	0	0	0	0	0	0	0	0	0	0	6	0	0	0	0
Bakery	8	0	12	109	1	2	0	0	0	0	0	0	0	0	0	0	1	0	16	0			
Medical Battalion	49	2	46	156	0	0	0	0	0	0	0	0	0	0	0	0	0	1	49	0	0	0	0
Traffic Control Platoon	1	0	3	29	0	0	0	0	0	0	0	0	0	0	0	0	1	0	2	0	0	0	0
other services	12	0	4	13	0	0	0	0	0	0	0	0	0	0	0	0	0	0	1	0	8	4	0

Table 1.3 Rifle division (TO 04/400-417), from April 1941.

earlier organization, although it seems likely that few divisions had their full complement of 37mm AA guns. The anti-tank battalion was clearly intended for decentralized direct support of the infantry, for it contained no signal assets at all, nor any ammunition supply or trains elements. The anti-aircraft battalion, on the other hand, had a well-developed communications net with each light battery having two radios and the heavy battery four radios, as well as linemen. For fire control the heavy battery's firing platoon included a 19-man fire control section with an optical rangefinder and a fire control system, while each 37mm gun was provided with a short-base rangefinder.

The division chemical company consisted of a small 14-man decontamination platoon and a 38-man flamethrower platoon, the latter with thirty backpack flamethrowers. The pioneer battalion was made up of three pioneer companies (each of three platoons, each with four 8-man squads), a technical platoon (with electric generating and sawmill sections), a bridging platoon (with twenty-four pontoons to create a 110m 3-ton bridge) and service elements.

Almost all of the supply and transport elements normally found throughout a division were here concentrated in the divisional motor transport battalion. This was divided into an ammunition platoon (eighty-five trucks), a food and fodder platoon (twenty-one trucks), a POL (petroleum, oil and lubricants) platoon (fourteen trucks), a repair platoon and supporting elements. The battalion was provided with a single radio to coordinate its activities.

The effort to streamline the clumsy divisions of the Russo-Finnish War cannot be regarded as entirely successful. True, personnel strength was cut to 14,454 men without sacrificing firepower. The number of bolt-action rifles declined from 13,000 to 6,627; but the number of semi-automatic rifles was increased from 530 to 3,405 and the number of sub-machine guns authorized climbed slightly to 1,195. The number of motor vehicles remained the same at 670 but the number of horses fell from 6,000 to 3,025. Service support, on the other hand, appears to have been ruthlessly slashed, particularly in the artillery. The manpower of division artillery was cut back, from 3,221 to 2,315, although part of the savings almost certainly came from the decision to motorize three of the artillery battalions instead of just one. On the other hand, the wide span of control and the disparate nature of the units under all the line commands continued to confound most of the commanders so recently quickly promoted as a result of the purges. The changes had not made the division any easier to command, only harder to sustain in combat.

The new style divisions did not fare well in the 1941 campaigns. The causes appear to have been the same as those affecting the Finnish campaign but the bulk of the blame can probably be laid on two primary problems. Firstly, large numbers of inexperienced officers had been quickly promoted beyond their level of competence to make up for the heavy losses of the Stalinist purges of the late 1930s. Secondly, compounding this, was a tactical communications net that looked good on paper, but which in practice was absolutely wretched for lack of radios, relying primarily on wire, and insufficiently manned even for that. The weak communications impacted particularly on the artillery support so necessary for infantry in modern combat. German accounts of the campaigns of the summers of 1941 (and 1942) make practically no mention of Soviet artillery except in those few instances when the Soviets were defending fixed positions.

Further exacerbating these problems were other shortcomings that rendered the

Soviet officers receive a briefing before operations from the battalion's commissars, seen here to the left with the notebooks. The role of commissars began to be weakened by the August 1940 reforms based on the Army's poor performance in Finland. The tasks of a Soviet officer were further hampered by the lack of a professional non-commissioned officer tradition in the Soviet Army which left the junior officers the tasks normally handled by NCOs in the German, British or American armies.

divisions, powerful as they looked on paper, almost impotent. As an example, the rifle divisions in the western military districts had only about half the motor vehicles and tractors called for in the TO&Es, with the remainder to come from requisitioned civilian stocks. Even in those few instances where requisitioning went smoothly, agricultural tractors proved less than ideal as artillery prime movers. Anti-aircraft defences for the rifle divisions (and corps) proved inadequate. The 12.7mm *DShK* machine guns were in short supply, as were the 37mm guns, leaving air defence to the elderly Maxim machine guns and a few inappropriate 76mm guns.

THE REDUCED STRENGTH DIVISIONS OF JULY 1941 (NO. 04/600–616)

Finding the leaders and equipment to fill out the new divisions mandated by the massive expansion of the summer and autumn of 1941 would clearly be impossible using the existing TO&Es. As a result, on 24 July 1941 a new set of TO&Es was issued for a 'reduced strength' rifle division. These were amended within a matter of weeks to even further reduce the division size. The infantry regiments were cut by 15 per cent and the whole division by slightly over 25 per cent. The most striking changes were to the infantry battalion and artillery component organization.

The changes to the rifle company were startling. Each rifle platoon was authorized only two light machine guns[4] and the August amendments further eliminated the 50mm mortar squad in one platoon per company. The medium machine gun platoon was dropped from the company entirely, yielding a company heavy weapons strength of six light machine guns and two 50mm mortars. Initially, high-explosive (HE) firepower was left unchanged, but in August the battalion mortar company was reduced to a 15-man platoon with two 82mm mortars; at the same time the regimental mortar battery was similarly reduced to a 21-man platoon with two mortars. Simultaneously, the regimental supply company lost one of its 20-man platoons, along with its twenty 2-horse wagons.

Anti-tank (AT) guns, considerably more difficult to produce than mortars, suffered similarly. The anti-tank platoon was deleted from the battalion structure, as was the divisional anti-tank battalion. This left only the six-gun regimental AT companies to provide anti-tank protection for the division. A later amendment to the TO&E added six AT rifles per infantry regiment, and these new weapons were first used in combat on 16 November 1941 by the 1075th Rifle Regiment. The only regimental unit to emerge unscathed from the new TO&E was the anti-aircraft company, which retained its earlier armament of six quad-mounted Maxim machine guns and three 12.7mm heavy machine guns.

The most dramatic downsizing came in the artillery component. The fifteen batteries held by the April 1941 division structure were reduced to a mere six. An artillery battalion consisted of two 76mm batteries, a 122mm battery, a 9-man HQ, a 10-man mounted reconnaissance section, a 21-man survey platoon, a 27-man signal platoon, a 29-man ammunition supply platoon (with sixteen 2-horse wagons) and trains elements.

The diminutive artillery regiment comprised two such battalions and supporting elements. The artillery component thus fell from sixteen 76mm guns, thirty-two 122mm howitzers and twelve 152mm howitzers, to sixteen 76mm guns and eight 122mm howitzers. Not only that, but the number of radios per battalion fell from twelve (three per battery plus three in the battalion HQ) to seven (two per battery plus one in battalion HQ), and wire communications were reduced as well, although not as dramatically. The artillery was thus not only smaller but less responsive as well.

Divisional reconnaissance was now provided by a single motorized company that consisted of a 7-man HQ (with the company's sole radio) and three platoons. Each of these platoons had a platoon leader, an assistant platoon leader and three rifle squads, with each squad consisting of a squad leader, four sub-machine gunners, four riflemen with semi-automatic rifles, a 2-man light machine gun team and a driver with a truck. The company HQ had no vehicles of its own, but instead was split up among the line platoon trucks as needed.

Under the original July TO&E each infantry regiment was to have included a 28-man flamethrower platoon with twenty backpack flamethrowers and three 2-horse wagons. This, however, was deleted in the August revisions. It was replaced by a divisional flamethrower platoon. The basic element of this unit was the 11-man squad with ten backpack flamethrowers. The platoon consisted of three such squads plus a 4-man HQ and four drivers with cargo trucks.

	Officers	Warrant & Political Officers	NCOs	Other Ranks	Submachine Guns	Light Machine Guns	Medium Machine Guns	Quad AA Machine Guns	Heavy Machine Guns	50mm Mortars	82mm Mortars	120mm Mortars	Anti-Tank Guns	Anti-Aircraft Guns	Infantry Guns	Artillery Pieces	Motorcycles	Field Cars	Trucks	Tractors	Horses	Wagons	Carts
Division Headquarters	26	49	14	37	0	0	0	0	0	0	0	0	0	0	0	0	0	2	4	0	24	6	0
Signal Battalion	17	15	47	184	0	0	0	0	0	0	0	0	0	0	0	0	3	1	18	0	27	1	13
Reconnaissance Company	4	1	15	101	0	0	0	0	0	0	0	0	0	0	0	0	0	0	9	0	0	0	0
Three Infantry Regiments, each	107	51	365	2,172	54	54	36	6	3	18	6	2	*6	0	4	0	0	0	9	0	477	154	41
Artillery Regiment	57	36	141	729	0	0	0	0	0	0	0	0	0	0	0	24	0	0	5	0	723	85	33
Anti-Aircraft Battalion	16	13	42	172	0	0	0	0	0	0	0	0	0	10	0	0	0	1	29	5	0	0	0
Pioneer Battalion	17	14	70	316	0	0	0	0	0	0	0	0	0	0	0	0	0	0	0	0	102	43	7
Chemical Platoon	1	0	4	33	0	0	0	0	0	0	0	0	0	0	0	0	0	0	3	0	0	0	0
Motor Transport Company	4	8	24	83	0	0	0	0	0	0	0	0	0	0	0	0	1	0	81	0	0	0	0
Medical Battalion	2	31	32	165	0	0	0	0	0	0	0	0	0	0	0	0	0	0	20	0	104	50	1
Bakery	0	4	12	144	0	0	0	0	0	0	0	0	0	0	0	0	0	0	18	0	45	20	1
other services	0	5	4	14	0	0	0	0	0	0	0	0	0	0	0	0	0	0	0	0	12	6	0

* also 6 AT rifles per regiment added later

Table 1.4 Rifle division (TO 04/600-616), from August 1941.

Other engineer support was provided by the divisional pioneer battalion that consisted of three companies. Each of these companies was built around three 34-man pioneer platoons (each of four squads) and a 9-man supply section with five 2-horse wagons for equipment. A 27-man equipment platoon (with twenty-two more wagons) was also provided in the battalion, but the former technical and bridging units were absent.

The new organization also shrank the divisional anti-aircraft battalion. All the radios and their crews were deleted. Gun strength was reduced by the simple, if unorthodox, process of eliminating one gun and its crew from one platoon in each light battery, leaving the battery with one platoon of two guns and one with only one gun. Otherwise, the battalion structure was virtually unchanged.

As before, selected divisions received a tank battalion, although such units were rare because of the need to concentrate all available tanks in the tank brigades. Such a unit, when it existed, was to consist of an 11-man HQ, a 10-man headquarters platoon, a medium tank company, two light tank companies and a 34-man support platoon. The HQ platoon consisted simply of two medium tanks for command use and a truck with a radio. The medium tank company consisted of two 12-man platoons (each with three medium tanks) and a 7-man HQ (with one medium tank) for a total of thirty-one men and seven tanks. The light tank company had three 6-man platoons (each with three light tanks) and a 4-man HQ (with a tenth light tank). The battalion support platoon provided one field car, ten cargo trucks, one workshop truck, three tractors and one motorcycle. The 'battalion' thus had a total strength of 15 officers, 14 political and warrant officers, 70 NCOs and 31 other ranks with 9 medium and 20 light tanks.

The July 1941 TO&Es reflected the shortages of equipment, particularly infantry heavy weapons and artillery, plaguing the Red Army but did not address the problem of poorly trained officers at the lower levels. The massive and hasty, almost panic-stricken, mobilization of the second half of 1941 did not permit more than the most cursory of

Although ill prepared for winter warfare in the 1939–40 war with Finland, the experience forced the Red Army to pay more attention to the needs for winter combat. By the time of the 1941 winter fighting, the Red Army was better prepared than were their German counterparts in terms of winter clothing and specialized equipment. Their winter camouflage coveralls were part of this trend, seen here during the fighting in winter 1944.

training for the new generation of platoon, company and battalion commanders. It quickly became apparent that this new generation of officers was incapable of efficiently integrating the efforts of direct- and indirect-fire weapons on the battlefield. In response, the People's Commissariat for Defence on 12 October 1941 ordered all mortars withdrawn from the infantry battalions and concentrated in a single regimental mortar battalion. At the same time the former heavy (120mm) mortar units were withdrawn from the infantry regiments

and formed into a single divisional mortar battalion.

This modification, which was applied to divisions using both the pre-war (04/401) and July (04/601) infantry regiment TO&Es, resulted in the creation in each regiment of a battalion of three companies, each with two light and two medium platoons. A light platoon consisted of the platoon leader, a 4-man ammunition section with two 1-horse carts and four 3-man squads each with a 50mm mortar The medium platoon had a platoon leader and four 7-man squads, each with an 82mm mortar and a cart. Severely limiting the usefulness of the battalion was its lack of modern communications. The battalion included only a single radio and relied primarily on land lines for its signal net, with each company having a 5-man telephone team, while the battalion signal platoon included eight wiremen. For fire direction duties a simple celluloid plotting device was issued to each platoon leader, assistant company commander and company commander, as well as to the battalion commander and the assistant battalion commander. The organization of the regimental mortar battalion allowed a mortar company to be assigned to each line battalion or, if required, the mortars could be concentrated in support of one or two battalions.

The divisional mortar battalion consisted of a very small 18-man HQ, a 30-man supply platoon (with 18 wagons), a 6-man trains group and three 68-man batteries. Each battery was made up of a 12-man HQ (including a 4-man telephone team with a cart) and two 28-man platoons with three 120mm mortars and three 2-horse wagons. Notable here was the complete absence of motor vehicles to move the heavy 120mm mortars and the reliance on wire communications, for there was not a single radio in the battalion.

At the same time a sub-machine gun company was added to each infantry regiment on the July (04/601) TO&E, although apparently not to the pre-war regiments. This new company consisted of a 7-man HQ and three 31-man platoons, with all personnel being armed with *PPSh*-41 sub-machine guns. A sub-machine gun platoon consisted simply of a lieutenant platoon leader and three squads each of two sergeants and eight privates. The company HQ consisted of the company CO (a captain), the executive officer (a first

lieutenant), the political officer, the first sergeant, a medic sergeant, a runner and a wagoner with a 2-horse wagon.

CONSOLIDATION: THE DECEMBER 1941 TO&ES (NO. 04/750–769)

On 6 December 1941 a new infantry regiment TO&E (No. 04/751) was issued that incorporated the October changes to the July TO&E with only minor modifications. The most important change was the issuance of three more light-machine guns to each rifle company, permitting three of the four squads in each platoon to be so equipped. Production of anti-tank rifles and ammunition had also increased to the point where a company with three 9-gun platoons could be incorporated into the regimental structure. The battalion trains platoon was also strengthened slightly, to consist of an ammunition section (four 2-horse wagons) and a baggage train (two baggage wagons and four field kitchen wagons).

Signal assets, however, actually decreased. The radio net now consisted of a single transceiver in each battalion HQ with two more in the regimental signal company and the infantry gun battery, although the Model *6-PK* radios with a voice range of five miles were replaced by Model *RB* radios with a voice range of twenty-one miles.

Other divisional TO&Es were issued at the same time but existing divisions were apparently instructed to reorganize only their infantry regiments and the new divisional mortar battalions on the 700-series TO&Es initially. Finally, on 27 December, the People's Commissariat for Defence instructed existing divisions to reconfigure all their existing units on to the new TO&Es, although they were not to create the new units mandated by the 700-series TO&Es. Two such new units were called for in the December 1941 infantry division: the

	Officers	Political Officers	Warrant Officers	NCOs	Other Ranks	Light Machine Guns	Medium Machine Guns	Heavy Machine Guns	Anti-Tank Rifles	50mm Mortars	82mm Mortars	45mm Anti-Tank Guns	76mm Infantry Guns	Other Equipment & Notes
Regiment Headquarters	12	4	10	5	1	0	0	0	0	0	0	0	0	
Headquarters Company														
Headquarters Platoon	1	0	0	4	19	0	0	0	0	0	0	0	0	3 field kitchen wagons, 1 baggage wagon
Mounted Recnnaissance Platoon	1	0	0	3	18	0	0	0	0	0	0	0	0	(2 squads)
Infantry Reconnaissance Platoon	1	0	0	5	43	0	0	0	0	0	0	0	0	(4 squads)
Pioneer Platoon	1	0	0	5	34	0	0	0	0	0	0	0	0	(4 squads) 2 carts
Anti-Aircraft Platoon	1	0	0	6	9	0	0	3	0	0	0	0	0	3 trucks
Chemical Platoon	1	0	0	4	27	0	0	0	0	0	0	0	0	8 two-horse wagons
Flamethrower Platoon	1	0	0	3	21	0	0	0	0	0	0	0	0	(2 squads each 10 flamethrowers) 3 two-horse wagons
Band	0	0	1	1	11	0	0	0	0	0	0	0	0	
Signal Company														
Company HQ & Platoon	3	1	0	4	15	0	0	0	0	0	0	0	0	2 wire equipment carts
Radio Platoon	1	0	0	2	5	0	0	0	0	0	0	0	0	2 RB transceivers, 1 receiver, 1 cart
1st Wire/Optical Platoon	1	0	0	2	10	0	0	0	0	0	0	0	0	2 wire equipment carts
2nd Wire/Optical Platoon	1	0	0	2	8	0	0	0	0	0	0	0	0	2 wire equipment carts
Three Infantry Battalions, each														
Battalion Headquarters	4	0	0	0	0	0	0	0	0	0	0	0	0	
Signal Platoon	1	0	0	4	13	0	0	0	0	0	0	0	0	1 RB transceiver, 2 wire equipment carts
Three Rifle Companies, each														
Company Headquarters	2	1	0	2	3	0	0	0	0	0	0	0	0	
Medical Squad	0	0	0	1	4	0	0	0	0	0	0	0	0	
Three Rifle Platoons, each	1	0	0	9	37	3	0	0	0	0	0	0	0	(4 squads)
Machine Gun Company														
Company Headquarters	2	1	0	2	1	0	0	0	0	0	0	0	0	
Three MG Platoons, each	1	0	0	8	20	0	4	0	0	0	0	0	0	2 two-horse wagons
Medical Platoon	0	0	1	1	5	0	0	0	0	0	0	0	0	1 two-horse wagon
Trains Platoon	1	0	0	3	19	0	0	0	0	0	0	0	0	10 two-horse wagons
Mortar Battalion														
Battalion Headquarters	4	1	0	1	0	0	0	0	0	0	0	0	0	
Signal Platoon	1	0	0	2	11	0	0	0	0	0	0	0	0	1 "RB" receiver, 1 wire equipment cart
Three Mortar Companies, each														
Company Headquarters	2	1	0	1	5	0	0	0	0	0	0	0	0	1 wire equipment cart
Two Light Platoons, each	1	0	0	9	6	0	0	0	0	4	0	0	0	2 one-horse wagons
Two Medium Platoons, each	1	0	0	9	20	0	0	0	0	0	4	0	0	4 one-horse wagons
Trains Platoon	1	0	0	3	19	0	0	0	0	0	0	0	0	15 two-horse wagons
Submachine Gun Company														
Company Headquarters	2	1	0	2	2	0	0	0	0	0	0	0	0	
Three SMG Gun Platoons, each	1	0	0	6	24	0	0	0	0	0	0	0	0	(3 squads) 31 submachine guns
Anti-Tank Rifle Company														
Company Headquarters	2	1	0	2	2	0	0	0	0	0	0	0	0	2 two-horse wagons
Three AT Rifle Platoons, each	1	0	0	7	16	0	0	0	9	0	0	0	0	(3 squads) 1 two-horse wagon
Anti-Tank Battery														
Battery Headquarters	2	1	0	1	2	0	0	0	0	0	0	0	0	
Three Anti-Tank Platoons, each	1	0	0	4	12	0	0	0	0	0	0	2	0	2 two-horse wagons
Infantry Gun Battery														
Battery Headquarters	3	1	0	3	12	0	0	0	0	0	0	0	0	2 RB3 transceivers, 2 wire equipment carts
Two Infantry Gun Platoons, each	1	0	0	4	19	0	0	0	0	0	0	0	2	2 four-horse wagons
Ammunition Platoon	1	0	0	2	15	0	0	0	0	0	0	0	0	9 two-horse wagons
Trains	0	0	0	2	8	0	0	0	0	0	0	0	0	3 two-horse wagons
Medical Company	0	0	7	7	35	0	0	0	0	0	0	0	0	9 two-horse wagons, 2 carts
Veterinary Hospital	0	0	2	1	3	0	0	0	0	0	0	0	0	2 two-horse wagons
Weapons Repair Shop	0	0	3	7	4	0	0	0	0	0	0	0	0	
Trains Shop	0	0	0	1	10	0	0	0	0	0	0	0	0	
Supply Company	5	1	0	8	57	0	0	0	0	0	0	0	0	54 two-horse wagons

Table 1.5 Infantry regiment (TO 04/750), from December 1941.

Soviet infantry equipment was spartan and old-fashioned for the most part. The one exception was the heavy use of sub-machine guns such as the *PPSh*, being used by the soldier to the right, another lesson of the Finnish campaign. The machine gun is the same Maxim Model 1910 in use in the First World War – a heavy and cumbersome weapon compared to its German counterparts – seen here in action in the northern Caucasus in the summer of 1942.

restoration of the anti-tank battalion and a rocket-launcher battalion. The anti-tank battalions were added, however, to existing divisions as weapons became available.

The new rocket-launcher battalion was to take advantage of the 82mm M-8 and the 132mm M-13 multiple rocket launchers (MRL). The battalion had two batteries each with four truck-mounted multiple rocket-launcher units. Although potent weapons, their usefulness when diluted to eight systems for each infantry division was probably questionable. In any event few divisions seem to have actually received these weapons in

the short period before they were deleted from the divisional organization.

The emergency divisional organization of July 1941 had eliminated the pre-war anti-tank battalions from the divisional structure and the anti-tank platoons from the infantry battalions, leaving only the regimental batteries. As weapons to replace the horrendous losses of 1941 finally became available the divisional anti-tank battalions were restored in the December TO&Es, although the battalion AT platoons, clearly the lowest priority, still had to await further equipment deliveries. The battalion, actually

	Officers	Warrant & Political Officers	NCOs	Other Ranks	Submachine Guns	Light Machine Guns	Medium Machine Guns	Heavy Machine Guns	Anti-Tank Rifles	Flamethrowers	50mm Mortars	82mm Mortars	120mm Mortars	Anti-Aircraft Guns	Anti-Tank Guns	Infantry Guns	Artillery Pieces	Motorcycles	Field Cars	Trucks	Horses	Wagons	Carts
Division Headquarters	39	45	34	95	0	1	0	0	0	0	0	0	0	0	0	0	0	0	3	3	22	0	0
Signal Battalion	16	9	32	128	0	0	0	0	0	0	0	0	0	0	0	0	0	3	1	3	48	8	11
Reconnaissance Company	5	1	15	100	0	0	0	0	0	0	0	0	0	0	0	0	0	0	0	9	0	0	0
Three Infantry Regiments, each	153	52	630	2,122	184	81	36	3	27	20	24	24	0	6	0	4	0	0	0	3	515	190	44
Artillery Headquarters	5	1	11	51	0	0	0	0	0	0	0	0	0	0	0	0	0	0	0	3	25	1	2
Field Artillery Regiment	64	56	147	565	0	0	0	0	0	0	0	0	0	0	0	0	24	0	0	0	675	93	29
Anti-Tank Battalion	15	6	37	93	0	0	0	0	0	0	0	0	0	0	12	0	0	0	1	16	0	0	0
Anti-Aircraft Battery	6	1	17	56	0	0	0	0	0	0	0	0	0	6	0	0	0	0	0	9	0	0	0
Mortar Battalion (Horsed)*	18	8	45	206	0	0	0	0	0	0	0	0	18	0	0	0	0	0	0	0	216	46	5
Mortar Battalion (Motorized)*	19	6	45	143	0	0	0	0	0	0	0	0	18	0	0	0	0	0	0	27	0	0	0
Rocket Launcher Battalion	14	7	45	125	0	4	0	3	0	0	0	**8	0	0	0	0	0	0	1	42	0	0	0
Pioneer Battalion	14	8	31	188	0	0	0	0	0	0	0	0	0	0	0	0	0	0	0	0	37	15	2
Chemical Company	6	1	11	40	0	3	0	0	0	0	0	0	0	0	0	0	0	0	0	1	12	6	0
Motor Transport Company	5	8	24	101	0	0	0	0	0	0	0	0	0	0	0	0	0	1	0	100	0	0	0
Medical Battalion	3	27	20	63	0	0	0	0	0	0	0	0	0	0	0	0	0	0	0	15	0	0	0
Bakery	0	4	7	91	0	0	0	0	0	0	0	0	0	0	0	0	0	0	0	0	53	23	1
other services	0	9	3	15	0	0	0	0	0	0	0	0	0	0	0	0	0	0	0	0	10	5	0

* division may have either or both type of mortar battalion
** 82mm M-8 or 132mm M-13 multiple rocket launchers

Table 1.6 Rifle division (TO 04/750-769), from December 1941.

a company by Western standards, was a motorized formation with twelve AT guns in three batteries. Nominally the weapons were to be the new 57mm M.1941 but few of these were available to the infantry divisions so the 45mm remained the standard weapon.

The primary divisional fire support element remained the artillery regiment. This was unchanged from the July organization of two battalions each with two batteries of 76mm guns and one of 122mm howitzers. The divisional artillery HQ was reinstated, presumably to coordinate the efforts of the rapidly proliferating indirect-fire units, which now included not only the artillery regiment and the rocket-launcher battalion but also one or two battalions of 120mm mortars. Each of these mortar battalions comprised three batteries of six 120mm weapons, with one battalion being horse-drawn and the other motorized.

The anti-aircraft component was reduced by eliminating the 76mm guns, which had proven unwieldy on the front and of limited usefulness in such small numbers. The remaining six 37mm guns were consolidated into a single battery with nine trucks. The air defence component of the infantry regiment was also reduced by eliminating the marginally useful quad-mounted 7.62mm Maxim guns and instead relying solely on the 12.7mm truck-mounted heavy machine guns.

These new organization tables clearly still bore the hallmarks of emergency mobilization. The standard Soviet work on the subject notes of the December 1941 TO&Es that 'although the division's firepower gradually rose, its mobility fell noticeably. The load-carrying capacity of the division's transport equipment compared unfavourably with that of the pre-war division. Even before December 1941, the rifle division could move almost all of its unit reserves in one trip with its own transport equipment. In 1942, this was no longer possible.'[5]

THE FINE-TUNING OF MARCH 1942 (NO. 04/200–216)

The 700-series TO&Es remained in effect through 1942 for most of the divisions activated before March of that year, although it seems likely that authorization for the rocket-launcher battalion was withdrawn soon after issuance. In March 1942 a new set of TO&Es (Nos 04/200–216) was issued for subsequent rifle divisions that fine-tuned the earlier tables.

The rifle companies were finally fully equipped with light machine guns, one being provided for each of the twelve squads in the company. Sniper rifles were also added to the company, a characteristic which would remain prominent in Soviet rifle company organization to the end of the war. At the battalion level an anti-tank rifle company was added, made up of two platoons each of four 2-gun squads. The battalion trains platoon, however, was reduced to only three general-purpose wagons and four field kitchen wagons.

The infantry regimental structure was not significantly changed, although once again the trains elements here were reduced, with the supply company losing eleven wagons. The regimental signal net remained unchanged.

A precursor of things to come, the new organization authorized an increase in strength for units that had been awarded the honorific 'guards' title. Each infantry regiment in a guards division was allotted a second sub-machine gun company, although there were no other changes in unit structure.

The divisional structure was strengthened through the addition of a third battalion to the field artillery regiment. This third battalion, however, was not a full-strength unit since it had only one gun and one howitzer battery. Proportional reductions were also made in the signal, survey and trains elements. Nevertheless, this diminutive battalion certainly compensated for the absence of the multiple rocket-launcher battalion, since this latter was only rarely present in actuality.

Another change to the artillery organization was the replacement of draft horses by tractors as the motive force for the 122mm howitzers. Motor vehicles remained in extremely short supply, so their use could be justified only where the use of horses was clearly extravagant. This was apparently only felt to be the case in towing the 122mm howitzers, for the five tractors (including one reserve) allocated to each howitzer battery were the only significant holdings of motor vehicles in the artillery regiment.

In the divisional anti-tank battalion the specified weapon was once again the 45mm anti-tank gun, the 57mm weapons having been appropriated to the GHQ anti-tank brigades. An AT rifle company was added to the battalion, this consisting of four platoons each with three 3-gun squads. The company was not provided with any organic transport and probably rode in the trucks of the AT batteries as available or walked with the supported elements.

The number of heavy mortar battalions was reduced to one by eliminating the horse-drawn unit, while the anti-aircraft component remained unchanged at a single battery of six 37mm guns.

This organization did not remain in force for long, however. A series of modifications to the TO&Es was published in almost monthly instalments through July. Revisions in May, June and July 1942 completely reorganized the infantry regiment, although the nominal TO&E designation (04/204) remained the same.

	Officers	Political Officers	Warrant Officers	NCOs	Other Ranks	Weapons, equipment & notes
Division Headquarters						10 SMG, 3 field cars, 2 trucks
Command Element & HQ Co	30	20	32	26	52	8 SMG, 3 field cars, 2 trucks
NKVD Rifle Platoon	1	0	0	4	19	2 SMG
Signal Battalion						
Battalion HQ & trains elements	5	1	4	7	6	1 field car, 5 wagons
Headquarters Company	5	1	0	17	47	5 radios, 3 m/c, 2 trucks, 3 wagons, 3 carts
Wire Company	6	1	0	11	67	10 carts
Reconnaissance Company	3	1	0	15	91	(3 plts each 3 sqds) 12 SMG, 1 radio
Three Infantry Regiments, each						
Regiment HQ & Platoon	15	4	10	6	10	2 wagons
Mounted Reconnaissance Platoon	1	1	0	3	13	(2 squads) 2 SMG
Infantry Reconnaissance Platoon	1	1	0	5	43	(4 squads) 2 SMG
Signal Company	5	1	0	9	35	(radio sec & 2 wire plts) 2 radios, 6 wire equipment carts
Anti-Aircraft MG Company	1	0	0	6	9	3 HMG, 3 trucks
Chemical Platoon	1	0	0	4	25	6 wagons
Pioneer Platoon	1	0	0	5	33	1 wagon
Anti-Tank Mortar Platoon	1	0	0	8	14	6 AT mortars, 2 wagons
Band	0	0	1	1	11	
Three Infantry Battalions, each						
Battalion Headquarters	4	1	0	0	0	
Signal Platoon	1	0	0	4	12	1 radio, 1 wire equipment cart
Three Rifle Companies, each	6	1	0	39	144	(3 rifle & 1 mortar plt) 11 sniper rifles, 9 SMG, 12 LMG, 4 50mm Mort
Machine Gun Company	5	1	0	19	51	(3 plts each 3 sqds) 9 MG, 6 wagons
AT Rifle Company	4	1	0	19	24	(2 plts each 4 sqds) 16 AT rifles
Mortar Company	6	1	0	29	60	(6 plts), 12 82mm Mort, 12 wagons
Medical Platoon	0	0	1	1	5	1 cart
Trains Platoon	1	0	0	3	19	14 wagons
Submachine Gun Company	5	1	0	20	74	(3 plts each 3 sqds) 100 SMG, 1 wagon
Anti-Tank Rifle Company	5	1	0	22	48	(3 plts each 3 sqds) 27 AT rifles, 3 wagons
Anti-Tank Battery	5	1	0	13	38	(3 plts) 6 45mm AT guns, 6 caissons
Infantry Gun Battery	6	1	0	15	62	(2 gun plts) 4 76mm Inf Guns, 2 carts, 16 wagons
Mortar Company	6	1	0	21	43	(4 plts) 8 82mm Mort, 11 wagons
Mortar Battery	5	1	0	13	37	(3 plts) 6 120mm Mort, 7 trucks
Medical Company	0	0	7	7	34	2 carts, 9 wagons
Supply Company	4	1	0	8	46	(2 plts) 43 wagons
other services	0	0	4	9	6	1 wagon
Artillery Headquarters	5	1	0	10	46	2 radios, 2 carts, 3 trucks
Field Artillery Regiment						
Regiment HQ & Battery	15	5	9	12	40	(recon, signal & survey plts) 2 SMG, 1 radio, 3 carts, 5 wagons
Three Field Artillery Battalions, each						
Battalion HQ & trains elements	7	1	3	17	71	1 SMG, 2 radios, 5 carts, 28 wagons (24 ammo)
Two Field Gun Batteries, each	5	1	0	16	55	1 SMG, 4 76mm guns, 2 radios, 2 carts, 8 wagons
Field Howitzer Battery	5	1	0	20	52	1 SMG, 4 122mm How, 2 radios, 5 tractors, 1 cart, 8 wagons
Supply Platoon	1	0	0	3	22	2 trucks, 17 wagons
other services	0	0	6	9	15	1 truck, 1 cart, 4 wagons
Machine Gun Battalion						
Battalion HQ & trains elements	4	1	3	9	21	1 cart, 7 wagons
Three Machine Gun Companies, each	5	1	0	19	33	(3 plts) 9 MG, 6 wagons
Anti-Tank Battalion						
Battalion HQ & trains elements	3	1	4	8	14	1 radio, 1 field car, 5 trucks
Three Anti-Tank Batteries, each	4	1	0	9	25	(2 plts) 4 45mm AT guns, 4 trucks
Anti-Tank Rifle Company	6	1	0	26	61	(4 plts each 3 sqds) 4 SMG, 36 ATR
Anti-Aircraft Battery	6	1	0	17	55	(3 plts) 6 37mm AA, 9 trucks
Pioneer Battalion						
Battalion HQ & trains elements	5	1	5	5	8	1 cart, 2 wagons
Two Pioneer Companies, each	5	1	0	10	86	(3 plts each 3 sqds) 2 wagons
Division Services						
Chemical Company	4	1	1	10	38	(1 gas plt & 1 decon plt) 3 LMG, 6 trucks, 3 wagons
Motor Transport Company	5	1	7	20	60	(3 plts) 1 m/c, 61 trucks
Medical Battalion	3	2	25	19	54	13 trucks
Bakery	0	1	3	6	86	21 wagons
other services	0	1	8	3	14	4 wagons
Infantry Training Battalion	29	9	5	64	493	36 SMG, 24 LMG, 6 MG, 6 ATR, 4 50mm Mort, 4 82mm Mort, 9 wagons

Table 1.7 Rifle division (TO 04/200-216), from July 1942.

An infantry section advances under the covering fire of its automatic weapons: a Degtaryev *DP* light machine gun and a Tokarev *SVT*-40 automatic rifle being operated by the two prone soldiers. The squad itself is armed with the usual Moisin Nagant Model 1891/30 rifles. This is probably a staged training exercise. As the war went on, the proportion of automatic weapons in the squad continued to increase, most noticeably the more regular use of *PPSh* sub-machine guns.

These amendments abolished the regimental mortar battalions and finally returned control of the mortars to company and battalion line commanders, who were now apparently judged sufficiently proficient to use them effectively. Unlike the pre-war organization that provided a 50mm mortar to each rifle platoon, however, the new structure added a centralized mortar platoon to each rifle company that controlled four 3-man mortar crews. This brought rifle company strength up to 190 men, the highest that company strength would reach during the war.

Simultaneously, a medium mortar company with six 2-gun platoons of 82mm mortars was added to the infantry battalion. In keeping with prior practice, this unit was extremely austere, consisting of little more than the gun crews, a wagon for each mortar, and platoon and company commanders. To handle the extra ammunition loads imposed by the mortar units the battalion trains platoon was expanded to ten general-purpose wagons as well as the standard four kitchen wagons. In an apparent effort to keep battalion strength down somewhat the machine gun company lost one squad in each of its three platoons, reducing its strength to nine squads.

A new weapon introduced by the TO&E revisions was the anti-tank mortar (*ampulomet*). A platoon consisting of a lieutenant and two sections (each of a section leader, three 3-man teams and one man with a 2-horse wagon) was added to the infantry regiment structure.

The heavy mortars were decentralized as well, with the divisional mortar battalion being broken up and the companies distributed one to each infantry regiment. Strangely, each regiment also retained one 82mm mortar company as direct assets despite the allocation of these weapons to the battalions and the heavier 120mm weapons to the regiment. The former heavy mortar battalion was replaced in the divisional structure by a new machine gun battalion. This unit was entirely triangular, consisting of three companies each of three 3-squad platoons. The water-cooled Maxim machine guns, although cumbersome and heavy, were effective weapons but, lacking any combat support elements, the battalion could not be safely employed by itself. Instead the machine gun companies and platoons were parcelled out to the line infantry as needed for defensive and economy-of-force missions.

FURTHER MANPOWER REDUCTIONS: JULY 1942 (NO. 04/300–316)

On 28 July 1942 a whole new series of TO&Es (Nos 04/300–316) was issued for the infantry division. The main effect of these new organization tables was to enforce overall manpower reductions in the division without making major changes in its composition or that of its subordinate elements.

In the case of the rifle company that meant reducing squad size to two sergeants and seven privates, and deleting one squad from the 50mm mortar platoon. In the

machine gun company two privates were eliminated from each gun squad. Battalion fire support was reduced somewhat by reducing the AT rifle component from a company with two 8-gun platoons to a single platoon with three 3-gun sections, and by reducing the mortar company from the rather ungainly configuration of six 2-gun platoons to three 3-gun platoons.

At the regimental level the pioneer and infantry scout platoons each lost one squad, while the chemical platoon lost one of its two gas-detection squads. The only other significant change was in the communications net, where the radio team, with its 'RB' transceiver formerly held as a battalion asset, was deleted in favour of adding two teams to the regimental signal company for distribution as needed. The effect was to reduce the number of radios available to control line elements from five to four.

No major changes were made to the divisional structure except for the addition of an AT rifle company to the machine gun battalion and a return to the practice of providing only one gun battery to one of the field artillery battalions. Artillery communications were not improved, the divisional field artillery regiment disposing of a total of nineteen regular 'RB' transceivers, four 'RB' sets with special high antennas and one receiver. Motor transport for the regiment consisted of fifteen *STZ* tractors, two cargo trucks and one shop truck.

The anti-tank battalion remained one of the few motorized formations in the division, having thirteen ZiS-5/6 trucks as prime movers, four *GAZ* trucks and a shop truck in the trains, and a field car for the commander. For close-in defence the battalion held a total of 25 pistols, 148 rifles, 4 sub-machine guns and 36 AT rifles.

The former signal battalion was redesignated a signal company although the

	Political & Warrant Officers	Officers	NCOs	Other Ranks	Submachine Guns	Light Machine Guns	Medium Machine Guns	Anti-Tank Rifles	50mm Mortars	82mm Mortars	120mm Mortars	45mm AT Guns	37mm AA Guns	76mm Infantry Guns	76mm Field Guns	122mm Field Howitzers	Field Cars	Trucks	Tractors	Horses	Wagons	Carts
Division Headquarters																						
Command Element	26	48	12	33	2	0	0	0	0	0	0	0	0	0	0	0	0	0	0	0	0	0
NKVD Rifle Platoon	1	0	5	14	1	1	0	0	0	0	0	0	0	0	0	0	0	1	0	0	0	0
Signal Company	10	7	39	108	0	0	0	0	0	0	0	0	0	0	0	0	4	5	0	37	4	17
Reconnaissance Company	5	1	15	82	12	0	0	0	0	0	0	0	0	0	0	0	0	0	0	0	0	0
Three Infantry Regiments, each																						
Regiment HQ & Platoon	15	14	6	10	0	0	0	0	0	0	0	0	0	0	0	0	0	0	0	8	0	2
Mounted Reconnaissance Platoon	1	1	3	12	2	0	0	0	0	0	0	0	0	0	0	0	0	0	0	17	0	0
Infantry Reconnaissance Platoon	1	1	4	30	4	0	0	0	0	0	0	0	0	0	0	0	0	0	0	0	0	0
Signal Company	5	1	11	36	0	0	0	0	0	0	0	0	0	0	0	0	0	0	0	11	0	6
Anti-Aircraft MG Platoon	1	0	6	6	0	0	*3	0	0	0	0	0	0	0	0	0	0	3	0	0	0	0
Chemical Platoon	1	0	3	14	0	0	0	0	0	0	0	0	0	0	0	0	0	0	0	7	2	3
Pioneer Platoon	1	0	4	19	0	0	0	0	0	0	0	0	0	0	0	0	0	0	0	2	1	0
Anti-Tank Mortar Platoon	1	0	8	10	2	0	0	**6	0	0	0	0	0	0	0	0	0	0	0	4	2	0
Three Infantry Battalions, each																						
Battalion Headquarters	3	1	0	0	0	0	0	0	0	0	0	0	0	0	0	0	0	0	0	0	0	0
Signal Platoon	1	0	2	8	0	0	0	0	0	0	0	0	0	0	0	0	0	0	0	1	0	1
Three Rifle Companies, each	6	1	36	102	12	12	0	0	3	0	0	0	0	0	0	0	0	0	0	1	0	1
Machine Gun Company	5	1	19	33	0	0	9	0	0	0	0	0	0	0	0	0	0	0	0	12	6	0
AT Rifle Platoon	1	0	6	16	0	0	0	9	0	0	0	0	0	0	0	0	0	0	0	2	1	0
Mortar Company	5	1	19	36	0	0	0	0	0	9	0	0	0	0	0	0	0	0	0	9	0	9
Medical Platoon	0	1	1	3	0	0	0	0	0	0	0	0	0	0	0	0	0	0	0	1	0	1
Trains Platoons	1	0	2	9	0	0	0	0	0	0	0	0	0	0	0	0	0	0	0	14	4	3
Submachine Gun Company	5	1	20	94	100	0	0	0	0	0	0	0	0	0	0	0	0	0	0	0	0	0
Anti-Tank Rifle Company	5	1	19	48	0	0	0	27	0	0	0	0	0	0	0	0	0	0	0	6	3	0
Anti-Tank Battery	5	1	19	30	0	0	0	0	0	0	0	6	0	0	0	0	0	0	0	26	0	6
Infantry Gun Battery	6	1	14	58	0	0	0	0	0	0	0	0	0	4	0	0	0	0	0	49	12	3
Mortar Battery	5	1	13	37	0	0	0	0	0	0	6	0	0	0	0	0	0	7	0	0	0	0
Medical Company	0	7	5	26	0	0	0	0	0	0	0	0	0	0	0	0	0	0	0	17	5	6
Supply Company	4	1	8	34	0	0	0	0	0	0	0	0	0	0	0	0	0	0	0	64	31	1
other services	0	4	8	5	0	0	0	0	0	0	0	0	0	0	0	0	0	0	0	1	0	1
Field Artillery Regiment																						
Regiment Headquarters	10	12	3	0	0	0	0	0	0	0	0	0	0	0	0	0	0	0	0	6	0	0
Headquarters Battery	5	1	9	40	2	0	0	0	0	0	0	0	0	0	0	0	0	0	0	23	0	8
Three Field Artillery Battalions, each																						
Battalion HQ & trains elements	7	4	17	65	1	0	0	0	0	0	0	0	0	0	0	0	0	0	0	68	25	5
Two Field Gun Batteries, each***	5	1	16	52	3	0	0	0	0	0	0	0	0	0	4	0	0	0	0	54	8	1
Field Howitzer Battery	5	1	20	49	3	0	0	4	0	0	0	0	0	0	0	4	0	0	5	30	8	1
Supply Platoon	1	0	3	20	0	0	0	0	0	0	0	0	0	0	0	0	0	2	0	30	12	5
other services	0	6	8	13	0	0	0	0	0	0	0	0	0	0	0	0	0	1	0	9	4	1
Machine Gun Battalion																						
Battalion HQ & trains elements	4	4	8	20	0	0	0	0	0	0	0	0	0	0	0	0	0	0	0	20	6	2
Three Machine Gun Companies	5	1	19	33	0	0	9	0	0	0	0	0	0	0	0	0	0	0	0	12	6	0
Anti-Tank Rifle Company	4	1	15	21	0	0	0	12	0	0	0	0	0	0	0	0	0	0	0	6	3	0
Anti-Tank Battalion																						
Battalion HQ & trains elements	3	5	7	11	0	0	0	0	0	0	0	0	0	0	0	0	1	5	0	0	0	0
Three Anti-Tank Batteries, each	4	1	13	16	0	0	0	0	0	0	0	4	0	0	0	0	0	4	0	0	0	0
Anti-Tank Rifle Company	6	1	26	60	4	0	0	36	0	0	0	0	0	0	0	0	0	0	0	0	0	0
Anti-Aircraft Battery	6	1	17	53	0	0	0	0	0	0	0	0	6	0	0	0	0	9	0	0	0	0
Pioneer Battalion																						
Battalion HQ & trains elements	5	5	4	6	0	0	0	0	0	0	0	0	0	0	0	0	0	0	0	10	4	1
Two Pioneer Companies, each	5	1	10	64	0	0	0	0	0	0	0	0	0	0	0	0	0	0	0	2	1	0
Division Services																						
Chemical Company	5	2	12	33	0	0	0	0	0	0	0	0	0	0	0	0	0	6	0	4	2	0
Motor Transport Company	5	8	16	59	0	0	0	0	0	0	0	0	0	0	0	0	0	61	0	0	0	0
Medical Battalion	2	27	19	50	0	0	0	0	0	0	0	0	0	0	0	0	0	13	0	0	0	0
Bakery	0	3	6	56	0	0	0	0	0	0	0	0	0	0	0	0	0	0	0	26	10	4
Veterinary Hospital	0	3	0	8	0	0	0	0	0	0	0	0	0	0	0	0	0	0	0	2	1	0
Infantry Training Battalion	23	12	48	317	16	12	4	6	4	4	0	0	0	0	0	0	0	0	0	10	0	8

*heavy (12.7mm) machine guns
** anti-tank mortars
*** only one gun battery in one of the battalions, with proportional reductions in survey, signal, ammunition and trains elements.

Table 1.8 Rifle division (TO 04/300-314), from July 1942.

actual reductions in size, from 178 men to 164, and in capabilities were minimal. Where the old divisional signal battalion consisted primarily of its 70-man HQ company (comprising a radio platoon with five sets, one telegraph platoon and one messenger platoon) and a wire company (with ten telephone squads), the new signal company had a 27-man radio platoon (seven sets), a 19-man messenger platoon with bicycles and motorcycles, one telegraph section, and three wire platoons with a total of nine squads.

The chemical company, characteristic of Soviet divisions through the war, was little changed. It consisted of one 7-man HQ (including two chemical warrant officers), one gas-detection platoon (with a 2-man HQ and two 8-man teams), one general decontamination platoon (fourteen men with four *GAZ-AA* trucks for chlorine decontamination) and an equipment decontamination platoon (fifteen men with two trucks).

These changes, however, were enough to reduce overall division strength from 13,534 under the modified old (04/200-series) TO&Es to 10,393, a saving of 23 per cent.

STANDARDIZATION: DECEMBER 1942 (NO. 04/550-562)

The new July 1942 TO&Es were apparently intended to apply only to newly raised divisions, for by late 1942 the divisions serving on the front were using three sets of TO&Es: some were on the December 1941 tables (04/750-769), some on the March 1942 tables (04/200-216) and the remainder on the July tables (04/300-316). The proliferation of TO&Es was apparently proving cumbersome, so on 10 December 1942 the definitive set of infantry division TO&Es was published, to which all divisions would conform, although it took several

months for all divisions to reorganize. In fact, two sets of organization tables were actually promulgated: one for the regular infantry divisions (Nos 04/550-562) and one for guards infantry divisions (Nos 04/500-512).

The new rifle company TO&E featured greatly increased automatic weapons firepower. Two of the squads in each rifle platoon were issued a second *RPD* light machine gun, although with no increase in strength, and these tended to be used as a base of firepower against which the other two lighter squads could manoeuvre. The platoon thus had an overall strength of 40 men, armed with 4 *PPSh* sub-machine guns, 14 semi-automatic rifles, 6 light-machine guns and 2 sniper rifles, as well as the standard bolt-action rifles.

At the company level yet another of the squads was deleted from the mortar platoon, reducing it to two weapons, while a new medium machine gun squad was added to the company. The only other change to the company, as compared with the July (04/301) TO&E, was the elimination of all the runners (one in each rifle platoon and company HQ) and the removal of the cart from the mortar platoon to the new MG squad. Thus, while overall company strength actually fell slightly from 145 to 143, heavy weapons firepower was increased from twelve light MGs and three 50mm mortars to eighteen light MGs, one medium MG and two 50mm mortars.

The infantry battalion organization remained unchanged except for one significant addition: sufficient anti-tank guns were finally found to permit the restoration of the battalion anti-tank platoon that had been dropped in the July 1941 tables. The infantry division was thus returned to the level of anti-tank protection held by the pre-war divisions, e.g., a 2-gun platoon in each infantry battalion, a 6-gun battery in each infantry regiment, and a 12-gun battalion in

The relative lack of motor transport in the Red Army in 1941–3 meant that most deployments were conducted by rail. Here, a company takes a cigarette break.

	Political Officers	Officers	Warrant Officers	NCOs	Other Ranks	Submachine Guns	Light Machine Guns	Medium Machine Guns	Anti-Tank Rifles	50mm Mortars	82mm Mortars	120mm Mortars	45mm AT Guns	76mm Infantry Guns	Horses	Wagons	Carts
Regiment Headquarters	14	4	10	1	0	0	0	0	0	0	0	0	0	0	4	0	0
Headquarters Elements																	
Headquarters Platoon	1	0	0	3	9	0	0	0	0	0	0	0	0	0	4	0	2
Mounted Reconnaissance Platoon	1	0	0	2	8	2	0	0	0	0	0	0	0	0	11	0	0
Infantry Reconnaissance Platoon	1	1	0	4	19	4	0	0	0	0	0	0	0	0	0	0	0
Pioneer Platoon	1	0	0	4	15	0	0	0	0	0	0	0	0	0	2	1	0
Chemical Platoon	1	0	0	2	9	0	0	0	0	0	0	0	0	0	7	3	1
Signal Company																	
Company Headquarters	2	1	0	5	3	0	0	0	0	0	0	0	0	0	3	0	0
Headquarters Platoon	1	0	0	2	6	0	0	0	0	0	0	0	0	0	2	0	2
Radio Platoon	1	0	0	0	8	0	0	0	0	0	0	0	0	0	0	0	0
Wire Platoon	1	0	0	4	16	0	0	0	0	0	0	0	0	0	4	0	4
Three Infantry Battalions, each																	
Battalion Headquarters	3	1	0	0	0	0	0	0	0	0	0	0	0	0	0	0	0
Signal Platoon	1	0	0	2	7	0	0	0	0	0	0	0	0	0	1	0	1
Three Rifle Companies, each																	
Company Headquarters	2	1	0	2	0	0	0	0	0	0	0	0	0	0	0	0	0
Medical Squad	0	0	0	1	4	0	0	0	0	0	0	0	0	0	0	0	0
Three Rifle Platoons, each																	
Platoon HQ	1	0	0	1	2	0	0	0	0	0	0	0	0	0	0	0	0
Two Light Squads, each	0	0	0	2	7	1	1	0	0	0	0	0	0	0	0	0	0
Two Heavy Squads, each	0	0	0	2	7	1	2	0	0	0	0	0	0	0	0	0	0
Mortar Platoon	1	0	0	4	2	0	0	0	0	2	0	0	0	0	0	0	0
Machine Gun Squad	0	0	0	2	2	0	0	1	0	0	0	0	0	0	1	0	1
Machine Gun Company																	
Company Headquarters	2	1	0	1	0	0	0	0	0	0	0	0	0	0	0	0	0
Three Machine Gun Platoons, each																	
Platoon HQ	1	0	0	0	2	0	0	0	0	0	0	0	0	0	3	1	1
Three MG Squads	0	0	0	1	4	0	0	1	0	0	0	0	0	0	0	0	0
Anti-Tank Rifle Platoon																	
Platoon Headquarters	1	0	0	0	1	0	0	0	0	0	0	0	0	0	2	1	0
Three AT Rifle Squads, each	0	0	0	2	5	0	0	0	3	0	0	0	0	0	0	0	0
Anti-Tank Gun Platoon																	
Platoon Headquarters	1	0	0	1	3	0	0	0	0	0	0	0	0	0	0	0	0
Two AT Squads, each	0	0	0	2	4	0	0	0	0	0	0	0	1	0	4	1	0
Mortar Company																	
Company Headquarters	1	1	0	1	0	0	0	0	0	0	0	0	0	0	0	0	0
Three Mortar Platoons, each																	
Platoon HQ	1	0	0	0	3	0	0	0	0	0	0	0	0	0	3	0	3
Three Mortar Squads, each	0	0	0	1	4	0	0	0	0	0	1	0	0	0	0	0	0
Medical Platoon	0	0	1	1	3	0	0	0	0	0	0	0	0	0	1	0	1
Trains Platoon	1	0	0	2	9	0	0	0	0	0	0	0	0	0	14	4	3
Submachine Gun Company																	
Company Headquartes	2	1	0	2	2	7	0	0	0	0	0	0	0	0	0	0	0
Three Submachine Gun Platoons, each	1	0	0	6	24	31	0	0	0	0	0	0	0	0	0	0	0
Anti-Tank Rifle Company																	
Company Headquarters	2	1	0	1	0	0	0	0	0	0	0	0	0	0	0	0	0
Three Anti-Tank Rifle Platoons, each																	
Platoon Headquarters	1	0	0	1	1	0	0	0	0	0	0	0	0	0	2	1	0
Three AT Rifle Squads, each	0	0	0	1	6	0	0	0	3	0	0	0	0	0	0	0	0
Anti-Tank Battery																	
Battery Headquarters	2	1	0	1	0	0	0	0	0	0	0	0	0	0	2	0	0
Three Anti-Tank Platoons, each	1	0	0	4	12	0	0	0	0	0	0	0	2	0	8	1	0
Infantry Gun Battery	6	1	0	14	53	6	0	0	0	0	0	0	0	4	49	12	3
Mortar Battery	5	1	0	17	43	0	0	0	0	0	0	7	0	0	0	*8	0
Medical Company	0	0	7	4	22	0	0	0	0	0	0	0	0	0	16	6	3
Veterinary Hospital	0	0	1	1	1	0	0	0	0	0	0	0	0	0	1	0	0
Weapons Repair Shop	0	0	3	7	1	0	0	0	0	0	0	0	0	0	0	0	0
Trains Shop	0	0	0	0	3	0	0	0	0	0	0	0	0	0	0	0	0
Supply (Transport) Company	4	1	0	8	26	0	0	0	0	0	0	0	0	0	60	29	1

motor trucks

Table 1.9 Infantry regiment (TO 04/551), from December 1942.

	Officers	Political Officers	Warrant Officers	NCOs	Other Ranks	Submachine Guns	Anti-Tank Rifles	76mm Field Guns	122mm Howitzers	Trucks	Tractors	Horses	Wagons	Carts
Regiment Headquarters	15	3	4	2	0	0	0	0	0	0	0	6	0	0
Headquarters Battery	4	1	0	10	39	2	0	0	0	0	0	19	4	4
Two Artillery Battalions, each														
Battalion Headquarters	4	1	2	0	0	0	0	0	0	0	0	2	0	0
Reconnaissance Squad	0	0	0	1	3	1	0	0	0	0	0	4	0	0
Survey Platoon	1	0	0	3	8	0	0	0	0	0	0	3	0	2
Signal Platoon	1	0	0	5	18	0	0	0	0	0	0	4	0	2
Two Field Gun Batteries, each														
Battery HQ & Platoon	3	1	0	7	12	1	0	0	0	0	0	8	0	1
Two Firing Platoons, each	1	0	0	4	18	1	0	2	0	0	0	23	4	0
Field Howitzer Battery														
Battery HQ & Platoon	3	1	0	7	13	1	0	0	0	0	1	8	0	1
Two Firing Platoons, each	1	0	0	6	16	1	2	0	2	0	2	11	4	0
Ammunition Platoon	1	0	0	3	24	0	0	0	0	0	0	49	24	0
Trains	0	0	0	4	7	0	0	0	0	0	0	8	1	3
One Artillery Battalion														
Battalion HQ & Reconnaissance Squad				*as above*										
Survey Platoon	1	0	0	2	6	0	0	0	0	0	0	3	0	2
Signal Platoon	1	0	0	5	15	0	0	0	0	0	0	3	0	2
One Field Gun Battery				*as above*										
Field Howitzer Battery				*as above*										
Ammunition Platoon	1	0	0	2	20	0	0	0	0	0	0	41	20	0
Trains	0	0	0	4	5	0	0	0	0	0	0	5	1	2
Regimental Trains Elements	2	0	5	11	28	0	0	0	0	5	0	27	14	2

Table 1.10 Infantry division artillery regiment (TO 04/552), from December 1942.

each division. In fairness it should be pointed out, however, that these new divisions were substantially smaller (about 11,000 men compared with 14,500 for the pre-war divisions) and that the guns, although still 45mm, were being replaced by models with longer barrels.

The regimental structure was little changed aside from a further reduction in the size of the mounted scout platoon and the elimination of the marginally useful anti-tank mortar platoon.[6] Altogether the infantry regiment was reduced slightly in size, from 2,517 to 2,474. Light weapons firepower, however, was increased from 108 light and 27 medium MGs to 162 light and 36 medium MGs. The divisional artillery complement remained essentially unchanged, consisting of 2 full-strength battalions and one 2-battery battalion, for a total of twenty 76mm guns and twelve 122mm howitzers.

At the divisional level the main changes were the elimination of two units, the AA battery and the machine gun battalion. The former had been rendered less useful by the declining fortunes of the Luftwaffe. The latter had been partially replaced by the assignment to each rifle company of its own

Maxim gun while at the same time being less useful by virtue of the increasing Soviet emphasis on offensive operations.

The signal company was reduced further in strength, to 130 men, primarily through reduction in trains elements. The radio platoon held one Type 'RBS' high-power set for communications with corps or Army HQ, and six 'RB' sets for its internal net. Each of the three wire platoons held about 33 km of wire and eighteen telephones to establish communications with subordinate HQs.

The guards infantry division, which for the first time had its own unique set of TO&Es, differed from the regular division primarily in its assignment of infantry support weapons. In the rifle company the machine gun squad was enlarged to a platoon by the simple expedient of adding a platoon leader and a second gun squad. The machine gun company was also expanded by adding a fourth gun squad to each platoon. The battalion anti-tank rifle platoon was expanded to a small company of two 8-gun platoons. At the regimental level the practice of assigning a second sub-machine gun company to each regiment was continued, while the heavy mortar battery received an eighth weapon.

At the division level the main changes were the expansion of the third battalion in the artillery regiment to full 3-battery strength through the addition of a second 76mm gun battery, and expansion of the training company to a battalion. The pioneer battalion was also expanded: to 254 men in three companies, each of three platoons. The battalion was armed with 26 pistols and 152 rifles, but was not well equipped with engineer equipment, having only six horses and three trucks for transport, and two small rafts for water-crossing operations.

With these changes the Red Army had finally found the basic organizational format that would see them through the rest of the war in Europe.

NEW DIRECTIONS: 1943–4

Just as the issuance of standard sets of TO&Es for the regular and guards infantry divisions reflected a growing awareness of the need to stabilize the army organizationally after its often haphazard expansion of late 1941 and early 1942, so too did another change in policy reflect a new phase of Soviet thinking about maintaining their army structure. Previously, the emphasis had been on forming new divisions and brigades to replace those lost so disastrously in the German offensives, but as the situation stabilized more attention was paid to maintaining existing formations so as to take advantage of their now-experienced leadership and unit integrity.

Even the ruthless mobilization of all assets by Stalin could not both expand and maintain the huge Red Army. Although the mobilization of new units was dramatically trimmed between late 1942 and the autumn of 1943, it proved impossible to pass enough replacements to the existing divisions to keep them up to strength. This was a different problem from that of late 1941, and even the summer of 1942, when large numbers of entire divisions simply disappeared in the encirclement battles. Instead of amputations, the Red Army was now facing a bleeding process that gradually attritted, but did not destroy, the field units.

With insufficient replacements available to keep these units up to full strength, the Stavka adopted the only other recourse available: an official acceptance of reduced size. On 22 August 1943 a 'reduced strength' variant of the basic infantry regiment TO&E (No. 04/550) was authorized. Under this new table the basic building block, the rifle platoon, was reduced to the platoon leader and three squads, each of a sergeant and ten privates. Each squad was provided with a single light machine gun, to give the rifle

Food was a constant problem for the Red Army, especially in 1941–3 when the Germans occupied so much of the best farmland. Black bread, soup and *kasha* (a grain porridge) were the staples, livened up by an occasional delicacy such as a 'soldier's sandwich' – a slab of fat on black bread.

Shortages of weapons led to considerable irregularity in infantry firepower. This platoon has been equipped with the dismounted version of the Degtaryev *DT* tank machine gun instead of the usual *DP* light machine gun. The unit is otherwise well equipped, including at least one *SVT*-40 automatic rifle evident. The soldier in the foreground wears the ubiquitous fur pile cap, called 'fish fur' by Russian troops since the enlisted men's caps were made of synthetic rather than natural fur.

company a total of nine such weapons, compared to eighteen in the original organization. The company's 50mm mortar platoon was deleted entirely from the organization, although the machine gun section remained.

At the battalion level the machine gun company and the mortar company were both reduced to two platoons (six weapons), while less significant changes were made to the regimental elements. In sum, the infantry regiment was reduced from its original strength of 2,443 men to 2,017.

Few changes were made in the division base, with the artillery regiment remaining unchanged, while the reconnaissance company pioneer battalion, signal company and chemical company each lost ten men; and the motor transport and medical battalions each lost five.

It is not clear if this reduced TO&E was applied only to combat-weary divisions for which a low priority in replacements had been assigned, or whether new divisions were actually formed on this TO&E, but the latter seems unlikely, and in any event

	Officers	Political Officers	Warrant Officers	NCOs	Other Ranks	Submachine Guns	Anti-Tank Rifles	Anti-Tank Guns	Field Cars	Trucks
Battalion Headquarters	4	1	2	0	0	0	0	0	0	0
Headquarters Platoon	1	0	0	3	8	3	0	0	0	1
Three Anti-Tank Batteries, each										
Battery Headquarters	1	0	1	5	6	1	0	0	0	1
Two Anti-Tank Platoons, each	1	0	0	6	8	12	0	2	0	2
Anti-Tank Rifle Company										
Company Headquarters	1	0	0	2	0	0	0	0	0	0
Four AT Rifle Platoons, each	1	0	0	6	15	13	8	9	9	9
Ammunition Platoon	0	0	2	1	4	0	0	0	0	3
Trains	0	0	0	2	3	0	0	0	1	2

Table 1.11 Divisional anti-tank battalion (TO 04/569), from December 1943.

not many rifle divisions were formed subsequently.

Another pressing need was a requirement to upgrade the anti-tank protection held by the rifle divisions. By mid-1943 the 45mm gun was clearly marginal as a tank-killer, although its small size and light weight made it useful as a battalion (and even regimental) weapon. First priority for the heavier weapons had been given to the independent anti-tank divisions and brigades but by late 1943 enough had been produced to begin considering supplying them to the infantry divisions. Thus, in mid-December 1943 a new TO&E (No. 04/569) was issued for a divisional anti-tank battalion equipped with 76mm guns.

The new battalion was notable not only for the introduction of the new, more powerful, gun but for other features as well. The earlier 45mm battalion had held only one radio, in the battalion signal platoon. The new 76mm battalion not only had two

radios in the battalion signal platoon, but two more in each gun battery, making the unit much more responsive. In addition, the gun crews were provided with sub-machine guns to enable them to defend their pieces better against enemy close-assault infantry.

This new TO&E notwithstanding, it seems unlikely that many rifle divisions actually received the 76mm guns since first priority continued to go to the separate anti-tank units, with mechanized formations apparently receiving second priority.

Anti-tank protection was not the only concern of the organization department; apparently they had been premature in their dismissal of the Luftwaffe. On 30 May 1944 a new TO&E (No. 04/578) was issued for a divisional anti-aircraft machine gun company. This unit was composed of a 7-man headquarters platoon, six AA MG platoons and a 6-man trains. Each of the 14-man firing platoons was provided with three trucks, each mounting a 12.7mm heavy machine gun on its rear bed. The trains group had another truck, while the company HQ held a field car and the company's only radio. Each infantry division received one such company for air defence purposes, although the heavy machine guns probably served well in the ground-support role as well.

By this time, however, it was becoming apparent that the Soviet force structure of 500-plus divisions simply exceeded their capacity to support it. Replacement personnel could not be found to make up for combat losses and the field formations, particularly the rifle divisions, began shrinking rapidly. The reduction in strength authorized in late 1943 had managed to keep up the pretence that all was well for a while, but by mid-1944 more drastic action was necessary. Either some of the rifle divisions would have to be demobilized and their personnel used to fill out other units, or divisional strengths far below the envisioned norms would have to be accepted. The *Stavka* opted for the latter alternative.

Authority to promulgate emergency TO&Es for understrength units was delegated to the front commanders. One example of the result was the order issued by the First Baltic Front in July 1944. This provided for a four-stage reduction in division strength; the smallest option being 4,400 men, with intermediate levels at 5,327, 6,245 and 7,189 men. The reductions in division strength were realized primarily through reducing the size of the infantry regiments – not surprising since these units invariably took the vast majority of the casualties and thus tended to operate well below strength with any shortage of replacements.

In divisions where the strength had fallen to about 7,189 men, and for which replacements were not expected, the infantry

regiments were to be reorganized slightly by losing the mounted scout platoon and the AT rifle company, along with proportional personnel reductions in other elements. At the battalion level the machine gun company lost three of its twelve squads, while the mortar company lost three of its nine weapons. In the rifle company the 2-gun mortar platoon was deleted entirely, while each rifle platoon lost one squad.

When division strength fell to about 6,245 the regiment was again reorganized, with the AT battery this time being reduced from six guns to four. The rifle company was dramatically decreased in size, falling to two platoons each of three squads. When division strength fell to about 5,327 the rifle company structure returned to three triangular platoons (albeit with one less man per squad), but the regiment now consisted of only two battalions. In the final and smallest configuration the regiment consisted of two battalions each with two rifle companies, each in turn of two 3-squad platoons. This reduced regimental strength to 900 men, a battalion-size formation by any other standards, although well supported by heavy weapons.

Another example of a reduced-strength authorization table was that issued by the Third Ukrainian Front in October 1944. This differed in format in that it defined the personnel who were to be deleted from the original TO&Es rather than the remaining structure, the route taken by the First Baltic Front.

Under the first strength reduction (to reach an 8,000-man division) the rifle companies each lost their platoon sergeants, snipers, a crewman for each 50mm mortar, a machine gun crewman and a medic. The machine gun company lost one of its platoons and three men in each of the remaining two platoons, while the mortar company lost one crewman per mortar. At

An archetypal Soviet infantry section advances in the rubble of yet another shattered Russian city. The *PPSh* sub-machine gun was the preferred weapon in close-in streetfighting, and was a popular trophy by German infantry who prized its rugged construction.

the regimental level the mounted scout platoon and the AT rifle company were deleted entirely. To reach a 7,000-man division each rifle company was further reduced by one squad per platoon. To reach the next step down the mortar company lost a full platoon.

Despite the adoption of these temporary TO&Es enough divisions were apparently kept on the original full-strength versions to warrant continued fine-tuning of the organization. Two changes to the divisional structure were ordered in October 1944. The first expanded the pioneer battalion from two companies to three, enhancing the assault,

river-crossing and mine warfare capabilities of the division. The second change was more apparent than real: on 25 October the divisional signal company TO&E was replaced by a new one (No. 04/548) for a signal battalion; in fact, with a total strength of only 143 men, this battalion represented little more than a minor reorganization of existing assets. The new battalion consisted of a 7-man headquarters, a 62-man HQ company (with switchboard, radio and messenger platoons), a 62-man wire company (with four 15-man platoons) and a 12-man trains element.

The old 130-man signal company included a radio platoon with an '*RBS*' transceiver for use in the corps/Army net and six 'RB' transceivers for the division net. The new battalion added only a single receiver to this structure. The old signal company had three wire platoons while the new signal battalion had four, but these latter held a total of only nine wire squads (each with a one-horse cart) so the actual increase in capabilities was probably not great. In addition, some further changes were made locally; an apparently popular one was to rearm one platoon in each rifle company entirely with sub-machine guns – in some cases such platoon kept its *DP* light machine guns and in others these were dropped.

THE FINAL CONFIGURATION: DECEMBER 1944

In December 1944 a new set of TO&Es for the infantry division was issued. Little detail is available on this new organization but it clearly made the division much more powerful. The anti-tank rifle company was finally dropped from the infantry regiment structure and an AA machine gun platoon added. A second sub-machine gun company was authorized for all infantry regiments, bringing them all up to the strength of guards regiments.

The artillery component was expanded to a brigade consisting of three artillery regiments, each with two battalion HQs and a total of five 4-gun batteries. One regiment was equipped with 76mm guns, one with 122mm howitzers and the third with mortars (120mm in practice, 160mm planned). The anti-tank battalion was finally standardized as a battalion with three 4-gun batteries of 76mm guns. The anti-aircraft battalion was restored to the division, this consisting of three 4-gun 37mm batteries and a heavy machine gun company.

An *SU*-76 assault gun battalion (with sixteen vehicles) was added to the guards divisions, replacing the former towed anti-tank

battalion. This was eventually applied to the standard rifle division TO&E in June 1945.

This new organization was not used extensively in Europe, seeing only trials usage, but was the standard organization (with some minor modifications ordered in June 1945) for the operations in Manchuria in August 1945, although few divisions appear to have had their new, expanded artillery component.

During the four years of combat the Soviet infantry division had gone from a heavy and well-balanced, if somewhat cumbersome, organization at the start of the war, through a desperate transitional phase that reflected shortages of both equipment and trained tactical leadership, to an extremely lean and offensively oriented formation. Characteristic of the later division structures was a high ratio of infantry support weapons, such as mortars, machine guns and anti-tank weapons to riflemen, although the organic division artillery was rather weak, the Soviets preferring instead to concentrate the available artillery into massed GHQ reserve elements. Another characteristic of the later divisions, although not an inherent organizational one, was an inability to maintain these divisions at near full strength, the Army having simply expanded beyond the ability of the available manpower pool to support it. This was not remedied until after Germany's fall when the Soviets were able to concentrate smaller forces against the Japanese Kwantung Army in 1945. The evolution of rifle division strength during the war is shown in Table 1.12.[7]

RIFLE BRIGADES: EXTEMPORIZING FIELD FORMATIONS

At the start of the war there were five rifle brigades on the strength of the Red Army: the 1st, 4th and 5th in the Far East, the 3rd as a garrison for the Baltic islands and the 8th on the Hango peninsula in Finland. The

	13-Sep-39	5-Apr-41	29-Jul-41	6-Dec-41	18-Mar-42	28-Jul-42	10-Dec-42	15-Jul-43	18-Dec-44	Jun-45
Personnel	18,841	14,483	10,859	11,626	12,725	10,386	9,435	9,380	11,706	11,780
Submachine Guns	0	1,204	171	582	655	711	727	1,084	3,594	3,557
Rifles & Carbines	n/a	10,420	8,341	8,565	9,375	7,241	6,474	6,274	6,330	6,188
Light Machine Guns	578	392	162	251	352	337	494	494	337	383
Medium Machine Guns	162	166	108	108	114	112	111	111	166	158
Quad AA MG	15	15	18	0	0	0	0	0	0	0
DShK Machine Guns	18	18	9	12	9	9	0	0	18	18
50mm Mortars	81	84	54	72	76	85	56	56	0	0
82mm Mortars	36	54	18	72	76	85	83	83	89	136
120mm Mortars	12	12	6	18	18	18	21	21	38	
AT Rifles	60	0	0	89	279	228	212	212	107	111
45mm AT Guns	54	54	18	18	30	30	48	48	18	66
57mm AT Guns	0	0	0	12	0	0	0	0	18	
37mm AA Guns	8	8	6	6	6	6	0	0	12	12
76mm AA Guns	4	4	4	0	0	0	0	0	0	0
76mm Guns	38	34	28	28	32	32	32	32	44	32
122mm Howitzers	28	32	8	8	12	12	12	12	20	20
152mm Howitzers	12	12	0	0	0	0	0	0	0	0
76mm SP Guns	0	0	0	0	0	0	0	0	0	13
Cars & Trucks	725	558	203	248	154	149	123	124	419	445
Tractors	92	99	5	0	15	15	15	15	0	0

Table 1.12 Rifle division evolution, 1939–45.

composition of those in the Far East is not known but each of the others was built around two infantry regiments and a light artillery regiment, presumably on the standard TO&Es of the time.

The great expansion of the brigades, however, came shortly after the war began. The new, simpler divisions of July 1941 had been mandated in order to speed up the activation of new units. Such was the need for new infantry units to slow down the German blitzkrieg, however, that an even quicker expedient was needed. The result was a new type of formation in the Soviet Army – the infantry brigade. This organizational format was purely a stopgap measure designed to field combat-capable infantry units in a shorter period of time than it took to organize and train the more complex infantry divisions.

The personnel for these units were found from a variety of sources. Of 250 rifle brigades

formed by the Red Army, thirty-seven were Navy rifle brigades made up of sailors[8] and nineteen were student or cadet (kursantskie) rifle brigades formed by conversion of training units. Establishment of these expedient formations began in September 1941 and, except for a few anomalous units, the process ended in April 1942.

Essentially, an infantry brigade was one-third of an infantry division, consisting of an infantry regiment, an artillery battalion and smaller support units. Most of the early TO&Es for an infantry brigade are not available; they appear, however, simply to have taken a close variant of the standard divisional infantry regiments (TO&Es Nos 04/401, 04/601 and 04/751) as their baseline, modifying them by centralizing the mortars in accordance with the October 1941 amendment to the standard TO&Es and adding some support units.

Besides the regular Red Army, the Germans also had to contend with a sizeable partisan force in their rear areas. The partisan units depended on Soviet soldiers who had escaped from the encirclements early in the war, added to by young men trying to escape wholesale German round-ups for forced labour back in the Reich. Aside from tying down substantial numbers of German security troops, partisan formations caused serious problems for the Wehrmacht during operations in 1943. They contributed in no small way to the catastrophic defeat in Belorussia in the summer of 1944.

OCTOBER 1941: THE INITIAL EFFORTS

An example is provided by the infantry brigade organization mandated by TO&Es 04/730-744 of 15 October 1941 for the *kursantskie* brigades.[9] The basis for this structure was a hybrid of the infantry regiment mandated in July (TO&E 04/601) and December (04/751) of 1941.

The rifle company was similar to that of the July infantry regiment, having only two light machine guns (for four squads) per platoon, but lacking the mortar squads and with a greater number of sub-machine guns. The brigade anticipated the December infantry regiment, however, with its inclusion of a sub-machine gun company and an anti-tank rifle company. This was the smallest of the brigade organizations in use at the end of 1941, with a total strength of only 4,356 men. Other organizational forms were also used. Thus, the 79th Infantry Brigade had the following structure in mid-December 1941:

	Political Officers	Officers	Warrant Officers	NCOs	Other Ranks	Submachine Guns	Light Machine Guns	Medium Machine Guns	Heavy Machine Guns	Anti-Tank Guns	Anti-Tank Rifles	50mm Mortars	82mm Mortars	120mm Mortars	45mm AT Guns	76mm Field Guns	Field Guns	Field Cars	Trucks	Horses	Wagons	Carts
Brigade Headquarters																						
Command Group	18	10	21	9	21	1	0	0	0	0	0	0	0	0	0	0	0	3	2	13	0	0
NKVD Rifle Platoon	1	0	0	6	29	3	1	0	0	0	0	0	0	0	0	0	0	0	0	0	0	0
Anti-Aircraft MG Platoon	1	0	0	6	9	0	0	0	3	0	0	0	0	0	0	0	0	0	3	0	0	0
Signal Battalion																						
Battalion HQ & trains elements	4	1	5	9	9	0	0	0	0	0	0	0	0	0	0	0	0	1	5	0	0	0
Headquarters Company	5	1	0	11	38	0	0	0	0	0	0	0	0	0	0	0	0	0	5	4	0	0
Wire Company	5	1	0	8	49	5	0	0	0	0	0	0	0	0	0	0	0	0	3	4	0	4
Reconnaissance Company																						
Company Headquarters	2	1	0	4	3	0	0	0	0	0	0	0	0	0	0	0	0	0	0	2	1	0
Two Rifle Platoons, each	1	0	0	3	16	5	0	0	0	0	0	0	0	0	0	0	0	0	0	0	0	0
Chemical Platoon	1	0	0	2	18	0	0	0	0	0	0	0	0	0	0	0	0	0	0	4	2	0
Three Infantry Battalions, each																						
Battalion Headquarters	7	3	3	2	0	0	0	0	0	0	0	0	0	0	0	0	0	0	0	10	0	0
Signal Platoon	1	0	0	4	19	0	0	0	0	0	0	0	0	0	0	0	0	0	0	2	0	2
Infantry Reconnaissance Platoon	1	1	0	5	43	2	0	0	0	0	0	0	0	0	0	0	0	0	0	0	0	0
Submachine Gun Platoon	1	0	0	7	25	33	0	0	0	0	0	0	0	0	0	0	0	0	0	0	0	0
Anti-Tank Mortar Platoon	1	0	0	3	23	0	0	0	0	0	0	0	7	0	0	0	0	0	0	6	0	3
Three Rifle Companies, each																						
Company HQ	2	1	0	3	7	0	0	0	0	0	0	0	0	0	0	0	0	0	0	0	0	0
Three Rifle Platoons, each	1	0	0	9	41	10	2	0	0	0	0	0	0	0	0	0	0	0	0	0	0	0
Machine Gun Company																						
Company HQ	2	1	0	2	1	0	0	0	0	0	0	0	0	0	0	0	0	0	0	0	0	0
Three MG Platoons, each	1	0	0	8	20	0	0	4	0	0	0	0	0	0	0	0	0	0	0	4	2	0
Supply Platoon	1	0	0	4	29	0	0	0	0	0	0	0	0	0	0	0	0	0	0	54	27	0
other services	0	0	6	6	30	1	0	0	0	0	0	0	0	0	0	0	0	0	0	12	6	0
Mortar Battalion																						
Battalion HQ & trains elements	5	3	6	6	5	0	0	0	0	0	0	0	0	0	0	0	0	0	0	4	0	0
Signal Platoon	1	0	0	1	12	0	0	0	0	0	0	0	0	0	0	0	0	0	0	1	0	1
Three Mortar Companies, each																						
Company HQ	2	1	0	1	5	0	0	0	0	0	0	0	0	0	0	0	0	0	0	1	0	1
Two Light Platoons, each	1	0	0	8	8	0	0	0	0	0	0	4	0	0	0	0	0	0	0	4	2	0
Two Medium Platoons, each	1	0	0	8	20	0	0	0	0	0	0	0	4	0	0	0	0	0	0	8	4	0
Supply Platoon	1	0	0	3	32	0	0	0	0	0	0	0	0	0	0	0	0	0	0	59	28	3
Heavy Mortar Battalion																						
Battalion HQ & trains elements	3	1	3	3	16	0	0	0	0	0	0	0	0	0	0	0	0	0	0	*108	0	2
Two Mortar Batteries, each																						
Battery HQ	2	1	0	2	6	0	0	0	0	0	0	0	0	0	0	0	0	0	0	?	0	1
Two Mortar Platoons, each	1	0	0	4	16	0	0	0	0	0	0	0	0	2	0	0	0	0	0	?	2	0
Supply Platoon	0	0	1	3	11	0	0	0	0	0	0	0	0	0	0	0	0	0	0	16	8	0
Artillery Battalion																						
Battalion HQ & trains elements	5	3	8	8	25	0	0	0	0	0	0	0	0	0	0	0	0	0	0	*266	8	2
Signal Platoon	1	0	0	5	20	0	0	0	0	0	0	0	0	0	0	0	0	0	0	6	0	3
Two Field Gun Batteries, each	5	1	0	19	66	0	2	0	0	0	0	0	0	0	0	4	0	0	0	?	8	1
Infantry Gun Battery	5	1	0	12	53	0	0	0	0	0	0	0	0	0	0	0	4	0	0	?	0	9
Supply Platoon	1	0	0	3	24	0	0	0	0	0	0	0	0	0	0	0	0	0	0	30	15	0
Anti-Tank Battalion																						
Battalion HQ & trains elements	3	1	4	10	19	0	0	0	0	0	0	0	0	0	0	0	0	1	9	0	0	0
Three Anti-Tank Batteries, each																						
Battery HQ	2	1	0	1	3	0	0	0	0	0	0	0	0	0	0	0	0	0	0	0	0	0
Two AT Platoons, each	1	0	0	4	12	0	0	0	0	0	0	0	0	0	2	0	0	0	2	0	0	0
Anti-Tank Rifle Company																						
Company Headquarters	2	1	1	2	0	0	0	0	0	0	0	0	0	0	0	0	0	0	0	0	0	0
Four AT Rifle Platoons, each	1	0	0	9	24	0	0	0	0	0	12	0	0	0	0	0	0	0	0	8	4	0
Submachine Gun Company																						
Company Headquarters	2	1	0	2	2	7	0	0	0	0	0	0	0	0	0	0	0	0	0	2	1	0
Three SMG Platoons, each	1	0	0	6	24	31	0	0	0	0	0	0	0	0	0	0	0	0	0	0	0	0
Pioneer Company	5	1	2	18	94	0	0	0	0	0	0	0	0	0	0	0	0	0	0	20	7	1
Motor Transport Company	5	1	7	20	60	0	0	0	0	0	0	0	0	0	0	0	0	0	54	0	0	0
Medical Company	0	1	17	10	35	0	0	0	0	0	0	0	0	0	0	0	0	0	8	0	0	0

* total for all subordinate units.

Table 1.13 'Cadet' rifle brigade (TO 04/730-744), from October 1941.

Brigade HQ (3 AA heavy machine guns)
Signal company
  Three infantry battalions, each
    Three rifle companies, each (12 light machine guns)
    Machine gun company (12 machine guns)
Light mortar battalion
  Three light mortar companies, each (8 × 50mm mortars, 8 × 82mm mortars)
Heavy mortar battalion
  Three heavy mortar batteries, each (8 × 120mm mortars)
Artillery battalion
  Three batteries, each (4 × 76mm guns)
Anti-tank battalion
  Two AT companies, each (6 × 45mm anti-tank weapons)
  AT rifle company (unknown number of anti-tank rifles)
Sub-machine gun company
Pioneer company
Motor transport company (80-ton trucks)
Medical unit

This gave the brigade a strength of 399 officers, 868 NCOs and 3,213 other ranks, or a total of 4,480 men. Personal weapons were to include 2,837 bolt-action rifles, 1,173 semi-automatic rifles and 100 sub-machine guns. Other allocations included 868 horses, 163 trucks and 30 radios. This too was apparently one of the smaller types of infantry brigade, for the Soviets have noted that by the end of 1941 these units 'were maintained in accordance with three different tables of organization and equipment and had a strength of 4,356 to 6,000 men'.[10]

APRIL 1942: THE SECOND GENERATION (TO&E 04/230–241)

These infantry brigades were apparently successful short-term expedients, for they were raised in large numbers. On 17 April 1942 a new set of TO&Es (No. 04/230–241)

for the infantry brigade was published that added a fourth organizational format for these formations. These were closely derived from, but not exact copies of, the TO&Es issued a month earlier for the infantry division (Nos 04/200–212). Aside from increasing the allocation of light machine guns, adding an AT rifle platoon to each infantry battalion and subordinating the brigade's AT rifle company to the AT battalion, this new structure made only detail changes to the brigade organization of the previous October to save 168 men in strength.

The brigade's infantry battalions (officially denominated independent infantry battalions since there was no regimental HQ) were strengthened versions of those in the 04/200-series infantry division TO&Es. They included infantry scout, sub-machine gun and anti-tank mortar platoons not found in the standard infantry battalion, while the rifle companies had three times as many sub-machine guns, although ten fewer men. The brigade's light mortar battalion was similar to that found in the infantry regiment but had a supply platoon with twenty-five two-horse wagons lacking in the regular battalion.

The brigade's artillery battalion consisted of three 76mm gun batteries, two equipped with Model 1939 field guns and one with Model 1927 regimental guns. Like the 04/200-series TO&E infantry division, the 04/230-series TO&E infantry brigade included a heavy mortar battalion with the effective 120mm Model 1938 weapons. In the case of the brigade's heavy mortar battalion, however, there were only two 4-gun horse-drawn batteries in place of the normal three 6-gun motorized batteries.

The one element of the infantry brigade that was just as strong as that in the infantry division was, perhaps not surprisingly, the anti-tank battalion. In fact, the brigade's AT battalion was actually somewhat stronger

Anti-aircraft defence in Soviet infantry formations was poor and led to expedient solutions. The standard method was simply to use whatever weapons were at hand. This staged air raid drill reveals the usual motley selection of weapons found in a typical infantry unit in the middle of the war. The machine gun is a captured German *MG.34*, and besides the *PPSh* sub-machine guns, the soldier to the far left is armed with a captured German Schmeisser *MP.38*.

than the division's by virtue of having an extra 3-gun squad in each AT rifle platoon.

Radio communications were little changed from the divisional structure, with one radio assigned to each infantry, light mortar and AT battalion HQ, none in the heavy mortar battalion, three in each field gun battery, four in the infantry gun battery, two in the artillery battalion HQ and two in the radio platoon of the signal battalion.

Service support was somewhat more decentralized in the infantry brigade than in the division. Under the normal divisional structure an infantry battalion's supply platoon held three cargo wagons and four field kitchen wagons, while a light mortar battalion's supply platoon held seven cargo wagons and two field kitchen wagons, each pulled by two horses. In the brigade format, however, the infantry battalion supply platoon had sixteen wagons (plus five kitchens) and the light mortar battalion twenty-five wagons (and three kitchens). In lieu of the infantry regiment's supply company with forty-two 2-horse cargo wagons (and an expected one-third share of the divisional transport company's sixty-one

Unit	Political Officers	Officers	Warrant Officers	NCOs	Other Ranks	Submachine Guns	Light Machine Guns	Medium Machine Guns	Heavy Machine Guns	Anti-Tank Rifles	Anti-Tank Guns	50mm Mortars	82mm Mortars	120mm Mortars	45mm AT Guns	76mm Field Guns	Field Cars	Trucks	Horses	Wagons	Carts
Brigade Headquarters																					
Command Group	19	10	21	7	14	0	0	0	0	0	0	0	0	0	0	0	3	1	5	0	0
NKVD Rifle Platoon	1	0	0	4	13	3	1	0	0	0	0	0	0	0	0	0	0	0	0	0	0
Anti-Aircraft MG Platoon	1	0	0	6	9	0	0	0	3	0	0	0	0	0	0	0	0	3	0	0	0
Signal Battalion																					
Battalion HQ & trains elements	4	1	5	10	5	0	0	0	0	0	0	0	0	0	0	0	1	3	0	0	0
Headquarters Company	5	1	0	12	36	0	0	0	0	0	0	0	0	0	0	0	0	4	0	0	0
Wire Company	5	1	0	8	44	0	0	0	0	0	0	0	0	0	0	0	0	3	8	0	8
Reconnaissance Company																					
Company Headquarters	2	1	0	4	3	0	0	0	0	0	0	0	0	0	0	0	0	0	2	1	0
Two Rifle Platoons, each	1	0	0	3	16	5	0	0	0	0	0	0	0	0	0	0	0	0	0	0	0
Chemical Platoon	1	0	0	5	15	0	0	0	0	0	0	0	0	0	0	0	0	0	4	2	0
Three Infantry Battalions, each																					
Battalion Headquarters	7	3	3	2	0	0	0	0	0	0	0	0	0	0	0	0	0	0	3	0	0
Signal Platoon	1	0	0	4	17	0	0	0	0	0	0	0	0	0	0	0	0	0	2	0	2
Infantry Reconnaissance Platoon	1	1	0	5	42	3	0	0	0	0	0	0	0	0	0	0	0	0	0	0	0
Submachine Gun Platoon	1	0	0	7	25	33	0	0	0	0	0	0	0	0	0	0	0	0	0	0	0
Anti-Tank Mortar Platoon	1	0	0	3	19	0	0	0	0	0	0	7	0	0	0	0	0	0	5	0	3
Anti-Tank Rifle Platoon	1	0	0	9	12	0	0	0	0	8	0	0	0	0	0	0	0	0	0	0	0
Three Rifle Companies, each																					
Company HQ	2	1	0	3	6	3	0	0	0	0	0	0	0	0	0	0	0	0	0	0	0
Three Rifle Platoons, each	1	0	0	9	41	9	4	0	0	0	0	0	0	0	0	0	0	0	0	0	0
Machine Gun Company																					
Company HQ	2	1	0	1	0	0	0	0	0	0	0	0	0	0	0	0	0	0	0	0	0
Three MG Platoons, each	1	0	0	8	20	0	0	4	0	0	0	0	0	0	0	0	0	0	4	2	0
Medical Platoon	0	0	3	1	9	0	0	0	0	0	0	0	0	0	0	0	0	0	6	3	0
Supply Platoon	1	0	0	4	23	0	0	0	0	0	0	0	0	0	0	0	0	0	37	16	5
other trains	0	0	2	1	6	0	0	0	0	0	0	0	0	0	0	0	0	0	2	1	0
Mortar Battalion																					
Battalion HQ & trains elements	5	3	6	6	2	0	0	0	0	0	0	0	0	0	0	0	0	0	2	0	0
Signal Platoon	1	0	0	2	11	0	0	0	0	0	0	0	0	0	0	0	0	0	1	0	1
Three Mortar Companies, each																					
Company HQ	2	1	0	1	4	0	0	0	0	0	0	0	0	0	0	0	0	0	1	0	1
Two Light Platoons, each	1	0	0	8	8	0	0	0	0	0	0	4	0	0	0	0	0	0	4	2	0
Two Medium Platoons, each	1	0	0	8	20	0	0	0	0	0	0	0	4	0	0	0	0	0	8	4	0
Supply Platoon	1	0	0	3	29	0	0	0	0	0	0	0	0	0	0	0	0	0	54	25	3
Heavy Mortar Battalion																					
Battalion HQ & trains elements	3	1	3	3	14	0	0	0	0	0	0	0	0	0	0	0	0	0	10	1	2
Two Mortar Batteries, each																					
Battery HQ	2	1	0	2	6	0	0	0	0	0	0	0	0	0	0	0	0	0	2	0	1
Two Mortar Platoons, each	1	0	0	4	16	0	0	0	0	0	0	0	0	2	0	0	0	0	8	2	0
Supply Platoon	0	0	1	3	11	0	0	0	0	0	0	0	0	0	0	0	0	0	32	8	0
Field Artillery Battalion																					
Battalion HQ & trains elements	5	3	8	8	19	0	0	0	0	0	0	0	0	0	0	0	0	0	30	8	2
Signal Platoon	1	0	0	5	20	0	0	0	0	0	0	0	0	0	0	0	0	0	3	0	3
Two Field Gun Batteries, each	5	1	0	19	63	0	0	0	0	0	0	0	0	0	0	4	0	0	61	8	1
Infantry Gun Battery	5	1	0	12	56	0	0	0	0	0	0	0	0	0	0	4	0	0	52	8	1
Supply Platoon	1	0	0	3	19	0	0	0	0	0	0	0	0	0	0	0	0	0	52	13	0
Anti-Tank Battalion																					
Battalion HQ & trains elements	3	1	4	8	14	0	0	0	0	0	0	0	0	0	0	0	1	5	0	0	0
Three Anti-Tank Batteries, each																					
Battery HQ	2	1	0	1	1	0	0	0	0	0	0	0	0	0	0	0	0	0	0	0	0
Two AT Platoons, each	1	0	0	4	8	0	0	0	0	0	0	0	0	0	2	0	0	2	0	0	0
Anti-Tank Rifle Company																					
Company HQ	2	1	0	2	1	0	0	0	0	0	0	0	0	0	0	0	0	0	0	0	0
Four AT Rifle Platoons, each	1	0	0	9	20	1	0	0	0	12	0	0	0	0	0	0	0	0	0	0	0
Submachine Gun Company																					
Company Headquarters	2	1	0	2	2	7	0	0	0	0	0	0	0	0	0	0	0	0	2	1	0
Three SMG Platoons, each	1	0	0	6	24	31	0	0	0	0	0	0	0	0	0	0	0	0	0	0	0
Pioneer Company																					
Company HQ & Trains	2	1	2	3	8	0	0	0	0	0	0	0	0	0	0	0	0	0	17	6	1
Three Pioneer Platoons, each	1	0	0	5	24	0	0	0	0	0	0	0	0	0	0	0	0	0	0	0	0
Supply (Motor Transport) Company	4	1	7	18	47	0	0	0	0	0	0	0	0	0	0	0	0	47	0	0	0
Medical Company	0	1	17	10	35	0	0	0	0	0	0	0	0	0	0	0	0	8	0	0	0

* total for all subordinate units.

Table 1.14 Rifle brigade (TO 04/230-241), from April 1941.

trucks), the brigade had a supply and transport company with forty-seven trucks. The brigade, however, completely lacked the bakery and veterinary elements found in the division. These brigades were usually grouped together into infantry corps. Some three to five brigades made up a corps, giving it a strength of about 15,000 to 30,000 men.

In April 1942 a fourth infantry battalion was added to all infantry brigades, although without changing the rest of the brigade base. In July the brigades underwent the same reorganization as was applied to the divisional infantry. The light mortar battalions were dissolved and a 4-gun 50mm mortar platoon assigned to each rifle company and a 6-gun 82mm mortar company assigned to each infantry battalion. At about the same time a field bakery was assigned to the brigade. These changes brought the strength of the infantry brigade organized under TO&Es 04/230–241 up to 5,200 men.

JULY 1942: TO&E 04/330–341

Development of the infantry brigades continued in parallel with that of the infantry divisions. While the 04/200-series infantry division and 04/230-series infantry brigade TO&Es were being modified, two new sets of TO&Es were simultaneously being issued for subsequently raised infantry divisions (Nos 04/300–316) and infantry brigades (04/330–341), both issued in late July 1942.

The new brigades retained the square structure of four infantry battalions pioneered in April. As before, the independent infantry battalions of the infantry brigade were similar, but not identical, to the infantry battalions of the infantry division. The rifle companies under TO&E 04/331 lacked the 50mm mortar platoon found in their divisional equivalents but had three times as many sub-machine guns. The battalion mortar company was also

	Officers*	NCOs	Other Ranks	Submachine Guns	Bolt-Action Rifles	Semi-Automatic Rifles	Light Machine Guns	Medium Machine Guns	Heavy Machine Guns	Anti-Tank Rifles	Anti-Tank Guns	50mm Mortars	82mm Mortars	120mm Mortars	45mm AT Guns	76mm Guns	Horses
Brigade Headquarters	51	14	23	3	19	28	0	0	3	0	0	0	0	0	0	0	5
Signal Battalion	22	30	85	0	113	0	0	0	0	0	0	0	0	0	0	0	8
Reconnaissance Company	6	15	74	10	24	31	0	0	0	0	0	0	0	0	0	0	6
Four Infantry Battalions, each	58	193	677	126	220	403	36	12	0	8	7	12	6	0	0	0	89
Heavy Mortar Battalion	18	26	101	0	108	0	0	0	0	0	0	0	0	8	0	0	77
Artillery Battalion	35	66	240	4	0	263	0	0	0	0	0	0	0	0	0	12	244
Anti-Tank Battalion	30	73	170	0	199	0	0	0	0	48	0	0	0	0	12	0	0
Submachine Gun Company	6	20	74	100	0	0	0	0	0	0	0	0	0	0	0	0	17
Pioneer Company	8	18	80	0	6	0	0	0	0	0	0	0	0	0	0	0	0
Motor Transport Company	12	18	47	0	56	0	0	0	0	0	0	0	0	0	0	0	0
NKVD Platoon	1	4	13	0	0	14	0	0	0	0	0	0	0	0	0	0	0
Bakery	2	3	28	0	0	0	0	0	0	0	0	0	0	0	0	0	0

* includes political and warrant officers.
Note: transport assets other than horses not known.

Table 1.15 Rifle brigade summary (TO 04/230-243 as modified), from July 1942.

smaller, having only six 82mm weapons as opposed to the nine found in TO&E 04/301. On the other hand, the independent infantry battalion included several units not found in the divisional infantry battalion, in particular an AT mortar platoon (six AT mortars), a pioneer platoon and an infantry scout platoon. In addition, the anti-tank rifle platoon was expanded to a small company with two 9-gun platoons. Transport was inexplicably decreased – a sharp contrast from the earlier infantry brigades – and the battalion transport consisted of twenty-six 2-horse cargo wagons, eleven carts (including two for telephone wire-laying), four kitchen wagons and two trucks. All these elements gave the battalion a strength of 43 officers, 18 political officers, 194 NCOs and 649 other ranks, for a total of 904. This was considerably above the 609 men found in the divisional infantry battalion.

The rest of the brigade followed earlier practice, consisting of an artillery battalion, a heavy mortar battalion, an anti-tank battalion, reconnaissance and pioneer companies and service support. In addition, almost all new infantry brigades (and some older brigades) received either a machine gun battalion or a sub-machine gun battalion, or both. A machine gun battalion had a strength of 304 men divided into 3 companies, each with 9 medium-machine guns and 4 AT rifles. In a few cases the companies were expanded to twelve machine guns. The sub-machine gun battalion consisted of three or four sub-machine gun companies with the normal 100-man TO&E used in the infantry divisions.

No further infantry brigade TO&Es appear to have been issued, as this type of unit was falling out of favour once the initial war emergencies passed. They did, however, modify the AT mortar platoon organization in the autumn of 1942: in place of the original awkward 7-gun platoon held by the independent infantry battalions under TO&Es 04/740 and 04/231, a new TO&E was issued, presumably similar to that used in the new battalion TO&E (04/331). The new platoon consisted of a lieutenant, two sergeant section leaders, eighteen gun crew, and two privates for wagons. The platoon had six AT mortars and two 2-horse wagons.

No infantry brigades were raised after December 1942. The Germans claimed the outright destruction of only one infantry brigade in 1941, seven in 1942 and one in 1943. Instead, the vast majority were used to create new formations. A total of 114 rifle brigades were disbanded in 1943, of which about 75 were used in April–July to form 26 new rifle divisions, with another 16 brigades being used to form divisions later in the year. The remainder were mostly used to fill out depleted divisions.

MOUNTAIN INFANTRY

The Soviets also raised a number of specialized infantry formations, the largest of which was the mountain infantry division (*gornostrelkova divizia*). The Red Army had a total of nineteen mountain infantry divisions at the start of the war: six (44th, 58th, 60th, 72nd, 96th and 192nd) in the Special Kiev Military District (MD), one (28th) in the North Caucasus MD, seven (9th, 20th, 47th, 63rd, 76th, 77th and 138th) in the Transcaucasus MD, three (68th, 83rd and 194th) in the Central Asian MD, one (101st) in the Far Eastern MD and one (30th) in the independent 9th Army.

The mountain infantry division was a unique formation, consisting of four line regiments each of five line companies, with no intermediate battalion HQs. The original wartime TO&Es were drafted in August 1940 and thereafter subjected to periodic amendment, although no major changes were made during 1940–1. The mountain

Soviet weapon designers strove to keep the weight of new weapons to a minimum since transport was often scarce. Infantry support guns frequently had to be hauled by hand. This is a 76mm Model 1943 regimental gun in operation in the Malopolska region of south-eastern Poland during the 1944 summer fighting. This weapon used the lighter carriage of the standard 45mm anti-tank gun mated to a lightweight 76mm gun.

rifle squad, like its flatland contemporary, was provided with a single light machine gun, although in this case a pack horse was provided to carry the gun and ammunition. Each mountain rifle company also included a medium machine gun platoon with three squads, each with a Maxim machine gun and two pack horses.

For close-support weaponry the regiment was provided with a machine gun company and a mortar company, each with twelve weapons carried by pack horses. Also included was a mountain battery with four 76mm mountain guns (using a combination of pack horses to carry the guns and an immediate allocation of ammunition, and four ammunition wagons) and a pioneer company. Due to the difficulties of communications in the mountains the regimental signal company was far more capable than its counterparts in the flatland infantry. The radio platoon held twelve radio sets in two sections. The two wire/optical platoons each had four squads laying wire and manning shuttered lights for flashing messages. The company HQ platoon was made up of three squads: switchboard, air warning and messenger.

Divisional fire support was provided by two artillery regiments, one a mountain unit using primarily pack horses and one a draft 122mm howitzer unit. The 76mm mountain battery was composed of a 41-man headquarters element (with two radios), two 55-man firing platoons (each with two guns and fifty-two pack horses), a 4-man light-machine gun squad and a 12-man trains. The mortar battery was smaller, consisting of a 34-man HQ group (again with two radios), three 22-man firing platoons (each with two 107mm mountain mortars and twenty-six pack horses) and a 10-man trains. The battalion included two 76mm gun batteries and one 107mm mortar battery, along with a 37-man signal platoon that provided three

wire squads, one radio section (four radios) and one liaison squad.

Anti-tank protection for the division was allotted on a much-reduced scale in light of the natural protection from tanks afforded by rugged mountain terrain. In fact, the only AT weapons in the division were eight 45mm guns in the divisional AT battery. This unit was built around four 20-man platoons each with two guns, three trucks or tractors (one with a trailer) and one motorcycle. An ammunition platoon provided two more trucks with trailers, while the trains included two workshop trucks, two cargo trucks, one fuel truck and one kitchen trailer.

The divisional pioneer battalion's largest elements were its two pioneer companies. Each consisted of three platoons (one mounted on riding horses) but had no wagons or pack horses to carry equipment. Instead, this was mainly carried by the machinery company, which was motorized and included a suspension bridge platoon and two other equipment platoons.

Of the mountain infantry divisions in existence at the start of the war only one, the 9th of the North Caucasus MD, apparently distinguished itself. Those in the Special Kiev MD, of course, were completely out of their element in flat, rolling terrain and four were quickly destroyed, with the other two (the 58th and 96th) rebuilt as regular rifle divisions. Those in the mountains to the south, however, did not do much better. A post-war German account of fighting in the Caucasus stated:

In the mountains proper we encountered soldiers who said under interrogation that they were from mountain regiments, but these were not true *Gebirgsjaeger*. A number of them were quite elderly, more than thirty-five years of age, far too old for mountain warfare. Nor were these men Cherkassians but had come from low down on the Caspian Sea

	Officers	Political Officers	Warrant Officers	NCOs	Other Ranks	Light Machine Guns	Medium Machine Guns	Quad AA Machine Guns	50mm Mortars	82mm Mortars	76mm Mtn Guns	Field Cars	Trucks	Pack Horses	Draft Horses	Wagons	Carts
Regiment Headquarters	10	4	19	4	2	0	0	0	0	0	0	0	0	0	0	0	0
Headquarters Elements																	
Headquarters Platoon	1	0	0	6	28	1	0	0	0	0	0	1	1	11	0	0	0
Mounted Reconnaissance Platoon	1	0	0	3	21	3	0	0	0	0	0	0	0	4	0	0	0
Infantry Reconnaissance Platoon	1	0	0	5	44	4	0	0	0	0	0	0	0	6	0	0	0
Anti-Aircraft MG Platoon	1	0	0	3	12	0	0	3	0	0	0	0	3	0	0	0	0
Chemical Platoon	1	0	0	9	4	0	0	0	0	0	0	0	0	0	6	3	0
Band	0	0	1	1	11	0	0	0	0	0	0	0	0	0	0	0	0
Signal Company																	
Company HQ & trains elements	3	1	0	8	31	0	0	0	0	0	0	0	0	8	4	2	0
Radio Platoon	1	0	0	12	18	0	0	0	0	0	0	0	0	16	0	0	0
Two Wire/Optical Platoons, each	1	0	0	5	24	0	0	0	0	0	0	0	0	8	2	1	0
Five Rifle Companies, each																	
Company Headquarters	2	1	1	5	23	0	0	0	0	0	0	0	0	21	1	0	1
Three Rifle Platoons, each																	
Platoon HQ	1	0	0	1	2	0	0	0	0	0	0	0	0	0	0	0	0
Four Rifle Squads, each	0	0	0	1	11	1	0	0	0	0	0	0	0	1	0	0	0
Mortar Squad	0	0	0	1	3	0	0	0	1	0	0	0	0	0	0	0	0
Machine Gun Platoon																	
Platoon HQ	1	0	0	0	0	0	0	0	0	0	0	0	0	0	0	0	0
Three MG Squads, each	0	0	0	1	6	0	1	0	0	0	0	0	0	2	0	0	0
Machine Gun Company																	
Company HQ & trains elements	2	1	0	5	16	0	0	0	0	0	0	0	0	15	0	0	0
Three Machine Gun Platoons, each																	
Platoon HQ	1	0	0	0	0	0	0	0	0	0	0	0	0	0	0	0	0
Four MG Squads, each	0	0	0	1	6	0	1	0	0	0	0	0	0	2	0	0	0
Mortar Company																	
Company HQ & trains elements	2	1	0	3	14	0	0	0	0	0	0	0	0	7	0	0	0
Three Mortar Platoons, each																	
Platoon HQ	1	0	0	0	1	0	0	0	0	0	0	0	0	0	0	0	0
Four Mortar Squads, each	0	0	0	1	6	0	0	0	0	1	0	0	0	4	0	0	0
Mountain Battery																	
Battery HQ & trains elements	3	1	1	8	45	0	0	0	0	0	0	0	0	23	0	0	0
Two Firing Platoons, each	2	0	0	3	47	0	0	0	0	0	2	0	0	47	8	4	0
Pioneer Company																	
Company HQ & trains elements	2	1	0	3	7	0	0	0	0	0	0	0	0	0	10	5	0
Two Pioneer Platoons, each	1	0	0	5	32	0	0	0	0	0	0	0	0	0	0	0	0
Water Supply Squad	0	0	0	1	7	0	0	0	0	0	0	0	0	0	6	3	0
Medical Aid Station	0	0	6	10	38	0	0	0	0	0	0	0	0	3	16	7	2
Veterinary Section	0	0	2	4	9	0	0	0	0	0	0	0	0	2	4	2	0
Ammunition Supply Company	6	1	0	9	109	3	0	0	0	0	0	0	0	110	47	23	1
Trains Supply Company	4	1	0	4	44	0	0	0	0	0	0	0	0	20	1	0	1
Ordnance Section	0	0	3	1	10	0	0	0	0	0	0	0	0	0	0	0	0
other trains elements	0	0	0	3	13	0	0	0	0	0	0	0	0	0	0	0	0

NB: not shown, 91 riding horses, distribution not known.

Table 1.16 Mountain infantry regiment (TO 04/141), from August 1940 (as amended to October 1941).

As the Red Army shifted over to the offensive in the summer of 1943, river-crossing operations became increasingly important. Soviet tactics were seldom elegant but often effective. Instead of waiting for combat engineer equipment to arrive, infantry units were instructed to cross as quickly as possible using whatever means were available. Some specialized equipment, such as these inflatable assault craft, would be issued to units expected to reach the river, but commandeered boats were used as frequently.

. . . . Although the 20th was described as a mountain rifle division it had no formal training for that role and seemed to differ from a standard Red Army rifle division only in the large number of supply trains of mules and horses with which it was equipped.[11]

The original mountain divisions appear to have been allowed to wear down to a state of near uselessness, in much the same manner as the regular rifle divisions early in the war. The 28th Division was stricken from the rolls in September; the 194th Division was redesignated a rifle division in August 1941; and the 30th Division was rebuilt as a regular infantry division in October, followed by the 47th, 76th and 101st in December. In compensation two new mountain divisions were activated, both in the Caucasus, the 302nd in July and the 236th in December, although the latter was converted to a rifle division a month later. Thus, by the start of 1942 there remained only nine mountain divisions: the 9th, 20th, 63rd, 77th, 138th, 236th and 302nd in the Caucasus Front; and the 68th and 83rd in the Central Asian

Unit	Officers	Political Offs	Warrant Offs	NCOs	Other Ranks	Light MGs	Medium MGs	Quad AA MGs	Heavy MGs	107mm Mortars	45mm AT Guns	37mm AA Guns	76mm Mtn Guns	122mm Howitzers	Field Cars	Trucks	Riding Horses	Pack Horses	Draft Horses	Wagons	Carts
Division HQ	80			18	72	2	0	0	0	0	0	0	0	0	0	0	21	0	0	0	0
Signal Battalion																					
Battalion HQ & Company	10	4	6	19	76	0	0	0	0	0	0	0	0	0	2	5	*88	0	0	0	0
Radio Company	4	1	0	9	26	0	0	0	0	0	0	0	0	0	0	4	n/a	0	0	0	0
Wire/Optical Company	7	1	0	17	109	0	0	0	0	0	0	0	0	0	0	3	n/a	0	6	0	6
Battalion Trains	0	0	5	13	35	0	0	0	0	0	0	0	0	0	0	4	n/a	0	20	7	6
Mounted Recon Squadron	7	1	3	21	158	6	0	0	0	0	0	0	0	0	**5	1	150	32	12	4	4
Four Mountain Infantry Regiments	see separate table																				
Mountain Artillery Regiment																					
Regiment HQ & trains elements	14	5	25	43	2	0	0	0	0	0	0	0	0	0	1	0	*296	0	11	3	3
Two Mountain Artillery Battalions, each																					
Battalion HQ & trains elements	5	0	2	3	14	0	0	0	0	0	0	0	0	0	0	0	n/a	12	0	0	0
Recon Squad	0	0	0	1	8	0	0	0	0	0	0	0	0	0	0	0	n/a	1	0	0	0
FDC Squad	0	0	0	1	3	0	0	0	0	0	0	0	0	0	0	0	n/a	0	0	0	0
Signal Platoon	1	0	0	5	31	0	0	0	0	0	0	0	0	0	0	0	n/a	14	1	0	1
2 Gun Batteries, each	6	1	0	18	142	2	0	0	0	0	0	0	4	0	0	0	n/a	119	1	0	1
Mortar Battery	5	1	0	18	86	0	0	0	0	6	0	0	0	0	0	0	n/a	90	1	0	1
Ammunition Platoon	1	0	0	2	80	2	0	0	0	0	0	0	0	0	0	0	n/a	0	96	48	0
Supply Column	3	1	1	11	99	0	0	0	0	0	0	0	0	0	0	0	n/a	0	96	48	0
Howitzer Regiment																					
Regiment HQ & trains elements	17	5	26	33	113	2	0	2	0	0	0	0	0	0	1	3	*271	0	15	7	1
Two Howitzer Battalions, each																					
Battalion HQ	6	0	3	1	1	0	0	0	0	0	0	0	0	0	0	0	n/a	0	0	0	0
Recon Squad	0	0	0	1	11	0	0	0	0	0	0	0	0	0	0	0	n/a	0	0	0	0
FDC Squad	0	0	0	1	3	0	0	0	0	0	0	0	0	0	0	0	n/a	0	0	0	0
Signal Platoon	0	0	0	5	23	0	0	0	0	0	0	0	0	0	0	0	n/a	0	4	0	4
Liaison Squad	0	0	0	2	6	0	0	0	0	0	0	0	0	0	0	0	n/a	0	1	0	1
3 Howitzer Batteries, each	5	1	0	18	91	2	0	0	0	0	0	0	0	4	0	0	n/a	0	40	8	4
Ammunition Platoon	1	0	0	3	67	0	0	0	0	0	0	0	0	0	0	0	n/a	0	112	56	0
Battalion Trains	0	0	0	2	11	0	0	0	0	0	0	0	0	0	0	0	n/a	0	17	8	1
Supply Column	4	1	0	11	69	0	0	0	0	0	0	0	0	0	0	0	n/a	0	116	57	2
Anti-Tank Battery	6	1	4	18	88	0	0	0	0	0	8	0	0	0	1	19	0	0	0	0	0
Anti-Aircraft Battalion																					
Battalion HQ & trains elements	5	3	10	26	40	0	0	0	0	0	0	0	0	0	1	17	0	0	0	0	0
Two Anti-Air Batteries, each	5	1	0	10	54	0	0	0	0	0	0	4	0	0	0	7	0	0	0	0	0
Anti-Air MG Company	5	1	0	15	70	0	0	12	0	0	0	0	0	0	0	13	0	0	0	0	0
Ammunition Platoon	1	0	0	2	3	0	0	0	0	0	0	0	0	0	0	3	0	0	0	0	0
Pioneer Battalion																					
Battalion HQ & trains elements	4	3	8	14	31	0	0	0	0	0	0	0	0	0	1	8	*69	0	7	0	7
Signal Platoon	1	0	0	5	7	0	0	0	0	0	0	0	0	0	0	0	n/a	0	1	0	1
Technical Platoon	1	0	1	4	26	0	0	0	0	0	0	0	0	0	0	7	n/a	0	0	0	0
Two Pioneer Companies, each	4	1	0	15	98	3	0	0	0	0	0	0	0	0	0	0	n/a	0	0	0	0
Machinery Company	4	1	0	14	73	0	0	0	0	0	0	0	0	0	0	19	n/a	0	0	0	0
Special Platoon	1	0	1	2	20	0	2	0	0	0	0	0	0	0	0	0	n/a	0	16	0	8
Division Services																					
Motor Trans Company	4	1	4	17	64	2	0	0	0	0	0	0	0	0	0	34	0	0	0	0	0
Ammunition Supply Battalion																					
Battalion HQ & Trains	2	3	8	15	43	0	0	0	0	0	0	0	0	0	1	8	*26	0	13	5	1
Horsed Column	5	1	0	12	107	4	0	0	0	0	0	0	0	0	0	0	n/a	0	172	86	0
Motorised Column	4	1	1	23	71	3	0	0	0	0	0	0	0	0	0	70	0	0	0	0	0
Medical Battalion																					
Battalion HQ & Trains	1	1	10	14	44	2	0	0	0	0	0	0	0	0	2	21	*8	0	6	0	3
Medical Company	0	1	25	18	40	0	0	0	0	0	0	0	0	0	0	2	n/a	0	0	0	0
Stretcher/Ambulance Co	1	1	3	12	82	0	0	0	0	0	0	0	0	0	0	12	n/a	0	40	20	0
Chemical Platoon	0	0	7	7	26	0	0	0	0	0	0	0	0	0	1	7	n/a	0	0	0	0
Bakery	9			16	119	0	0	0	0	0	0	0	0	0	0	18	0	0	0	0	0
NKVD Rifle Platoon	1			3	32	1	0	0	0	0	0	0	0	0	0	3	0	0	0	0	0
Maintenance Workshop	8			18	20	0	0	0	0	0	0	0	0	1	1	6	0	0	0	0	0
Other Trains Elements	20			11	40	0	0	0	0	0	0	0	0	0	2	0	2	0	18	6	2
*total for all subordinate units																					
**BA-6 or BA-10 armored cars																					

Table 1.17 Mountain infantry division (TO 04/140-152), from August 1940 (as amended to October 1941).

District. In April 1942 the 63rd Mountain Division was lost and the 138th and 302nd divisions were converted to infantry divisions, then in July the 77th Division was also converted to a rifle division. For the rest of 1942 the mountain infantry force consisted of the 9th and 20th mountain divisions in the Transcaucasus Front (reinforced by the 242nd Mountain Division formed in August) and the 68th and 83rd in the Central Asian District, with the latter moving to the Transcaucasus in November. This force structure remained relatively intact through 1943, with the 3rd Corps of the North Caucasus Front being redesignated the 3rd Mountain Corps[12] in July to control the 9th, 83rd and 242nd divisions. The 9th Division was reorganized as a rifle division in September and the 20th Mountain Division replaced it in the 3rd Mountain Corps. In October the 83rd Division was redesignated the 128th Guards Mountain Division in recognition of its accomplishments in the Crimea, while the 68th Division moved to the Transcaucasus in early 1944.

Although the mountain infantry force was shrinking, changes to the organization continued to be issued. In 1942 an anti-tank mortar platoon was added to the mountain infantry regiment structure, but this was deleted again in January 1943. At about the same time the signal company was apparently reduced to platoon strength, with about forty-five men. In April 1943 the 50mm mortars and the machine gun platoon were dropped from the mountain rifle company's organization, although in partial compensation one rifle platoon in each company was issued sub-machine guns and a squad of six snipers was assigned to company HQ. The light mortars removed from the rifle companies were assigned to a regimental light mortar company with eighteen of these weapons. A sub-machine gun company and an anti-tank rifle company (with fifteen AT rifles) were added to the mountain infantry regiment strength, while the supply companies were consolidated into a single company with forty-five 2-horse wagons in lieu of the prior mix of pack horses and wagons. The centralization of the light mortars apparently did not work very well, for by September 1944 they seem to have been restored to the rifle companies.

Further confusing the issue of mountain organization was that by mid-1944 the surviving mountain regiments had been reorganized to consist of two infantry battalions, one artillery battery (four 76mm mountain guns), one mortar battery (four 107mm mortars), one sub-machine gun company (95 men), one AT rifle platoon (six AT rifles), one reconnaissance company, one pioneer company, one medical company and one transport company. Each of the infantry battalions comprised three rifle companies, one machine gun company (twelve medium machine guns) and one mortar company (six 82mm mortars). Each of the rifle companies now consisted of a 14-man HQ (including two snipers), a 36-man sub-machine gun platoon (with three 11-man squads), two 47-man rifle platoons (four 11-man squads) and one 9-man 50mm mortar section with one pack horse. This reorganization may have been ordered as early as 1942, but at least one division, the 242nd, still used a variant of the old regimental organization with five rifle companies and no battalion HQs as late as May 1944.

Divisional fire support was concentrated into a single artillery regiment of three battalions. Two of the battalions were mountain units similar to those earlier, while the third battalion was a howitzer unit with three 3-gun batteries of 122mm weapons.

The mountain troops' force structure continued with few changes through the rest of the war. The 20th Mountain Division was converted to a rifle division in May 1944 but

The horrendous losses suffered by the Red Army in 1941–3, and the German occupation of the heavily populated regions of western Russia, Belorussia and Ukraine, forced the Red Army to adopt draconian conscription methods. This also removed traditional barriers against employing women as soldiers. Although most female troops were used in roles away from the front line, such as in anti-aircraft units, many Russian women saw combat as mortar crews and snipers. The sniper teams, like this pair here, were often recruited from pre-war sporting clubs. One of the most important contributions of Russian women to the infantry during the war was as medics, and more women medics were decorated than in any other service.

was immediately replaced by a new 318th mountain division, so that for the remainder of the war the 3rd Mountain Corps consisted of the 128th Guards, 242nd and 318th Mountain Divisions, operating under the 4th Ukrainian Front, with the 68th Mountain Division independent in the Transcaucasus.

One mountain brigade, the 1st, was formed in the Leningrad District immediately after the start of the war, but nothing is known of its organization. Four naval rifle brigades and two ski brigades were redesignated to mountain brigades in January 1945 under the 126th and 127th light rifle corps, which were themselves then redesignated mountain rifle corps. Each of the two corps was supported by a mountain artillery regiment with 76mm howitzers and 120mm mortars.

SKI UNITS

While the mountain divisions were used mainly in the south, the cold weather in the north required a related, but different, type of infantry. Surprisingly, the Red Army had no ski units at the time of the attack on Finland. Finnish ski troops cut Soviet infantry to pieces in the deep snow and the Red Army began a programme in late December 1939 to throw together such ski units as could be formed hurriedly. For the most part, this took the form of simply culling out all the skiers in a given unit, such as a division, and forming them into an extemporized ski battalion.

The Finns identified sixteen army and one border guard ski battalions formed in this manner. Not surprisingly, given their genesis, there was no standard organization for a ski battalion; instead they were simply made up of whatever assets were available. Shortly after the Winter War the Finnish Army defined a 'typical' ski battalion as consisting of the following elements:

Battalion headquarters
Signal platoon (3 × 25-man squads: radio, wire and messenger)
Scout platoon (3 × 10-man squads)
Three rifle companies, each (c. 180 men with 5 sub-machine guns and 100 semi-automatic rifles)
    Company HQ (c. 8 men)
    Three or four rifle platoons (3 × 13-man squads with 2 light machine guns)
    Mortar squad (9 men with 2 mortars)
Machine gun company (4 medium machine guns)
    Company HQ
    Two platoons, each (2 × 9-man squads)

These elements gave the battalion a total strength of about 680 men with 400 semi-automatic rifles and 40 sub-machine guns, along with the heavier weapons. Such a battalion would have two *RB* radios for the battalion HQ and four *RRU* radios for the internal net.

The ski battalions did not perform well in the Winter War, undoubtedly due in large part to their hasty formation and lack of unit training. Following the conclusion of the war the ski units were disbanded and no new such units formed, although the Army did form several reserve ski regiments for training skiers.

Formation of the second batch of ski battalions began in the early winter of 1941. Some were drawn directly from the reserve ski regiments, and others were formed within divisions the same way as during the Winter War. Once again, there was considerable divergence in actual organization as a result. The official TO&E provided for a strength of 578 men, reduced in early 1942 to 556 men, and divided into a headquarters, three 126-man rifle companies and a 130-man mortar company. A ski rifle company consisted of

Another frequent role for Soviet women during the later years of the war was as traffic controllers and military police. Here, a female soldier armed with a *PPSh* sub-machine gun directs traffic as a ZiS-5 truck towing a ZiS-3 76mm divisional gun passes in the background.

three platoons each with three light-MGs. The mortar company was made up of three 50mm platoons and two 82mm mortar platoons, each with three mortars. The headquarters elements included a pioneer platoon, a signal platoon and an aid station.

Although little preparation had gone into the activation of this group, once the process got started the Soviets pursued it enthusiastically, raising no fewer than eighty-four ski battalions in December 1941, followed by seventy-seven in January 1942, then 135 more in February and March. For the most part these operated as separate battalions but in March the 1st Shock Army

consolidated ten of its ski battalions into the 1st and 2nd ski brigades, while the Karelian Front consolidated some of its battalions into the 2nd, 3rd, 4th, 5th and 6th ski brigades, followed by the 7th and 8th ski brigades in April. (The Karelian Front brigades appear to have consisted of only three ski battalions apiece.)

The disbanding of the ski brigades and battalions, which were essentially seasonal units, began in March 1942 and for the most part was completed by May, although the last twenty-three battalions in the north were not disbanded until August. Two ski brigades, the 5th and 6th, under the 14th Army north of

	Officers	Political Officers	Warrant Officers	NCOs	Other Ranks	Main Equipment
Battalion HQ Elements						
HQ Platoon	5	3	2	1	0	
Signal Platoon	1	0	0	6	9	2 radios
Pioneer Platoon	1	0	0	7	24	
Scout Section	0	0	0	2	8	
Three Ski Rifle Companies, each						
Company Headquarters	2	1	1	2	7	(incl 2 snipers)
Two Rifle Platoons, each						
Platoon HQ	1	0	0	0	0	
Three Rifle Squads, each	0	0	0	2	8	1 Light MG
Submachine Gun Platoon						
Platoon HQ	1	0	0	1	0	
Four SMG Squads, each	0	0	0	2	8	10 subMGs
Mortar Platoon						
Platoon HQ	1	0	0	0	0	
Three Mortar Squads, each	0	0	0	2	4	1 50mm mortar
Anti-Tank Rifle Platoon						
Platoon HQ	1	0	0	0	0	
Three ATR Squads, each	0	0	0	2	7	3 AT Rifles
Machine Gun Platoon						
Platoon HQ	1	0	0	1	2	
Three MG Squads, each	0	0	0	2	4	1 medium MG
Medical Platoon	0	0	1	1	6	2 wagons or sleds
Supply Platoon	1	0	0	6	14	15 wagons or sleds

Table 1.18 Ski battalion TO, October 1942.

the Arctic Circle, continued in existence through the summer and into the next autumn, being consolidated later into the new 31st Ski Brigade.

The third batch of ski units finally implemented lessons that should have been learned earlier. The units were formed well in advance of their intended employment to give them time to master basic infantry skills before training as units on skis. The 1st–35th, 37th–45th and 48th–50th ski brigades were formed in September 1942, followed by the 51st in October. In contrast, only three separate ski battalions were formed.

Due to the more systematized activation process these units appear to have been more uniform. The organization for a ski battalion showed three rifle companies, an AT rifle platoon and a machine gun platoon, but no medium or heavy mortars. A ski rifle company, with its strength of seven officers and 129 enlisted, was armed with 43 semi-automatic rifles, 55 sub-machine guns, 7 sniper rifles, 6 Degtyarev light machine guns and 3 50mm mortars. The basic load consisted of 8,026 rounds of rifle ammunition, 14,190 rounds of sub-machine gun ammunition and 168 mortar rounds. Each man was issued with a pair of skis and the company also held eighteen small man-pulled sleds (four of them as stretcher-carriers). Signal equipment was limited to three flare pistols and nine cloth aircraft signalling panels.

A ski brigade consisted of three such battalions, a reconnaissance company, a sub-machine gun company, a mortar company (six 82mm mortars), an anti-tank battalion (three 4-gun batteries of 45mm and an 18-gun AT rifle company), an AA machine gun platoon (three *DShK*), a medical company and a supply company.

Nevertheless, variations over time continued to exist. Thus, by early 1943 the 32nd Ski Brigade had the following composition:

Brigade HQ (130 men)
Signal company (60 men)
Reconnaissance company (100 men)
Three ski infantry battalions, each (580 men)
Battalion HQ (7 men)
   Signal platoon (13 men)
   Scout platoon (32 men)
   Three rifle companies, each (136 men with 6 × light machine guns and 3 × 50mm mortars)
   Mortar company (55 men with 9 × 82mm mortars)
   Machine gun platoon (16 men with 3 machine guns)
   Anti-tank rifle platoon (22 men with 9 anti-tank rifles)
   Pioneer section (10 men)
   Medical section (5 men)
   Trains platoon (12 men)
Machine gun company (65 men with 9 machine guns)
Mortar battalion (230 men)
   Battalion HQ
   Three mortar companies, each (8 × 82mm mortar)
Anti-tank battalion (230 men)
   Battalion HQ
   Three AT batteries, each (4 × 45mm anti-tank weapons)
   AT rifle company (27 anti-tank rifles)
Pioneer company (130 men)
Medical company (55 men)
Transport company (60 men)

By this time the number of radios at the battalion level appears to have increased to four, due to the unsuitability of wire systems for mobile ski operations. This was in contrast to the regular infantry battalion which only held one radio.

With the arrival of spring these units again became superfluous and were largely disbanded to provide fillers for other rifle units. Only the 31st, 32nd and 33rd ski brigades, operating in the far north of Finland with the 126th and 127th light rifle corps, continued to operate. In February 1944 a second 7th Ski Brigade (quickly redesignated 30th Ski Brigade) was formed in the same area, to bring the 127th Light Rifle Corps up to three ski brigades. The 30th and 33rd brigades were disbanded in the fall of 1944, and the other two brigades redesignated as mountain brigades in January 1945.

FORTIFIED REGIONS

Another type of infantry formation was the 'Fortified Region' (*Ukreplennye Raiony*).[13] During the first phase, 1928–38, a total of nineteen fortified regions were built

Soviet infantry tactics became more sophisticated as the war dragged on. The need for deep reconnaissance behind German lines became increasingly important as the Red Army surged forward after the summer of 1943. This led to the formation of special scout units, dubbed *razvedchiki* in Russia, who were the forerunners of contemporary *Spetsnaz* troops. These units were often provided with specialized camouflage battledress as seen here. These scouts are both armed with the ubiquitous *PPSh* sub-machine gun.

around Leningrad, Kiev, the borders of the Baltic states and the Far East. As tensions rose a further eight were built in 1938–9, again around Leningrad, the Baltic borders and Kiev. During 1939–40, however, the western borders of the Soviet Union shifted considerably, the Soviets having taken over the Baltic states and eastern Poland. Thus, in 1940 construction started on eleven more fortified regions, mostly around Leningrad and the new division line in Poland. Two more, in former Romanian

Bessarabia and Bukovina, were started in 1941. The fortified regions officially carried on the order of battle on 22 June 1941 were:

South Western Front: 1st–8th, 10th–13th, 15th and 17th

Northern Front: 23rd and 26th–29th

North Western Front: 41st, 42nd, 44th, 46th and 48th

Transcaucasus Military District: 51st and 55th

Western Front: 62nd–66th and 68th

9th Independent Army (Crimea): 80th, 81st, 84th and 86th
Odessa Military District: 83rd
Far Eastern Front: 101st–111th and Ust-Bure
Transbaikal Military District: Transbaikal

Such regions were essentially regiments or brigades in strength. An example of a pre-war fortified region was the 62nd (Brest) *UR*, which was composed of the 16th, 17th and 18th independent machine gun-artillery battalions (*otdelny pulemetno-artilleriiski batalonov*). Such a battalion had a strength of about 650 men and manned a variable number of concrete fortifications, typically 15–30 anti-tank positions (each with a 45mm gun and one or two machine guns), 10–15 machine gun positions, 5–10 artillery positions (each two or three 76mm guns or 122mm howitzers), 5–8 searchlight positions, and about a dozen smaller observation and communications posts.

New TO&Es were issued on 13 March 1942 that reoriented the machine gun-artillery battalions towards field formations, probably a reflection of the loss of most of the permanent fortifications to the advancing German armies. Under the new TO&Es a fortified region consisted of an 85-man headquarters and a variable number of 667-man machine gun-artillery battalions. A fortified region HQ could also control other field units as assigned, these including regular infantry battalions or regiments, field artillery battalions, and engineer and signal units.

The machine gun-artillery battalion consisted of a headquarters, a signal platoon (with two telephone squads and a 6-team radio section), a pioneer section, four machine gun-artillery companies and trains elements. The machine gun-artillery company was distinctive on several counts. First, the machine gun platoons contained only those men necessary to man the machine guns, two men per light machine gun and four men per medium machine gun, with no covering riflemen. Second, the mortar platoon mixed both light (50mm) and medium (82mm) mortars in its organization, both without benefit of any FDC (fire direction centre) or ammunition-carrying personnel. Third, and most distinctive, the company included a subordinate artillery battery which comprised a minuscule headquarters, a 45mm AT platoon and a 76mm field gun platoon, all consisting solely of the gun crews.

Horses were provided to move the anti-tank and field guns and one wagon was allotted for trains duties, but otherwise the company was completely immobile. Another limitation was the extreme decentralization of the 76mm guns. Although they were apparently used in the anti-tank role as often as general support weapons, the lack of dedicated signal assets and FDC personnel must have made indirect fire (not to mention coordination with other gun platoons) difficult.

In March 1943 an amendment was issued to the TO&E of the machine gun-artillery battalion that eliminated the battery HQs and 76mm gun platoons in the line companies and replaced them with a unified (if small) artillery group as a directly subordinate element under the battalion HQ. This new artillery group consisted of three 4-gun batteries, thus increasing not only the capabilities for centralized fire control, but also the number of guns from eight to twelve.

Finally, on 6 November 1943, a new TO&E for the machine gun-artillery battalion was published that incorporated the March amendment and made a few other small changes. In the machine gun-artillery company HQ the executive officer and political officer slots were deleted, leaving only the commanding officer and a 4-man

	Officers	Political Officers	Warrant Officers	NCOs	Other Ranks	Submachine Guns	Light Machine Guns	Medium Machine Guns	Anti-Tank Rifles	50mm Mortars	82mm Mortars	45mm AT Guns	76mm Field Guns	Field Cars	Trucks	Horses	Wagons	Carts
Battalion Headquarters	10	2	7	2	1	0	0	0	0	0	0	0	0	1	0	4	0	0
Signal Platoon	1	0	0	9	14	0	0	0	0	0	0	0	0	0	0	2	0	2
Pioneer Squad	0	0	0	1	8	1	0	0	0	0	0	0	0	0	0	0	0	0
Four Machine Gun-Artillery Companies, each																		
Company HQ & Signal Section	2	1	0	1	4	0	0	0	0	0	0	0	0	0	0	0	0	0
Four Machine Gun Platoons, each	1	0	0	6	6	0	2	2	0	0	0	0	0	0	0	0	0	0
Anti-Tank Rifle Platoon	1	0	0	4	12	2	0	0	7	0	0	0	0	0	0	0	0	0
Mortar Platoon	1	0	0	8	8	0	0	0	0	2	2	0	0	0	0	0	0	0
Artillery Battery																		
Battery HQ	2	1	0	1	3	0	0	0	0	0	0	0	0	0	0	1	0	0
AT Gun Platoon	1	0	0	6	2	0	0	0	0	0	0	2	0	0	0	4	0	0
Field Gun Platoon	1	0	0	4	10	1	0	0	0	0	0	0	2	0	0	8	0	0
Company Trains	0	0	0	6	2	0	0	0	0	0	0	0	0	0	0	2	1	0
Battalion Trains Elements																		
Medical & Veterinary Section	0	0	3	0	5	0	0	0	0	0	0	0	0	0	1	0	0	0
Ammunition & Supply Platoon	1	0	0	2	12	0	0	0	0	0	0	0	0	0	4	16	8	0
Field Trains Elements	0	0	0	3	10	0	0	0	0	0	0	0	0	0	1	8	4	0
TO&E 09/98 from March 1942																		
Battalion Headquarters	13	2	1	3	1	?	0	0	0	0	0	0	0	1	0	3	0	0
Signal Platoon																		
Platoon Headquarters	1	0	0	0	0	?	0	0	0	0	0	0	0	0	0	0	0	0
Two Wire Squads, each	0	0	0	1	4	?	0	0	0	0	0	0	0	0	0	1	0	1
Radio Section	0	0	0	7	6	?	0	0	0	0	0	0	0	0	0	0	0	0
Pioneer Squad	0	0	0	1	7	?	0	0	0	0	0	0	0	0	0	0	0	0
Four Machine Gun-Artillery Companies, each																		
Company Headquarters	1	0	0	1	3	?	0	0	0	0	0	0	0	0	0	0	0	0
Four Machine Gun Platoons, each																		
Platoon HQ	1	0	0	0	0	?	0	0	0	0	0	0	0	0	0	0	0	0
Two Light Teams, each	0	0	0	1	1	?	1	0	0	0	0	0	0	0	0	0	0	0
Two Medium Teams, each	0	0	0	1	3	?	0	1	0	0	0	0	0	0	0	0	0	0
Anti-Tank Rifle Platoon																		
Platoon HQ	1	0	0	0	0	?	0	0	0	0	0	0	0	0	0	0	0	0
One AT Rifle Squad	0	0	0	1	6	?	0	0	3	0	0	0	0	0	0	0	0	0
One AT Rifle Squad	0	0	0	1	8	?	0	0	4	0	0	0	0	0	0	0	0	0
Mortar Platoon																		
Platoon HQ	1	0	0	0	0	?	0	0	0	0	0	0	0	0	0	0	0	0
Light Squad	0	0	0	2	4	?	0	0	0	2	0	0	0	0	0	0	0	0
Medium Squad	0	0	0	2	8	?	0	0	0	0	2	0	0	0	0	0	0	0
Anti-Tank Gun Platoon																		
Platoon HQ	1	0	0	0	0	?	0	0	0	0	0	0	0	0	0	0	0	0
Two AT Squads, each	0	0	0	1	4	?	0	0	0	0	0	1	0	0	0	2	0	0
Company Trains	0	0	0	6	2	?	0	0	0	0	0	0	0	0	0	2	0	2
Artillery Group																		
Group Headquarters	3	0	0	1	0	?	0	0	0	0	0	0	0	0	0	3	0	0
Headquarters Platoon																		
Platoon Headquarters	1	0	0	0	0	?	0	0	0	0	0	0	0	0	0	0	0	0
Observer/Recon Squad	0	0	0	1	2	?	0	0	0	0	0	0	0	0	0	0	0	0
Signal Squad	0	0	0	1	6	?	0	0	0	0	0	0	0	0	0	3	0	0
Three Artillery Batteries, each																		
Battery HQ	1	0	0	5	4	?	0	0	0	0	0	0	0	0	0	2	0	0
Two Gun Platoons, each	1	0	0	2	12	?	0	0	0	0	0	0	2	0	0	8	0	0
Group Trains	0	0	0	4	2	?	0	0	0	0	0	0	0	0	0	4	2	0
Battalion Trains Elements																		
Medical Section	0	0	2	0	3	?	0	0	0	0	0	0	0	0	1	0	0	0
Veterinary Section	0	0	1	0	2	?	0	0	0	0	0	0	0	0	0	0	0	0
Ammunition Platoon	1	0	0	2	12	?	0	0	0	0	0	0	0	0	4	16	8	0
Field Trains Elements	0	0	0	3	9	?	0	0	0	0	0	0	0	0	1	8	4	0
TO&E 09/99 from November 1943																		

Table 1.19 Machine gun artillery battalions.

telephone squad. The machine gun, anti-tank rifle and mortar platoons were unchanged, while the 45mm AT platoon gained one more man per gun (although the prior rank-heavy structure was altered).

The new artillery group HQ was supported by a 3-man observer squad and a 7-man telephone squad. The battery headquarters was equally sparse, consisting of the commander, the first sergeant, a chemical NCO, a transport sergeant, a 2-man observer team and a 4-man telephone team. A gun platoon consisted simply of a lieutenant and two gun crews. As before, there were no dedicated FDC personnel to plan or coordinate fire.

Communications for the battalion were not improved, the radio section now operating five '*RB*' transceivers and one of the more powerful '*RBS*' models. The small arms of the battalion comprised 431 bolt-action rifles and nineteen sub-machine guns, together with about eighty pistols. The battalion trains provided four *GAZ*-AA trucks and eight 2-horse wagons for ammunition supply and one 12-ton truck and four wagons for trains duties.

The new type MG-artillery battalion was thus no more mobile than its predecessor. It should not be assumed, however, that once the Red Army moved over to the offence that these units disappeared. Although the bulk of the original battalions in the west had been destroyed in the initial German onslaught, many more were raised in 1942.

The fortified regions, largely immobile, had disappeared quickly in the west. By the end of 1941 there were only five *UR*s left facing the Germans (22nd, 23rd, 51st, 55th and 'Moscow'). In January 1942, however, six more (152nd–157th) were formed out of the former Moscow Region and one new region (158th) formed. Three more (159th–161st) were formed in February and no fewer than seventeen (52nd–54th, 69th–77th, 79th, 90th,

91st, 151st and 162nd) in April. Thereafter the pace slackened, with only one (78th) formed in May, two (14th and 17th) in July, one in August (16th), and one in October (13th). Thereafter, the *UR*s were, for most part, allowed to wither away or were broken up as replacements for rifle divisions, although seven more (2nd, 45th, 54th, 77th, 78th, 156th and 159th) were formed in early 1943.

Fortified region units accompanied the advancing Soviet Army westwards both as economy-of-force units on the flanks and in direct assault. During 1943 five fortified regions were credited by the Soviets with participation in the liberation of Soviet cities, while the list for 1944 was nine and in 1945 three participated in operations in Poland and Germany.[14] Only one region appears to have been redesignated with the 'guards' honorific, the 76th Fortified Region being retitled the 1st Guards Fortified Region in July 1943 and thereafter serving under the 3rd Ukrainian Front.

The fortified regions also played a major role in the Far East, where they screened the Soviet borders that had been all but denuded of manoeuvre troops in the desperate period of 1941–3. Between June and November 1941 there were two fortified regions in the Transbaikal District (31st and 32nd) and twelve more in the Far Eastern District (101st–111th and an unnumbered unit in the Ust Bureiskii Fortified Region). In November another *UR* (112th) was added to the Far East, and in early 1942 the unnumbered unit was dissolved and the 113th *UR* added. In late 1943 three more *UR*s were raised in the Far East (4th, 6th and 7th), followed by one (8th) in June 1944. Finally, two more *UR*s (150th and 162nd) were formed in May 1945.

By that time, at least, the Far Eastern fortified regions had grown substantially stronger than their counterparts in the west. According to the Japanese, for instance, the

Although the Red Army had traditionally frowned on the creation of special ethnic formations, by the middle of the war the practice was revived for political reasons. Among the ethnic units were a variety of infantry formations from the Baltic states. These are artillery forward observers serving with the Lithuanian 16th Rifle Division in 1944, identifiable by the special insignia on their arms.

102nd Fortified Region included three machine gun-artillery battalions (37th, 90th and 117th), three field artillery battalions (81st, 95th and 137th), one unidentified infantry unit and one signal company, and was responsible for an area 75 km wide and 1–8 km deep. The 106th Fortified Region held four machine gun-artillery battalions (26th, 80th, 98th and one other), one field artillery battalion (109th), one infantry regiment (158th), one anti-tank battalion (36th), one engineer battalion (134th) and one signal company to hold a position 35 km long and 2–8 km deep with 155 permanent pillboxes and 110 temporary field pillboxes. Other units found in the fortified regions were medium artillery battalions, anti-aircraft battalions, and motor transport and engineer units.

By August 1945, when the Soviets launched their lightning campaign against Manchuria, there were no fewer than 20 fortified regions in the theatre: two (31st and 32nd) under the Transbaikal Front, four (101st–104th) under the Second Far Eastern Front, and fourteen (6th, 7th, 8th, 105th–113th, 150th and 162nd) under the First Far Eastern Front. The single-digit fortified regions have also been referred to as 'field fortified units' and it is uncertain if this indicated a different organization. In any event, many of the fortified regions participated in the initial advance into Manchuria, undertaking assault tasks, although they appear to have been left behind once the initial breakthroughs occurred.

All of the machine gun-artillery battalions were subordinated to fortified regions at the time of the German invasion, but in the subsequent chaos a small number were separated from their parent regions and others, freshly raised, were sent into combat before they could be incorporated into a larger framework. This was generally a temporary expedient, and most were either disbanded or incorporated into fortified regions within a few months. Nevertheless, there were generally one or two dozen such battalions on the rolls at any given time during the first half of the war.

Notes

1. Nevertheless, it is doubtful whether many of these new weapons were actually ready for service when the organization tables were first published in 1939. The 1940 drill manual, for instance, still showed the old organization with no mortars in the rifle company. In fact, the manual specified an organization for the company identical to that shown in the 1938 edition, which in turn was based on the 1935 TO&Es. *Stroevoi ustav pekhoty* (1938 and 1940 eds).

2. The scale of issue of the sub-machine guns is not clear. A rifle regiment at peacetime strength of 2,698 men was authorized 341 sub-machine guns.

3. Production of these weapons never reached a level permitting this kind of distribution. In practice it would seem that most units provided semi-automatic rifles only to the squad leader, the light machine guns assistant gunner and two of the riflemen. Most of the rest of the personnel in the division used bolt-action rifles.

4. It is not clear whether this indicates a reduction in the number of rifle squads to two per platoon or whether, as is more likely, that only two of the four squads were issued machine guns.

5. Tyushkevich, 1978, p. 277.

6. In fact it is now estimated that only about a dozen German tanks were actually destroyed by this primitive weapon in the ten months it was in service.

7. Except for the September 1939 figures, data comes from Soviet sources. The data is in close, but not perfect, agreement with that shown earlier in the text, which comes primarily from German and Finnish sources. The differences are apparently due to the inclusion of some amendments and changes in the Soviet computations.

8. These are not to be confused with the naval infantry (*morskaya pekhota*) brigades raised by the Navy.

9. Although specifically designated for the *kursantskie* brigade, from the organizational structure, TO&E numbering system, and subsequent references it would appear that this set of TO&Es was actually used by all rifle brigades activated between mid-October and early December 1941.

10. Tyushkevich, 1978, p. 278.

11. Quoted in James Lucas, *Alpine Elite: German Mountain Troops of World War II*, Jane's, London and New York, 1980, p. 127.

12. The Karelian Front formed a few 'light mountain corps' in 1944, but these controlled ski, rather than mountain, troops.

13. Confusingly, the term *UR* was used to denote both the physical fortification system and the unit that manned it. To distinguish between the two the Soviets designated the actual physical systems by location name, while the units were designated with numbers. Thus, the fortifications of the Brest *UR* were manned by the personnel of the 62nd *UR*.

14. A summary prepared by German intelligence in April 1945 identified thirty-five fortified regions as encountered during 1943–5, with a total of 209 subordinate machine gun-artillery battalions, or an average of six per region. Also identified were seven regions with unknown subordinate units and twelve regions identified only by name.

CHAPTER 2

RED ARMY ARMOURED FORCE

The Army's portion of the 1938–42 five-year plan was approved on 28 December 1937 and showed no significant change over that period, envisioning a force of four tank corps, twenty-one independent tank brigades (renamed from mechanized brigades), three armoured car brigades and eleven training tank regiments, along with the tank units for the infantry and cavalry divisions. Expansion was planned, but in the form of enlarging the tank platoons from three to five tanks apiece.

THE PRE-WAR TANK CORPS

The new tank corps had 12,710 men with 560–600 tanks and 118 artillery pieces. It consisted of 2 light tank brigades and 1 motorized rifle machine gun brigade and 1 signal battalion. Each of its 2 light tank brigades had 4 tank battalions (each 54 light and 6 artillery tanks with 76mm guns), 1 reconnaissance battalion, 1 motor rifle battalion and service units for a total of 278 BT tanks or 267 T-26 tanks.

The Red Army's mechanized corps in 1941 were massive but poorly trained, poorly led and poorly maintained. Far more tanks were lost to mechanical breakdown or a lack of fuel than to combat action. Even when they did manage to encounter the Germans on the battlefield, the Soviet tank units were roughly handled by their more experienced opponents. Here, a company of T-26 light tanks lie burned out after an encounter with German panzers in the Ukraine in 1941.

		T-37	T-26	BT	T-28	Armoured Cars
Belorussian Front	15th Tank Corps	0	0	461	0	122
	6th Tank Brigade	0	0	248	0	0
	21st Tank Brigade	0	0	29	105	19
	22nd Tank Brigade	0	219	0	0	3
	25th Tank Brigade	0	251	0	0	27
	29th Tank Brigade	0	188	0	0	3
	32nd Tank Brigade	0	220	0	0	5
Ukrainian Front	25th Tank Corps	0	27	435	0	74
	10th Tank Brigade	0	10	30	98	19
	23rd Tank Brigade	0	8	209	0	5
	24th Tank Brigade	0	8	205	0	28
	26th Tank Brigade	0	228	0	0	22
	36th Tank Brigade	0	301	0	0	24
	38th Tank Brigade	4	141	0	0	4

Table 2.1 Tank strength in the invasion of Poland, 1939.

An independent BT-equipped brigade was similar but the independent T-26 brigades were to be smaller, with only three tank battalions, plus a motorized rifle battalion, a maintenance battalion, and signal and trains elements for a total of 2,745 men with 145 T-26 tanks, 56 artillery and flamethrower tanks, 28 armoured cars, 482 cars and trucks and 39 tractors. Most T-26 brigades appear to have been expanded to four tank battalions when the vehicles became available.

The heavy tank brigades were similar but platoon size was reduced from five tanks to three, with a concomitant reduction in overall numbers. Most of the heavy brigades were provided with 136 T-28s, 37 BT tanks and 10 flamethrowers, but the unique 5th Tank Brigade was authorized 94 T-35s plus 44 BTs and 10 flamethrower tanks.

A number of the tank units participated in the brief Polish campaign of September 1939. The two major units were the 15th Tank Corps (27th and 45th light tank brigades and

the 20th Motorized Brigade) and the 25th Tank Corps. A complete picture of the tank forces used in the advance into Poland is not available, but the major units and their actual tank strengths were as shown in Table 2.1.[1]

THE END OF THE TANK CORPS

Due to the lack of substantive Polish resistance the armoured forces did not get a chance to show their mettle in combat. Nevertheless on 23 October Marshal Voroshilov recommended abolishing the tank corps, along with the motorized rifle brigades and in November 1939 the Main Military Council pronounced the performance of the tank corps unsatisfactory and ordered them disbanded. At the same time the tank brigades were ordered to concentrate their efforts on infantry and cavalry cooperation and support rather than on independent operations. The new order of battle for the tank forces was to be:

	Personnel	Light Machine Guns	Medium Machine Guns	AA Machine Guns	45mm Anti-Tank Guns	Armored Cars	T-37 Light Tanks	BT or T-26 Tanks
Brigade Headquarters	?							
Signal Company	130					5		
Headquarters Protection Platoon	33	2						
Reconnaissance Battalion								
Battalion Headquarters	13							
Signal Platoon	18							
Motorized Rifle Company	44		2	2				
Armored Car Company	55					16		
Light Tank Company	40						16	
Battalion Trains	43							
Three Tank Battalions, each								
Battalion Headquarters	14							3
Signal Platoon	24							
Reconnaissance Platoon	10					1	1	
Three Tank Companies, each	53							17
Battalion Trains	60							
Motorized Rifle Battalion								
Battalion Headquarters	19							
Signal Platoon	32							
Three Rifle Companies, each	160		9	2				
Anti-Tank Platoon	31				3			
Anti-Aircraft MG Platoon	19			3				
Battalion Trains	78							
Anti-Air MG Platoon	30			5				
Chemical Company	90							
Pioneer Company	280							
Motor Transport Battalion	200							
Maintenance Battalion	200							
Reserve Tank Company	100							8
Medical Company	60							
Other Trains Elements	200							

Table 2.2 Light tank brigade (three battalion type), from November 1939.

1. 16 BT tank brigades, each of 238 tanks; with 13 brigades manned at 2,562 men apiece, and 3 at 2,907 apiece.
2. 16 T-26 tank brigades, each of 238 tanks; with 13 brigades manned at 1,610 men apiece and 3 at 2,217 apiece.
3. 3 T-28 tank brigades, each of 117 T-28 and 39 BT tanks, and 1,979 men.
4. 1 T-35 tank brigade with 32 T-35 and 85 T-28 tanks with 2,156 men.
5. 10 light tank regiments, 8 at 1,050 men each and 2 (Far Eastern and Transbaikal)

at 425 men each. One was equipped with BT tanks, the other nine with T-26.
6. 4 motorcycle battalions, each of 600 men.

The basic unit was the platoon of five T-26 or BT tanks. Three such platoons plus a headquarters with two more tanks made up the tank company. A battalion consisted of a headquarters (three more tanks, for a total of fifty-four), three tank companies and trains, for a total strength of slightly over 250 men. A brigade was to have four such

	Personnel	Light Machine Guns	AA Machine Guns	BA-20 Armored Cars	BT Tanks	T-28 Tanks
Brigade HQ	?					2
Headquarters Company	130				5	
Headquarters Protection Platoon	33	2				
Reconnaissance Company	70				10	6
Three Tank Battalions, each						
Battalion Headquarters	84					
Signal Platoon	23				2	3
Reconnaissance Platoon	9				3	
Three Tank Companies, each	73					10
Anti-Air MG Platoon	30		5			
Chemical Company	90					
Pioneer Company	200					
Motor Transport Battalion	200					
Maintenance Battalion	200					
Reserve Tank Company	100					?
Medical Company	60					
other trains elements	200					

Table 2.3 Heavy tank brigade, from November 1939.

battalions, although some had three and others five.

The brigade's reconnaissance battalion was built around an armoured car company of three platoons, a similar light tank company, and a small motorized rifle company with one 2-squad rifle platoon and a 2-squad machine gun platoon. The motorized rifle battalion had three rifle companies, each with three 44-man rifle platoons and a 13-man machine gun platoon, plus anti-tank and anti-aircraft machine gun platoons. The brigade also included AA-machine gun, pioneer and chemical units but no artillery.

A heavy tank brigade, equipped with T-28 multi-turret tanks, had a slightly different composition. At the most basic organizational level the platoon had only three tanks, rather than five, all commanded by officers. A tank company had three platoons plus a tenth tank in the company HQ. A heavy tank battalion was made up of one headquarters, three companies, one signal platoon, one reconnaissance platoon and one trains group. The signal platoon had three BT tanks, two BA-20 armoured cars, three radio trucks and five motorcycles. The scout platoon was provided with three BA-20s. The trains group consisted of one supply platoon (eleven trucks), one technical platoon, one medical platoon (two trucks), and one trains platoon (four trucks).

The heavy tank brigade, in turn, consisted of three heavy tank battalions and small support units. The reconnaissance company was divided into two armoured car platoons and a tank platoon with one more tank in the company HQ. The T-28s, like the light tanks, were due for replacement by a new model, in this case the KV heavy tank. Only a few prototypes were completed, however, by the conclusion of the Russo-Finnish War.

A new Army force structure approved in early May 1940 provided for an armoured branch of 96,785 men divided into one T-35/KV heavy tank brigade, three T-28 heavy tank brigades, sixteen BT light tank brigades for deep operations, eighteen T-26 light tank brigades for infantry support, three armoured car brigades for the Transbaikal Military District, six independent tank regiments for training and some smaller demonstration units. The new heavy tank brigades, with their KV tanks, would consist of three battalions totalling 156 tanks (including thirty-nine BTs).

THE RETURN OF THE CORPS STRUCTURE

Before further progress could be made, however, the German blitzkrieg over France brought home to the Soviets the need for their own large armoured units. The obvious could no longer be ignored, even in the make-believe world of Stalin's Moscow. In June 1940 the People's Commissariat for Defence authorized the reactivation of the mechanized corps as a major manoeuvre element, and the structure was ratified in July.

The new structure called for eight mechanized corps (each to consist of two tank divisions and one motorized division) plus two separate tank divisions. Each tank division would have 315 tanks and each mechanized corps 888 tanks. To create these formations twelve BT tank brigades, four T-28 tank brigades, three flamethrower tank brigades, two T-26 regiments and the tank battalions of all the rifle divisions except those in the Far East were disbanded. They were to have been formed with KV and T-34 tanks but these were not yet available, so BTs and, to a lesser extent, T-26s were substituted. Even so, the required numbers could not be found and by 1 October 1940 the mechanized corps averaged only 680 tanks apiece.

Remaining in the force structure after the formation of the eight corps were twenty

The massive T-35 breakthrough tank looked very impressive in the annual Red Square parades but most were lost in a few days of operations in the Ukraine due to mechanical problems. This was in many respects symptomatic of the Red Army of 1941: very advanced on paper in terms of doctrine and equipment but inept on the battlefield.

brigades of T-26s for infantry support. Each of these brigades had a strength of 1,994 men with 292 tanks (including one 54-tank battalion of flamethrower tanks), 11 cars, 155 trucks, 14 tractors and 23 motorcycles.

Plans called for the creation of one tank brigade for each rifle corps (except those in the Far East), which generated a requirement for an additional twenty-five brigades. Once the newer tanks became available, the older T-26s would be handed over from the mechanized corps to create these additional infantry support brigades. This was planned for completion by 1 June 1941. These plans

went awry, however: a ninth mechanized corps was formed in December and in February 1941 the decision was made to form an additional twenty mechanized corps and abolish all the remaining tank brigades. New TO&Es were prepared at the same time. Although there were not nearly enough modern tanks to fill out these formations, the new tables actually increased the authorized tank holdings of the corps.

Under these new TO&Es a mechanized corps was to consist of two tank divisions, a motorized division (see tables opposite), a motorcycle regiment, a signal battalion, an

Motorized Division
Division HQ
Signal Battalion
Reconnaissance Battalion
    Armoured Car Co (15 Arm Cars)
    Light Tank Co (17 T-40)
    Motorcycle Rifle Co (12 LMG, 3×5cm Mort)
Tank Regiment
    Five Light Tank Battalions, each
        Battalion HQ (3 BT)
        Three Cos, each (17 BT)
    Maintenance Company
    Supply Company
Two Motorized Infantry Regiments, each
    Signal Company
    Reconnaissance Co (10 Arm Cars)
    AA Machine Gun Company (6 AAMG)
    Three Infantry Battalions, each
        Three Rifle Cos, each (12 LMG, 2 MG, 3×5cm Mort)
        Machine Gun Co (6 MG)
        Mortar Platoon (2×82mm Mort)
        Anti-Tank Platoon (2×45mm AT)
    Infantry Gun Battery (4×76mm Inf Guns)
Artillery Regiment
    Field Gun Battalion
        Three Batteries, each (2 LMG, 4×76mm Guns)
    Light Field Howitzer Battalion
        Three Batteries, each (2 LMG, 4×122mm How)
    Heavy Field Howitzer Battalion
        Three Batteries, each (2 LMG, 4×152mm How)
Anti-Tank Battalion
    Three Batteries, each (6×45mm AT)
Anti-Aircraft Battalion
    Two Light Batteries, each (4×37mm AA)
    Heavy Battery (4×76mm AA)
Pioneer Battalion
    Two Pioneer Companies
    One PMP bridge Company

Tank Division
Division HQ
Signal Battalion
Reconnaissance Battalion
    Armoured Car Co (15 Arm Cars)
    Light Tank Co (17 T-40)
    Motorcycle Rifle Co (12 LMG, 3×5cm Mort)
Two Tank Regiments, each
    Regiment HQ (1 T-34, 3 AAMG)
    Reconnaissance Co (13 Arm Cars)
    Heavy Tank Battalion
        Battalion HQ (1 KV, 3 Arm Cars)
        Three Cos, each (10 KV)
    Two Medium Battalions, each
        Battalion HQ (1 T-34, 3 Arm Cars)
        Three Cos, each (17 T-34)
    Flamethrower Battalion
        Battalion HQ (1 T-26, 3 Arm Cars)
        Three Cos, each (3 T-26, 9×flamethrower T-26)
    Maintenance Company
    Supply Company
Motorized Infantry Regiment (as in motorized division)
Artillery Regiment
    Regiment HQ (1 KV tank, 3 AAMG)
    Light Field Howitzer Battalion
        Three Batteries, each (2 LMG, 4×122mm How)
    Heavy Field Howitzer Battalion
        Three Batteries, each (2 LMG, 4×152mm How)
Anti-Aircraft Battalion
    Three Light Batteries, each (4×37mm AA)
Pioneer Battalion

Motorized and Tank Divisions, June 1941.

	Political Officers	Officers	NCOs	Other Ranks	Light Machine Guns	Medium Machine Guns	Quad AA Machine Guns	50mm Mortars	82mm Mortars	45mm AT Guns	76mm Infantry Guns	Armored Cars
Regiment Headquarters & Platoon	18	6	9	29	1	0	0	0	0	0	0	0
Signal Company												
Company HQ & Platoon	3	1	4	17	0	0	0	0	0	0	0	0
Radio Platoon	1	0	3	16	0	0	0	0	0	0	0	0
Wire/Optical Platoon	1	0	3	10	0	0	0	0	0	0	0	0
Reconnaissance Company												
Company Headquarters	1	1	2	2	0	0	0	0	0	0	0	2
Motorcycle Scout Platoon	1	0	1	8	4	0	0	0	0	0	0	0
BA-20 Armored Car Platoon	1	0	3	8	0	0	0	0	0	0	0	4
BA-10 Armored Car Platoon	1	0	3	12	0	0	0	0	0	0	0	4
Anti-Aircraft Machine Gun Company												
Company Headquarters	2	1	1	3	0	0	0	0	0	0	0	0
Two AA Machine Gun Platoons, each	1	0	3	12	0	0	3	0	0	0	0	0
Three Motorized Infantry Battalions, each												
Battalion Headquarters	3	1	2	0	0	0	0	0	0	0	0	0
Signal Platoon	1	0	3	17	0	0	0	0	0	0	0	0
Motorcycle Scout Platoon												
Platoon HQ	1	0	0	0	0	0	0	0	0	0	0	0
Two Scout Sections, each	0	0	1	7	1	0	0	0	0	0	0	0
Three Rifle Companies, each												
Company Headquarters	1	1	1	7	0	0	0	0	0	0	0	0
Transport Group	0	0	1	11	0	0	0	0	0	0	0	0
Three Rifle Platoons, each												
Platoon HQ	1	0	1	1	0	0	0	0	0	0	0	0
Four Rifle Squads, each	0	0	1	10	1	0	0	0	0	0	0	0
Machine Gun Platoon												
Platoon HQ	1	0	1	0	0	0	0	0	0	0	0	0
Two MG Squads, each	0	0	1	6	0	1	0	0	0	0	0	0
Mortar Section	0	0	1	10	0	0	0	3	0	0	0	0
Machine Gun Company												
Company Headquarters	1	1	2	4	0	0	0	0	0	0	0	0
Transport Group	0	0	1	6	0	0	0	0	0	0	0	0
Three MG Platoons, each												
Platoon HQ	1	0	0	0	0	0	0	0	0	0	0	0
Two MG Squads, each	0	0	1	8	0	1	0	0	0	0	0	0
Mortar Platoon	1	0	2	8	0	0	0	0	2	0	0	0
Anti-Tank Platoon	1	0	2	14	0	0	0	0	0	2	0	0
Supply Platoon	1	0	3	22	0	0	0	0	0	0	0	0
Regimental Gun Battery	*65				0	0	0	0	0	0	4	0
Engineer Platoon	1	0	5	26	2	0	0	0	0	0	0	0
Traffic Control Platoon	1	0	2	16	0	0	0	0	0	0	0	0
total all personnel (breakdown by rank unknown)												

Table 2.4 Motorized infantry regiment (TO 05/71), from April 1941.

engineer battalion and an air squadron. It would have a strength of over 36,000 men with 1,031 tanks (including 546 KV or T-34 models), 268 armoured cars and 358 guns and mortars.

A motorized division totalled 11,600 men. Its reconnaissance battalion was built around a light tank company, an armoured car company and a motorized rifle company of three rifle platoons and a mortar section. The tank regiment contributed five battalions each with fifty-four BT tanks. The motorized infantry regiments followed the pattern of the non-motorized infantry but lacked the regimental anti-tank battery while adding trucks.

As would be true of all the mechanized formations, the motorized divisions were never fully equipped. Not only were tanks in short supply, but the motorized divisions as a whole had only 39 per cent of their authorized trucks, 44 per cent of the tractors and 17 per cent of the motorcycles. The artillery component rarely exceeded 40 per cent of the authorized levels and the divisions held only about 29 per cent of the repair equipment needed. The motorized divisions, in fact, often moved on foot.

The other major mechanized formation was the tank division, which totalled 11,343 men with 210 T-34 medium tanks, 63 KV heavy tanks, 26 BT-7 light tanks, 22 T-26 light tanks, 54 flamethrower T-26 tanks, 56 BA-10 heavy and 39 BA-20 light armoured cars, 28 field guns, 12 AA guns and 54 mortars.

The internal organization of the tank division has been the subject of considerable speculation, for the official sources have had little to say. The information shown in Table 2.5 represents one author's estimate and seems to conform to what is known. Even the massive holdings of the Soviet Army could not possibly fill out this new structure. The armoured vehicle requirements generated by the TO&Es and the estimated actual holdings of armoured vehicles on 22 June 1941 are shown in Table 2.5.

It should further be noted that of the total available some 4,060 were already committed to the organic tank units of the infantry, cavalry and airborne divisions. Exacerbating this problem was the woeful state of readiness of most of the equipment. Emphasis on the production of new tanks to the exclusion of spare-parts production often rendered unserviceable what tanks were available. By 1941 29 per cent of the tanks in the Red Army inventory required a major overhaul

	Requirement	Actual
KV heavy tanks	3,528	508
T-34 medium tanks	11,760	967
T-28 obsolete tanks	0	500
BT light tanks	7,840	6,000
T-26 light tanks	5,880	11,000
T-37/38/40 scout Tanks	476	4,222
Total Tanks	29,484	23,197
Armoured Cars	7,448	4,819

Table 2.5 Requirements and holdings of tanks, 22 June 1941.

and 44 per cent required rebuilding, leaving 27 per cent, or about 7,000 tanks, as combat-worthy vehicles.

Rounding out the mechanized corps as a combat unit was the motorcycle regiment for use as a reconnaissance element. Such a unit, actually a battalion in strength, consisted of a headquarters and four rifle companies, each of these consisting of 150 men with twelve light machine guns and sixty-two motorcycles.

In addition to the corps there were three independent tank divisions (the 57th and 61st in the Transbaikal Military District and the 59th in the Far Eastern Front) and two independent motorized divisions (the 69th under the Far Eastern Front and the 82nd in the Transbaikal Military District). These units, with the exceptions of the 51st Tank Division, appear to have been at or close to full strength, albeit entirely with older model tanks.

The mechanized corps proved a failure in combat. Leadership was poor, communications weak, equipment unreliable and tactics unschooled. The numerically weaker German panzer divisions slashed them to pieces in short order. It was not that the Soviet tanks were that bad, for even the older

The staff of a Red Army tank regiment prepare for action in the summer of 1941. The two senior officers to the left are the unit's commissar and the unit commander, while the two tankers to the right are lieutenants. The unit is equipped with T-26 light tanks, an adequate tank by 1941 standards, but plagued by its age and the lack of spare parts.

T-26 and BT-7 had thoroughly respectable armament for the time and the latter, at least, a good turn of speed; instead, 'the weakness of the Soviet mechanized corps lay not in the design of their equipment, but rather in its poor mechanical state, the inadequate training of their crews, and the abysmal quality of Soviet military leadership in the first months of the war.'[2]

The two mechanized corps in the Special Baltic Military District had been destroyed by 24 June, while the five in the Special Kiev Military District fought hard in the Ukraine starting on 25 June, but within a week they too had been destroyed. The six mechanized corps in the Special Kiev MD were trapped in vast encircling battles by Army Group Centre and were all but wiped out by mid-July.

THE SECOND GENERATION TANK DIVISIONS

The inability to handle such massive formations of tanks had become clear and on 15 July the remaining mechanized corps were officially disbanded. The motorized divisions were converted to regular rifle divisions. Tanks were now to be formed into smaller

Division headquarters	
Reconnaissance battalion	10 T-40s, 26 armoured cars, 1 motorcycle company
Two Tank Regiments, each	
HQ & elements	3 armoured cars, 3 quad anti-aircraft machine guns
Medium tank battalion	1 heavy company (10 KV), 2 medium companies (each 10 T-34)
Two light tank battalions, each	3 light companies (each 10 T-26 or BT)
Motorized infantry regiment	
HQ & elements	3 armoured cars
Three infantry battalions, each	3 rifle companies, machine gun company (12 machine guns), mortar company (6 × 82mm)
Anti-tank battery	6 × 45mm anti-tank weapons
Mortar battery	4 × 120mm mortars
Gun battery	4 × 76mm regimental guns
Artillery regiment	
Three battalions, each	2 gun batteries (each with 4 × 76mm guns), one howitzer battery (4 × 122mm guns)
Light anti-aircraft battalion	3 light batteries (each with 4 × 25mm or 37mm AA guns)
Division services	Transport, maintenance and medical battalions

Table 2.6

divisions. The new structure was similar to the earlier formations, but reduced components gave it the appearance shown in Table 2.6.

The main change was a significant reduction in tank platoon size from five vehicles to three, and a reduction in company strength from seventeen to ten. The rifle companies were also made smaller, to purely triangular formations of three rifle platoons each of three rifle squads, for a total of 131 men with nine light machine guns and three 50mm mortars. Ten such divisions were formed, all numbered in the 101–112 series. By early October only three remained and by May 1942 only two divisions survived, the 61st Division (a pre-war formation) and the 111th (a second-generation unit), both in the Transbaikal Front.

LOWERED EXPECTATIONS: THE TANK BRIGADES

The new tank divisions represented an organizational dead-end. Of far more significance for the future conduct of the war were the tank brigades. The TO&Es for the tank brigade (TO 010/75–83) were issued on 23 August 1941 and provided for a small unit of only 1,943 men with 7 KV heavy tanks, 22 T-34 medium tanks and 64 T-40 light tanks.

Manpower requirements were kept to a minimum and the tank companies were little more than the crews needed to man the tanks. One tank in each medium and heavy platoon was equipped with a radio, as were all the tanks in company and battalion HQ elements, light and medium/heavy; the light tank platoons apparently had no radios. The regimental HQ company was made up of a motorcycle

The scourge of the Wehrmacht in 1941 was the KV-1 tank, named after defence minister Klimenti Voroshilov. This tank was substantially better armoured and better armed than any German design, and was the inspiration for the later German Tiger tank. It was rushed into service too soon and suffered from serious powertrain problems during the 1941 fighting.

security/scout platoon (with six sidecar motor-cycles and two light machine guns) and a signal platoon (with two truck-mounted type 5-*AK* radios and four motorcycle dispatch riders).

The brigade's infantry battalion included not only a large conventional AT company but also a unique tank-destroyer company that utilized extemporized close-in anti-tank weapons such as hand grenades, flamethrowers, 'Molotov cocktails' and engineer demolition material. The battalion's trains company included a motor transport platoon to carry the rifle companies, which were without organic transport. The brigade had no indirect-fire

support other than the mortars of the infantry battalion. In deference to the Luftwaffe, however, it did include an anti-aircraft battalion – a battery by western standards.

It quickly became apparent that the regimental HQ was a superfluous level of command and it was deleted from the TO&E in September. At the same time one of the light tank battalions was also deleted, although six of the tanks were apparently shifted elsewhere (perhaps to the re-connaissance company), for Soviet sources give the September 1941 tank brigade a total of 7 *KV*s, 22 T-34s and 38 light tanks.[3]

	Political Officers	Officers	Warrant Officers	NCOs	Other Ranks	Light Machine Guns	Medium Machine Guns	Heavy Machine Guns	50mm Mortars	82mm Mortars	Flamethrowers	45mm AT Guns	37mm AA Guns	Light Armored Cars	Heavy Armored Cars	Light Tanks	Medium Tanks	Heavy Tanks	Motorcycles	Field Cars	Trucks	Tractors
Brigade Headquarters	11	7	15	9	12	2	0	0	0	0	0	0	0	0	0	0	0	0	0	0	0	0
Headquarters Company																						
Company Headquarters	1	1	3	4	4	0	0	0	0	0	0	0	0	0	0	0	0	0	4	0	0	0
Armored Car Platoon	1	0	0	2	11	0	0	0	0	0	0	0	0	2	3	0	0	0	0	0	0	0
Traffic Control Platoon	1	0	0	3	20	0	0	0	0	0	0	0	0	0	0	0	0	0	5	0	1	0
Signal Platoon	1	0	0	8	34	0	0	0	0	0	0	0	0	0	0	0	0	0	0	0	5	0
Pioneer Platoon	1	0	0	4	32	0	0	0	0	0	0	0	0	0	0	0	0	0	0	0	0	0
Chemical (Decontamination) Platoon	1	0	0	2	17	0	0	0	0	0	0	0	0	0	0	0	0	0	0	0	1	0
Supply & Transport Platoon	0	0	1	3	20	0	0	0	0	0	0	0	0	0	0	0	0	0	0	7	8	0
Reconnaissance Company																						
Company Headquarters	1	1	2	4	7	0	0	0	0	0	0	0	0	0	0	0	0	0	4	0	1	0
Heavy Armored Car Platoon	1	0	0	6	13	0	0	0	0	0	0	0	0	0	5	0	0	0	0	0	0	0
Light Armored Car Platoon	1	0	0	4	10	0	0	0	0	0	0	0	0	5	0	0	0	0	0	0	0	0
Motorcycle Rifle Platoon	1	0	0	4	44	3	0	0	0	0	0	0	0	0	0	0	0	0	23	0	0	0
Tank Regiment																						
Regiment Headquarters	6	4	12	5	1	0	0	0	0	0	0	0	0	0	0	0	0	0	0	0	0	0
Headquarters Company	3	1	0	6	25	2	0	0	0	0	0	0	0	0	0	0	0	0	10	0	2	0
Medium/Heavy Tank Battalion																						
Battalion Headquarters	3	1	2	9	2	0	0	0	0	0	0	0	0	0	0	0	2	0	0	1	1	0
Heavy Tank Company	7	1	3	25	0	0	0	0	0	0	0	0	0	0	0	0	0	7	0	0	0	0
Two Medium Tank Companies, each	4	1	1	30	6	0	0	0	0	0	0	0	0	0	0	0	10	0	0	0	0	0
Battalion Trains	0	0	1	6	6	0	0	0	0	0	0	0	0	0	0	0	0	0	0	0	1	3
Two Light Tank Battalions, each																						
Battalion Headquarters	3	1	2	5	2	0	0	0	0	0	0	0	0	0	0	2	0	0	0	1	1	0
Three Tank Companies, each	4	1	1	16	0	0	0	0	0	0	0	0	0	0	0	10	0	0	0	0	0	0
Battalion Trains	0	0	1	6	6	0	0	0	0	0	0	0	0	0	0	0	0	0	0	0	1	3
Regimental Trains Company	3	1	10	25	91	0	0	0	0	0	0	0	0	0	0	0	0	0	1	3	49	3
Medical Company	0	0	3	3	10	0	0	0	0	0	0	0	0	0	0	0	0	0	0	0	4	0
Infantry Battalion																						
Battalion Headquarters	6	3	8	1	4	0	0	0	0	0	0	0	0	0	0	0	0	0	3	0	0	0
Headquarters Platoon	1	0	0	4	19	0	0	0	0	0	0	0	0	0	0	0	0	0	0	0	1	0
Three Rifle Companies, each																						
Company Headquarters	1	1	0	4	5	0	0	0	0	0	0	0	0	0	0	0	0	0	0	0	0	0
Three Rifle Platoons, each	1	0	0	4	29	4	0	0	0	0	0	0	0	0	0	0	0	0	0	0	0	0
Machine Gun Platoon	1	0	0	2	8	0	2	0	0	0	0	0	0	0	0	0	0	0	0	0	0	0
Tank Destroyer Company																						
Company Headquarters	1	1	0	1	0	0	0	0	0	0	0	0	0	0	0	0	0	0	0	0	0	0
Hand Grenade Platoon	1	0	0	2	14	0	0	0	0	0	0	0	0	0	0	0	0	0	0	0	0	0
Flamethrower Platoon	1	0	0	2	14	0	0	0	0	0	16	0	0	0	0	0	0	0	0	0	0	0
Incendiary Platoon	1	0	0	2	14	0	0	0	0	0	0	0	0	0	0	0	0	0	0	0	0	0
Demolitions Section	0	0	0	1	9	0	0	0	0	0	0	0	0	0	0	0	0	0	0	0	0	0
Mortar Company																						
Company Headquarters	1	1	0	2	5	0	0	0	0	0	0	0	0	0	0	0	0	0	0	0	1	0
Light Mortar Platoon	1	0	0	3	23	0	0	0	6	0	0	0	0	0	0	0	0	0	0	0	0	0
Two Medium Mortar Platoons, each	1	0	0	3	13	0	0	0	0	3	0	0	0	0	0	0	0	0	0	0	2	0
Anti-Tank Company																						
Company Headquarters	1	1	0	1	0	0	0	0	0	0	0	0	0	0	0	0	0	0	0	0	0	0
Four AT Platoons, each	1	0	0	2	12	0	0	0	0	0	0	2	0	0	0	0	0	0	0	0	2	0
Transport & Trains Company	3	1	3	19	61	0	0	0	0	0	0	0	0	0	0	0	0	0	0	1	52	0
Medical Platoon	0	0	2	2	3	0	0	0	0	0	0	0	0	0	0	0	0	0	0	0	0	0
Anti-Aircraft Battalion																						
Battalion Headquarters	3	3	1	2	0	0	0	0	0	0	0	0	0	0	0	0	0	0	0	0	0	0
Headquarters Platoon	0	0	0	2	7	0	0	0	0	0	0	0	0	0	0	0	0	0	0	0	1	0
Anti-Aircraft MG Platoon	1	0	0	3	24	0	0	6	0	0	0	0	0	0	0	0	0	0	0	0	6	0
Two Anti-Aircraft Batteries, each	3	1	0	6	39	0	0	0	0	0	0	0	4	0	0	0	0	0	0	0	5	0
Trains Group	0	0	3	9	18	0	0	0	0	0	0	0	0	0	0	0	0	0	0	1	12	0
Maintenance Company	2	1	10	23	55	0	0	0	0	0	0	0	0	0	0	0	0	0	2	0	25	0
Motor Transport Company	4	1	8	11	50	0	0	0	0	0	0	0	0	0	0	0	0	0	1	0	44	0
Medical Platoon	0	0	8	4	16	0	0	0	0	0	0	0	0	0	0	0	0	0	0	0	7	0

Table 2.7 Tank brigade (TO 10/75-83), from August 1941.

The best tank design of 1941 was the new T-34 tank. Although intended as a cavalry tank to replace the BT series for deep operations, the failure of the T-50 infantry tank led the Red Army to adopt the T-34 for both roles. One of the main shortcomings of Soviet tank tactics throughout the war was poor coordination of the tank and infantry units, stemming in part from the lack of mechanized infantry vehicles comparable to the German or American half-track infantry transporters.

In December a whole new set of TO&Es (Nos 010/345–352) were issued. Two changes were immediately apparent. The first was that overall tank strength in the brigade was reduced to forty-six (including sixteen light tanks), barely the strength of a conventional Western tank battalion. The second was that all three types of tanks – light, medium and heavy – were now integrated into each tank battalion.

A light tank company consisted of two platoons, each with three diminutive T-60 tanks, and the company HQ was provided with two more tanks – none of the eight tanks had a radio. The medium company had three 3-tank platoons plus a headquarters with one tank, of which only the company and platoon command tanks had radios. The heavy tank company had two platoons, each with two KV tanks, while the company HQ had a fifth tank. As with the medium company, the company HQ tank and the platoon leader tanks had radios. The battalion HQ did not have any tanks for command purposes, but did have two motorcycles for dispatch riders and two radios on a single truck.

The rifle companies had a unique organization, with each of the three rifle platoons consisting of three rifle squads (each with a light machine gun) and an anti-tank squad (with an anti-tank rifle), with a 2-gun medium machine gun platoon as the company firepower base. The sub-machine gun company was made up of three 25-man platoons, entirely equipped with sub-machine guns. These were intended as close protection for the tanks, with the sub-machine gunners riding on the tanks of the tank battalions, and thus rarely served under the infantry battalion HQ in combat.

THE RETURN OF THE CORPS

By the spring of 1942 it became apparent that larger groups than these diminutive tank brigades would be required if tanks were to make the decisive contribution to the Soviet war effort. On 31 March orders were issued

for the activation of the 1st–4th tank corps, each to consist of a headquarters, two tank brigades and a motor rifle brigade. These corps had an authorized strength of 5,603 men with 20 KV heavy tanks, 40 T-34 medium tanks (including 8 reserve tanks authorized but rarely present) and 40 T-60 or T-70 light tanks. The corps included no artillery, reconnaissance or engineer units, nor any service support elements.

The motorized rifle brigade was a new formation designed to hold captured terrain and protect the tanks from enemy infantry and anti-tank guns. Under the new TO&Es issued for this unit (Nos 10/370–380) the manoeuvre elements of the brigade were its three motorized infantry battalions. Each of the battalion's three rifle companies consisted of a HQ section, three rifle platoons (each of four squads) and a machine gun platoon (of two squads). Each rifle company was also provided with four

	Men	Main Weapons
Brigade Headquarters	22	
Headquarters Company	170	2 light machine guns
Two Tank Battalions, each		
Battalion HQ	20	
Light Tank Company	17	8 T-60
Medium Tank Company	43	10 T-34
Heavy Tank Company	27	5 KV
Trains Platoon	40	
Motorized Rifle Battalion		407
Battalion HQ		
Two Rifle Companies, each	108	9 light machine guns, 2 machine guns, 3 anti-tank rifles
Submachine Gun Company	79	
Mortar Company	42	6 × 82mm
Trains		
Anti-Aircraft Battery	47	3 heavy machine guns, 4 × 37mm
Trains & Medical		206

Table 2.8 Tank brigade (TO 10/345–352), from December 1941.

	Personnel	Pistols	Submachine Guns	Rifles	Light Machine Guns	Heavy Machine Guns	Medium Machine Guns	Anti-Tank Rifles	82mm Mortars	120mm Mortars	45mm AT Guns	37mm AA Guns	76mm Field Guns	Armored Cars	Motorcycles	Field Cars	Trucks
Brigade Headquarters	84	?	3	?	2	0	0	0	0	0	0	0	0	0	2	3	5
Headquarters Company	105	7	2	83	0	0	0	0	0	0	0	0	0	0	1	0	8
Reconnaissance Company	148	33	44	?	0	0	0	0	0	0	0	0	0	7	6	0	*10
Three Motorized Infantry Battalions, each	641	50	80	?	36	6	0	12	6	0	4	0	0	0	0	1	59
Submachine Gun Company	102	0	91	?	0	0	0	0	0	0	0	0	0	0	0	0	9
Anti-Tank Rifle Company	61	6	0	?	0	0	0	18	0	0	0	0	0	0	0	0	5
Mortar Battalion	195	27	2	?	0	0	0	0	12	4	0	0	0	0	0	1	20
Artillery Battalion	225	23	18	?	0	0	0	0	0	0	0	0	12	0	0	1	23
Anti-Aircraft Battalion	195	22	0	?	0	0	3	0	0	0	0	12	0	0	0	1	20
Trains Company	80	6	1	?	0	0	0	0	0	0	0	0	0	0	1	1	29
Medical Platoon	33	3	0	?	0	0	0	0	0	0	0	0	0	0	0	0	7

* armored trucks

Table 2.9 Motorized rifle brigade (TO 10/370-380), from April 1942.

sniper rifles. Also included in the motorized rifle battalion was an AT rifle company with eighteen weapons, a 6-gun 82mm mortar battery, an anti-tank battery with four 45mm guns, a 32-man sub-machine gun platoon and a pioneer platoon.

The brigade held two indirect-fire support elements: a mortar battalion and an artillery battalion. The former consisted of two 6-gun 82mm batteries and a 4-gun 120mm battery, the latter three 4-gun batteries of 76mm guns. The brigade reconnaissance company was composed of an armoured car platoon, two platoons in armoured trucks, a sub-machine gun platoon and a headquarters.

The tank corps was actually an armoured division, and a small one at that, by Western standards. Several factors limited its usefulness. One obvious problem was the tank mix. A third of its tanks were light T-60 models, with thin armour, weak armament, an inefficient 2-man crew and no radios. The T-34 medium and KV heavy models were effective fighting machines, but the three types of tanks in each battalion had such widely differing characteristics that coordination proved almost impossible. The T-60s and T-34s quickly left the KVs behind during road marches, with these behemoths also ruining roads and crushing bridges. Once the battalion left the roads the T-60s, in turn, were left behind by the T-34s. As a result, the arrival of a tank battalion at an interim objective in one piece was rarity.

Changes to the authorized composition of the brigade were made almost immediately. In mid-April a third tank brigade was added to the corps, along with an independent engineer-mine company. The lack of service support, which had limited the usefulness of the tank corps for an independent role, was partially rectified by the addition in June of a fuel transport company to the corps structure.

Two larger elements were added to the tank corps in July. The first was a rocket-launcher battalion of 250 men consisting of two batteries each with four BM-13 rocket-

One of the more curious armoured weapons to see service on the Eastern Front were armoured trains. These had proved a very valuable form of mobile firepower during the Russian Civil War of 1918–20, but their utility was severely limited by the advent of attack aircraft and tanks. Nevertheless, they remained in use in small numbers for most of the war, being especially useful in providing artillery firepower. Later in the war, anti-aircraft armoured trains became more common to protect railroad convoys.

launcher systems. An extremely useful weapon, the effectiveness of the rocket launchers was limited by the small number deployed. There was no shortage of artillery weapons in the Army as a whole and the Soviets were certainly believers in the value of artillery. The real problem lay in an inability to use artillery in a fluid battle. The kind of firepower employment brought to near-perfection by the American forces, featuring crushing salvos delivered on-call anytime and anywhere, required a modern, extensive and flexible communications net and sophis-

ticated personnel not available to the Red Army, as well as a decentralization of authority that was alien to their political and military dogma. Although the problem of divergent tank types would be solved quickly, that of indirect-fire support would continue to plague Soviet mechanized forces until the end of the war and would cost them dearly in tank losses. The second addition of July 1942 was a motorcycle reconnaissance battalion with 208 men divided into a motorcycle company and an armoured car company, the latter with twenty armoured cars.

Detail changes were made at the same time to the motorized rifle brigade. The 120mm mortar company in the brigade's mortar battalion was expanded to six weapons, while a 9-gun machine gun company was added to each of its rifle battalions. These served to increase brigade strength to about 3,370 men.

ENFORCING STANDARDIZATION

A serious problem was the lack of consistency in even nominal brigade strength. The tank brigades were still organized on three different TO&Es, and in addition an *NKO* order of 29 May had authorized the formation of corps in which one of the brigades was equipped primarily with heavy KV tanks. As a result, the number of tanks

authorized for the various corps varied from 150 to 180 depending on which TO&E their constituent tank brigades were on. To remedy this a new standard tank brigade organization table was published on 31 July 1942, to which all tank brigades were directed to conform, although in some cases this took time.

The new tank brigade TO&Es (Nos 10/270–277) was substantially similar to the earlier except for the tank component and the replacement of the AA battery by an anti-tank battery with four 76mm guns. The tank component for these new brigades consisted of two battalions: one light and one medium. In each case a company consisted of three 3-tank platoons plus a tenth tank in company HQ.

These and other minor changes to the brigade base gave the new tank brigades a

	Men	Main Weapons
Brigade HQ & Company	147	1 T-34
Medium Tank Battalion	151	
Battalion HQ & Platoon	24	1 T-34
Three Medium Tank Companies, each	44	10 T-34
Supply & Trains Group	39	
Light Tank Battalion	146	
Battalion HQ & Platoon		1 T-60/70
Two Light Tank Companies, each		10 T-60/70
Supply & Trains Group		
Motorized Rifle Battalion	403	
Battalion HQ & Platoon		3 armoured cars
Two Rifle Companies, each	112	9 light machine gun, 2 machine gun, 3 anti-tank rifle
Submachine Gun Company	79	
Mortar Company	43	6 × 82mm
Trains Company		
Anti-Tank Battery	52	4 × 76mm
Trains Company	101	
Medical Platoon		

Table 2.10 Tank brigade (TO 10/270–277), from July 1942.

Lend-Lease supplies of tanks were a useful, though not essential, addition to the Red Army. This Red Army unit is equipped with American M3 Stuart light tanks, and the tanker in the foreground is armed with a Thompson sub-machine gun and wears the standard US Army pattern tanker's helmet.

total of 1,038 men with twenty-one light and thirty-two medium tanks from July 1942. For communications each platoon leader and company commander's T-34 carried a radio, while the brigade also had four '*RB*' radios with tall antennas, one *RSB* radio and four *RBS* radios (the latter for the rifle battalion net).

A total of twenty-five tank corps were activated between April and September 1942, largely from existing assets. All of the tank brigades involved had already been fielded and the process simply involved gathering them together, although this was not always easy in practice, as many were heavily committed to combat. The motorized rifle

brigades were new, although it is not clear whether any were simply redesignations of existing rifle units. The final addition to authorized corps strength in 1942 came in December when two maintenance companies were added.

Interestingly, few of the corps actually had their specified combat support units during 1942. Only five motorcycle reconnaissance battalions were actually activated and each of these survived only a few months. No rocket-launcher or anti-aircraft battalions were actually formed for the corps during 1942. The corps thus contained only the headquarters, constituent brigades and a small base of service elements.

	Personnel			Personal Weapons		Main Weapons
	Officers	NCOs	Other	SMGs	Rifles	
Corps Headquarters	56	38	36	5	27	3 medium tanks
Three Tank Brigades, each	229	423	464	490	225	21 light & 32 medium tanks, 18 LMG, 4 MG, 6 ATR, 6 × 82mm mortar, 4 × 76mm guns
Motorized Rifle Brigade	390	1,187	1,960	1,364	1,396	110 LMG, 18 MG, 3 HMG, 54 ATR, 30 × 82mm and 4 × 120mm mortars, 12 × 45mm AT, 12 × 37mm AA, 12 × 76mm guns
Reconnaissance Battalion	41	146	21	50	56	20 armoured cars
Rocket Launcher Battalion	30	56	164	5	104	8 rocket launchers
Pioneer Mine Company	9	20	77	36	60	
Fuel Transport Company	8	9	58	0	51	
Two Maintenance Companies, each	9	13	53	10	20	
NKVD Section	11	6	32	10	20	
Total	1,250	2,757	3,846	2,068	3,126	

Table 2.11 Tank corps, end 1942.

An effort was finally made in December to provide reconnaissance for the corps and at that time ten tank corps received their reconnaissance units. Only one, however, received its rocket-launcher battalion and only one got its anti-aircraft battalion.

Soviet losses of tanks during 1942 were staggering, reaching 2,000–3,000 per month during mid-year and only declining to about 1,000 per month for the rest of the year. Thus only three more corps were formed during the last quarter of 1942. Another reason for the sudden slowdown in the activation of tank corps was the diversion of tanks to a new organizational form starting in the September 1942: the mechanized corps, discussed later.

The first half of 1943 saw a flurry of activity, starting with the addition of an anti-aircraft battery (with four 37mm and four *DShK* machine guns) to the tank brigade structure. Further additions resulted from a 10 January *NKO* order on strengthening tank and mechanized forces. That order immediately added a mortar regiment, an assault gun regiment and a reserve tank detachment to the corps TO&E, and also enlarged the fuel transport company. The mortar regiment used the standard motorized configuration with two battalions each of three 6-gun batteries of 120mm mortars. The usefulness of these very effective weapons, however, was limited by the still primitive communications allotted to them, one radio per 6-gun battery and two more in each battalion HQ. The assault gun regiments were of the early 6-battery type with seventeen SU-76 and eight SU-122. The reserve tank detachment provided 40 spare tanks (33 T-34 and 7 T-70) and 147 crewmen as replacement vehicles, but was probably only rarely filled in practice.

In February 1943 the engineer-mine company was expanded to a pioneer battalion; and in March the AA batteries of the subordinate brigades were consolidated into a corps AA battalion (sixteen 37mm guns) and the signal company expanded to a battalion. Replacing the AA batteries in the tank brigade was an AA-machine gun company with nine *DShK* weapons. In April a tank-destroyer artillery regiment (twenty 45mm guns) was added, along with an air signal platoon.

In May a tank-destroyer artillery battalion (twelve 76mm or 85mm guns) was added, and the SP regiment converted to a heavy SP regiment with twelve SU-152 vehicles. The two towed anti-tank units were replaced in August by two SP regiments, one with twenty-one SU-76s and the other with sixteen SU-122s.

One of the primary weaknesses of the tank corps had been its lack of high-explosive firepower with which to attack defending German infantry and anti-tank guns. Conventional indirect-fire artillery was still beyond Soviet capabilities in fluid battle, so the Red Army developed alternatives. The most notable was the SU-152 mounting the 152mm ML-20 Model 37 gun/howitzer on the chassis of the KV tank. Although its flexibility in support was nowhere near that of conventional artillery, because of its need to see its target, its main gun shell was devastating and Soviet troops learned almost immediately that it performed excellently in the anti-tank role as well.

THE 1943 TANK BRIGADE

A new tank brigade TO&E (No. 10/500–506) was issued in November 1943 that eliminated light tanks completely from the organization. The brigade was now built around three tank battalions, each with two companies of T-34s.

The tank brigade's motorized rifle battalion was reconfigured as a sub-machine gun battalion. This made few changes to the battalion organization, the only notable ones being that the two former rifle companies were converted to purely triangular organization (three platoons each of three squads) and re-equipped with sub-machine guns. Unlike the sub-machine gun companies in other roles, however, these units kept their crew-served machine guns for long-range fire. The third (original) sub-machine gun company kept its prior organization and role of riding into combat on the tanks of the

	Personnel	Submachine Guns	Rifles & Carbines	Light MGs	Medium MGs	Heavy MGs	82mm Mortars	AT Rifles	45mm AT Guns	Armored Cars	Medium Tanks	Motorcycles	Field Cars	Trucks
Brigade Headquarters	54	0	8	0	0	0	0	0	0	0	2	3	0	1
Headquarters Company	164	41	97	4	0	0	0	0	0	3	0	9	0	10
Three Tank Battalions, each	148	30	43	0	0	0	0	0	0	0	21	0	1	12
Motorised Submachine Gun Battalion	507	280	50	18	4	0	18	6	4	0	0	0	0	30
Anti-Air Machine Gun Company	48	1	37	0	0	9	0	0	0	0	0	0	0	9
Trains Company	123	10	113	0	0	0	0	0	0	0	0	0	1	58
Medical Platoon	14	0	14	0	0	0	0	0	0	0	0	0	0	2

Table 2.12 Tank brigade (10/500-506), from November 1943.

	Officers	NCOs	Other	Main Weapons
Battalion HQ	13	3	5	
Two SMG Companies, each	5	22	74	9 LMG, 2 MG
One SMG Company	4	10	81	
Mortar Company	3	13	26	6 × 82mm mortars
AT Rifle Company	53 (total)			18 AT rifles
AT Battery	4	15	25	4 × 45mm AT
Trains Platoon	2	14	29	
Medical Detachment	1	1	3	

Table 2.13 Motorized rifle battalion, from November 1943.

brigade. This gave the battalion the strength shown in Table 2.13.

The tank corps' mortar, rocket-launcher and engineer units also received new TO&Es, although these apparently made only detail changes to their organization. The new engineer battalion TO&E (No. 010/562) authorized 474 men in HQ and trains platoons, 3 pioneer companies (each of 3 platoons) and 1 mine company (3 platoons) armed with 72 pistols, 160 sub-machine guns

Corps Headquarters	32
Signal Battalion	253
Motorcycle Battalion	451
Three Tank Brigades, each	1,362
Motorized Rifle brigade	3,222
Heavy Assault Gun Regiment (SU-152)	374
Assault Gun Regiment (SU-85/100)	318
Light Assault Gun Regiment (SU-76)	225
Light Artillery Regiment	625
Rocket Launcher Battalion	203
Mortar Regiment	596
Anti-Aircraft Regiment	397
Pioneer Battalion	455
Trains elements	298

Table 2.14 Tank corps, January 1945.

and 272 rifles, and provided with 39 1½-ton and two 2½-ton trucks.

In February 1944 all the assault gun regiments were organized on a uniform basis with twenty-one vehicles, and this served to increase tank corps strength from forty-nine assault guns to sixty-three. The attempt to bring indirect fire to the support of mobile forces was manifested in mid-June with the introduction of an artillery commander into the corps headquarters to coordinate artillery fire. In August a light artillery regiment (twenty-four 76mm guns) was added to the corps structure. In a few cases a heavy tank regiment with IS-2 heavy tanks replaced the heavy assault gun regiment with its SU-152s.

This tank brigade and corps organization apparently proved satisfactory, for it remained in effect through the end of the war. The only change noted was an addition of one man per tank when the T-34/85 models were introduced, these having 5-man crews instead of the 4-man crews of the basic model T-34.

MECHANIZED CORPS

The tank corps, with its limited line-infantry strength (fifteen small rifle companies), and virtually non-existent artillery support, was

The KV-1 heavy tank lost favour by the summer of 1942 due to lingering technical problems and the tactical difficulties imposed by its heavy weight. In the autumn of 1942, KVs were withdrawn from tank brigades and the new tank corps and segregated into separate tank regiments for infantry support missions. One common Soviet solution to the lack of infantry transporters was to carry the infantry into combat on board the tanks. While often effective, it could also be a very costly tactic against a well-prepared enemy with artillery support.

simply incapable of holding the ground it had gained. A new approach was needed. The response was the mechanized corps, built around three mechanized brigades.

A mechanized brigade consisted of three motorized infantry battalions and supporting units. The infantry battalions were similar to those in the motorized infantry brigade, but added a machine gun company and expanded the anti-tank rifle company by 50 per cent. The mechanized brigade itself was nearly identical to the motorized infantry brigade. One important difference was the addition of an attached tank 'regiment' of thirty-nine tanks, initially only to the independent mechanized brigades (those not assigned to corps), but shortly thereafter expanded to all mechanized brigades.

The tank regiment's tank companies were triangular, equipped with either three T-34s or five T70s per platoon. The maintenance platoon was divided into a workshop section of seventeen men with three truck-mounted shops, and a 10-man electrical section with a

	April 42	January 43	January 44	May 45
Personnel	5,603	7,853	12,010	11,788
Armour — T-60 Light	40	0	0	0
T-70 Light	0	70	0	0
T-34 Medium	40	98	208	207
KV Heavy	20	0	1	0
SU-76	0	0	21	21
SU-85	0	0	16	21
SU-152/ISU-152	0	0	12	21
Guns & Mortars — 82mm Mortars	42	48	52	52
120mm Mortars	4	4	42	42
45mm AT Guns	12	12	12	12
57mm AT Guns	0	0	16	16
37mm AA Guns	20	2	18	16
76mm Guns	20	24	12	36
M-13 Rocket Launchers	0	8	8	8

Table 2.15 Tank corps authorized strength, 1942-5.

truck-mounted battery charging set. The trains company consisted of a transport platoon for fuel and ammunition with thirty-two trucks, and an administrative platoon with five trucks.

The first two mechanized corps were ordered formed on 8 September 1942 and by the end of the year no fewer than eight had been formed. They were formed from disparate elements, the original two being created from scratch, the 3rd–6th from the remnants of nearly destroyed tank corps, and the 1st and 2nd guards from guards rifle divisions. As a result, the initial batch of mechanized corps had differing organizations. The rifle strength and brigade base remained constant, consisting of three mechanized brigades supported by an anti-tank artillery regiment, an air defence (*PVO*) regiment, a rocket-launcher battalion, an armoured car battalion, an engineer

battalion, a maintenance battalion, an engineer-mine company and a fuel and lubricants transport company. The tank elements, however, differed considerably. In the 1st and 2nd mechanized corps these were formed into a tank brigade, in the 3rd two tank brigades, and in the remainder two tank regiments. As a result, authorized tank strength for the 1st and 2nd corps was 175, for the 3rd it was 224 and for the rest 204.

The corps organization was subjected to continual fine-tuning during the first year. An *NKO* order of 17 September added a motorcycle battalion. It should be noted, however, that through the end of 1943 only one mechanized corps, the 1st, actually had an armoured car battalion (and that only from August 1943), so the motorcycle battalions were, in fact, the corps reconnaissance units.

	1-Jul-42	1-Jan-43	1-Jul-43	1-Jan-44	1-Jul-44	1-Jan-45	1-May-45
Tank Corps HQs	22	20	24	24	24	24	24
Tank Brigades	63	58	72	72	72	72	72
Motor Rifle Brigades	20	19	23	24	24	24	24
Mechanized Brigades	0	3	0	0	0	0	0
Motorcycle Battalions	1	2	13	24	24	23	24
Armored Car Battalions	0	11	1	2	0	0	0
Assault Gun Regiments	0	0	13	42	42	52	58
Mortar Regiments	0	0	20	21	24	23	24
Anti-Tank Regiments	0	0	18	16	11	4	4
Anti-Tank Battalions	0	0	16	22	13	1	0
Rocket Battalions	0	2	4	19	24	22	24
Anti-Aircraft Regiments	0	1	16	21	22	22	23

Table 2.16 Assets actually assigned to Tank Corps on representative dates.

	Officers	NCOs	Other Ranks	Submachine Guns	Carbines	Semi-Automatic Rifles	Rifles	Light Machine Guns	Medium Machine Guns	Heavy Machine Guns	Anti-Tank Rifles	82mm Mortars	120mm Mortars	45mm AT Guns	37mm AA Guns	76mm Field Guns	Armored Trucks	Armored Cars	Light Tanks	T-34 Tanks
Brigade Headquarters	42	17	24	3	6	12	3	2	0	0	0	0	0	0	0	0	0	0	0	0
Headquarters Company	8	25	72	20	52	13	26	0	0	0	0	0	0	0	0	0	0	0	0	0
Reconnaissance Company	9	81	58	82	13	0	7	0	0	0	0	0	0	0	0	0	0	10	7	0
Three Motorized Rifle Battalions, each	66	242	399	276	134	114	61	36	15	0	18	6	0	4	0	0	0	0	0	0
Tank Regiment	86	137	134	34	0	136	0	3	0	0	0	0	0	0	0	0	0	0	16	23
Submachine Gun Company	6	86	10	91	9	0	4	0	0	0	0	0	0	0	0	0	0	0	0	0
Anti-Tank Rifle Company	6	21	49	37	4	0	0	0	0	0	27	0	0	0	0	0	0	0	0	0
Mortar Battalion	29	49	132	2	154	0	78	0	0	0	0	12	6	0	0	0	0	0	0	0
Artillery Battalion	31	69	125	60	88	0	34	0	0	0	0	0	0	0	0	12	0	0	0	0
Anti-Aircraft Battalion	25	56	105	0	104	0	42	0	0	0	12	0	0	0	8	0	0	0	0	0
Trains Company	7	24	49	1	46	0	23	0	0	0	0	0	0	0	0	0	0	0	0	0
Medical Platoon	9	5	19	0	9	0	0	0	0	0	0	0	0	0	0	0	0	0	0	0

notes:
(a) "officers" includes political and warrant officers
(b) the tank regiment includes 2 field cars and 54 trucks (including 9 special trucks)
(b) distribution of the brigade's other 11 field cars, 308 cargo trucks and other transport is unknown.

Table 2.17 Mechanized brigade summary (TO 10/370-380), from September 1942.

In January 1943 the tank regiment was made a permanent part of the brigade. A new TO&E was published for the tank regiment (No. 10/414) that increased the number of T-34 medium tanks at the expense of the less capable T-70 light tanks. The new organization called for a small headquarters (the commander, commissar, technical officer, staff officer, operations officer, a radioman and four clerks), three medium tank companies (each of three 3-tank platoons plus one tank in the HQ), a light tank company (two 3-tank platoons plus one tank in the HQ), a headquarters company (pioneer, scout and administrative platoons) and a trains company with thirty trucks. In addition, a sub-machine gun company and an anti-tank rifle platoon were added to the

	Officers	NCOs	Other Ranks	Submachine Guns	Carbines	Semi-Automatic Rifles	Light Machine Guns	Medium Machine Guns	Heavy Machine Guns	Anti-Tank Rifles	82mm Mortars	120mm Mortars	45mm AT Guns	76mm Field Guns	Armored Trucks	Armored Cars	Light Tanks	Medium Tanks	Motorcycles	Field Cars	Trucks
Brigade Headquarters	39	15	26	3	8	19	2	0	0	0	0	0	0	0	0	0	0	0	0	2	4
Headquarters Company	5	17	51	0	60	0	0	0	0	0	0	0	0	0	0	0	0	0	6	0	5
Reconnaissance Company	7	72	62	79	14	0	0	0	0	0	0	0	0	0	10	7	0	0	6	0	4
Tank Regiment	89	194	187	143	95	57	2	0	0	0	0	0	0	0	0	3	7	32	4	2	70
Three Motorized Rifle Battalions, each	48	212	389	273	99	138	36	15	0	18	6	0	4	0	0	0	0	0	1	1	26
Submachine Gun Company	4	22	68	88	5	0	0	0	0	0	0	0	0	0	0	0	0	0	1	0	1
Anti-Tank Rifle Company	4	20	45	37	0	0	0	0	0	27	0	0	0	0	0	0	0	0	0	0	0
Mortar Battalion	23	47	127	2	0	147	0	0	0	0	12	6	0	0	0	0	0	0	0	0	20
Artillery Battalion	24	67	123	60	100	9	0	0	0	0	0	0	0	12	0	0	0	0	0	1	25
Anti-Aircraft MG Company	4	23	21	0	32	0	0	0	9	0	0	0	0	0	0	0	0	0	0	0	12
Pioneer Mine Company	8	23	90	53	10	50	0	0	0	0	0	0	0	0	0	0	0	0	0	0	6
Trains Company	6	28	38	1	43	0	0	0	0	0	0	0	0	0	0	0	0	0	1	0	31
Medical Platoon	8	5	19	0	9	0	0	0	0	0	0	0	0	0	0	0	0	0	0	0	5

Table 2.18 Mechanized brigade summary (TO 10/420-432), from February 1943 (as amended to September 1943).

structure to provide close-in support for tanks. Not all regiments, however, immediately changed to this organization and the older format of two medium companies and one large light company remained in use in some units well into 1944.

Also in January a mortar regiment, a mixed self-propelled artillery regiment (either light with 25 SU-76 or mixed with 17 SU-76 and 8 SU-122), and a reserve tank detachment were added to the corps structure, identical to those added to the tank corps at the same time. The introduction of a self-propelled artillery regiment with SU-76 guns to the corps relieved the tanks of much of their mobile anti-tank and infantry overwatch roles, freeing them for offensive employment.

Building on the new tank regiment organization, a new set of TO&Es (Nos 10/420–432) was issued in February for the mechanized brigade. The motorized infantry battalion was not significantly changed, although the number of officers and NCOs was reduced, apparently to ameliorate the drain on trained leadership. The anti-aircraft

regiment was deleted, replaced by a small company with nine 12.7mm *DShK* heavy machine guns on trucks. The corps pioneer company, which specialized in mine-laying and removal, had proved very useful and as a result it was disbanded and replaced by a similar company in each brigade. A motor transport company was added to the mechanized brigade, a consolidation of the transport assets previously held by the infantry battalions.

In March the air defence regiment (from the *PVO*) was replaced by an Army anti-aircraft regiment consisting of four gun batteries (each with two 2-gun platoons of 37mm guns), an AA machine gun company (four platoons each of four 12.7mm machine guns) and trains elements, and the signal company was expanded to a battalion. In April the corps anti-tank regiment was redesignated a tank-destroyer artillery regiment, although without any substantive change in organization. In May a separate anti-tank battalion was added to the corps, identical to those added to the tank corps at the same time.

	8 September 42	1 January 43	1 January 44	1 May 45
Personnel	15,581	15,018	16, 370	16,438
Armoured Vehicles				
Light Tanks	69	42	21	0
Medium Tanks	101	162	176	183
Heavy Tanks	5	0	0	0
Light Assault Guns	0	17	21	21
Medium Assault Guns	0	0	16	21
Heavy Assault Guns	0	8	12	21
Guns & Mortars				
82mm Mortars	102	94	100	100
120mm Mortars	48	54	54	54
45mm AT guns	36	36	36	36
57mm AT guns	0	0	8	8
37mm AA guns	40	26	18	16
76mm guns	40	36	36	36
BM-13 rocket launchers	8	8	8	8

Table 2.19 Mechanized corps authorized strength, 1942–5.

As a result of these changes, not only was the 1943 mechanized corps twice the size of the contemporary tank corps (15,018 men versus 7,800 men), but it actually had more tanks (42 light and 162 medium in the mechanized corps versus 70 light and 98 medium in the tank corps). The mechanized corps was thus not only capable of holding ground seized by the marauding tank corps, but was an extremely potent offensive weapon in its own right.

Also during this time the process of standardizing the tank component of the mechanized corps at a single brigade was begun. In March 1943 the 5th Mechanized Corps and the 5th Guards Mechanized Corps (formerly the 6th Mechanized Corps) reorganized their tank regiments into a tank brigade; in April the 3rd Guards (ex-4th Mechanized Corps) and 4th Guards (ex-13th

Tank Corps) followed suit. In May the 2nd Guards Mechanized Corps did the same, followed by the 1st Guards Mechanized Corps in July. The 7th and 8th Mechanized Corps did not convert until October, while the 9th Mechanized Corps did not convert to the brigade organization until January 1945.

In the meantime, small numbers of mechanized corps continued to be activated, the 7th–9th in January–February 1943, the 6th Guards in June 1943 and the 10th in December 1944. The 6th Guards Mechanized Corps was not simply a redesignation of an existing unit but a conversion and consolidation of the 3rd Guards Motorized Rifle Division and the 49th Mechanized Brigade.

Further organizational changes came in August 1943. At that time the self-propelled component of the corps was redefined as

A tank crew is greeted by a Russian peasant family during the summer offensives of 1943. The workhorse of the Soviet tank corps during the war was the T-34 medium tank. This is a T-34 Model 1943, the final evolution of the family with the 76mm gun. In 1942–3, the emphasis in the T-34 programme was to simplify the design to enable maximum production. Technical improvements in armour and firepower were sacrificed for production quotas, and the technological balance on the Eastern Front began slipping in favour of the Wehrmacht.

three regiments. One regiment was equipped with SU-76s, one with SU-85s and one with the powerful SU-152. Early next year these regiments were reorganized to twenty-one vehicles apiece. At the same time the tank-destroyer artillery regiment was rearmed with 76mm ZiS-3 guns and the separate anti-tank battalion abolished. In fact, as can be seen from Table 2.19, the anti-tank regiments never formed a part of most mechanized corps and it took until the end of the war before most had their full complement of three assault gun regiments.

The November 1943 reorganization of the armoured force had affected the mechanized corps as well. The new tank brigade organization was adopted, although some corps continued to use the earlier organization, which included light tanks, into 1945. The mechanized corps thus nominally included 183 T-34 medium tanks: 39 in each of three mechanized brigades, 65 in the tank brigade and 1 in the corps HQ. The mechanized brigade, however, apparently remained unchanged (except for the usual continual detail changes) from its February 1943 TO&E.

	1-Jan-43	1-Jul-43	1-Jan-44	1-Jul-44	1-Jan-45	1-May-45
Mechanized Corps HQs	8	13	13	13	14	14
Mechanized Brigades	24	39	39	39	39	39
Tank Brigades	6	9	11	11	12	12
Tank Regiments	8	4	6	4	7	8
Assault Gun Regiments	0	0	21	22	30	32
Motorcycle Battalions	6	9	13	12	13	13
Armored Car Battalions	5	0	0	0	0	0
Mortar Regiments	0	8	13	10	13	13
Anti-Tank Regiments	5	8	7	4	2	1
Light Artillery Regiments	1	0	0	0	0	0
Anti-Aircraft Regiments	0	5	9	12	13	13
Rocket Battalions	7	7	11	13	13	13
Anti-Tank Battalions	2	5	12	6	1	1
note: 1945 columns include 10th Mech Corps in Far East with no subordinate units.						

Table 2.20 Assets actually assigned to mechanized corps on representative dates.

A T-34 Model 1943 of the 5th Guards Tank Corps at the time of the titanic tank battles of the Kursk salient in the summer of 1943. By the time of the Kursk battle, Russian tank designs had slipped in quality compared to their German counterparts as the Soviet industry focused on equipping the growing tank force. However, Soviet proficiency in the use of tank formations, and the tactical skills of the Soviet tank units, had continued to improve compared to their lacklustre performance in 1942.

	Personnel	Pistols	Submachine Guns	Rifles & Carbines	Light Machine Guns	Maxim Machine Guns	12.7mm Machine Guns	AT Rifles	82mm Mortars	120mm Mortars	37mm AA Guns	57mm AT Guns	76mm Field/AT Guns	100mm Field/AT Guns	BM-13 Rocket Launchers	T-34/76 Tanks	T-34/85 Tanks	IS-2 Tanks	SU-57 Assault Guns	SU-76 Assault Guns	SU-85 Assault Guns	ISU-122 Assault Guns
VI Gds Tank Corps	12010	2276	3744	5094	211	57	52	195	52	42	16	28	36	0	8	0	207	0	0	21	21	21
VII Gds Tank Corps	12010	2276	3744	5094	211	57	52	195	52	42	16	28	36	0	8	0	207	0	0	21	21	21
IX Mechanized Corps	16442	2802	5139	7168	381	139	52	297	100	54	16	44	36	0	8	0	182	0	0	21	21	21
50th Motorcycle Regiment	n/a	120	517	432	36	12	0	18	12	0	0	8	4	0	0	0	10	0	0	0	0	0
1381st AA Regiment	396	43	42	250	0	0	16	0	0	0	16	0	0	0	0	0	0	0	0	0	0	0
1394th AA Regiment	396	43	42	250	0	0	16	0	0	0	16	0	0	0	0	0	0	0	0	0	0	0
91st Rocket Launcher Regiment	695	77	35	492	8	0	0	24	0	0	0	0	0	0	24	0	0	0	0	0	0	0
16th Assault Gun Brigade	1112	302	397	391	4	0	9	0	0	0	0	0	0	0	0	0	0	0	0	65	0	0
199th Light Artillery Brigade	n/a	221	379	1231	35	0	0	68	0	0	0	0	48	20	0	0	0	0	0	0	0	0
57th Guards Heavy Tank Regiment	374	120	144	110	1	0	0	0	0	0	0	0	0	0	0	0	1	21	0	0	0	0
90th Engineer Tank Regiment	n/a	75	87	72	0	0	0	0	0	0	0	0	0	0	0	18	4	0	0	0	0	0
19th Engineer Mine Brigade	n/a	116	643	284	30	0	0	0	0	0	0	0	0	0	0	0	0	0	0	0	0	0
Army Troops	n/a	1512	718	4770	52	12	3	16	6	2	0	2	1	0	0	0	20	0	0	1	1	1

Table 2.21 3rd Guards tank army authorized strength, 28 January 1945.

THE TANK ARMIES

The answer to the German panzer corps was to be the tank army. The first two, the 3rd and 5th, were ordered formed on 25 May 1942. Each had two tank corps, a separate tank brigade and support units. In addition, the 3rd Tank Army had two rifle divisions and the 5th Tank Army one. The 1st and 4th tank armies followed in July. With the creation of the mechanized corps the rifle divisions were no longer needed and the composition was standardized at two tank corps and a mechanized corps, plus supporting units. In April 1943 *Stavka* directed that each tank army receive 2 AT artillery regiments (each 20 × 76mm), 2 mortar regiments (each 36 × 120mm), 2 assault gun regiments (each 9 × SU-76 and 12 × SU-122), 2 AA regiments (each 16 × *DShK* and 16 x 37mm) and 1 rocket launcher regiment (24 × *BM*-13). In early 1944 each tank army was also given a light assault gun brigade (60 × SU-76 and 5 × T-70) and a light artillery brigade (48 × 76mm and 20 × 100mm). There was, of course, some variation among the tank armies, but the authorized strength of the 3rd Guards Tank Army was typical. It is noteworthy that the army was actually at or close to full strength at the time in all weapons except the obsolescent AT rifle.

INDEPENDENT TANK UNITS

At the time of the German invasion there was only one separate tank battalion in the *RKKA* order of battle and large-scale activation of such units did not start until August, when fifty battalions were activated followed by twenty-four more the following month. The TO&E for a separate tank battalion, published on 23 August, called for 130 men divided into a headquarters (2 T-34s), a medium tank company (7 T-34s), two light tank companies (each with 10 T-60s) and a trains platoon. Although designed to support the infantry without requiring diversion of tank brigades to this role, they proved to have too light a mixture of tanks.

A new TO&E was published in November that made the battalion a heavier organization. It provided a 2-platoon heavy company, a 3-platoon medium company and two 3-platoon light companies. Officers commanded the KVs and T-34s and all tank crew were NCOs. This TO&E was applied to the eighty separate tank battalions raised in

	Officers	NCOs	Other ranks	Equipment
Battalion Headquarters	14	5	4	1 T-34, 2 m/c, 1 truck
Heavy Tank Company	7	19	0	5 KV tanks
Medium Tank Company	13	30	0	10 T-34 tanks
Two Light Tank Companies, each	7	16	0	10 T-40 or T-60 tanks
Trains elements	5	12	47	1 m/c, 1 car, 22 cargo trucks, 6 shop trucks, 4 tractors

Table 2.22 Separate tank battalion (TO 10/302), from November 1941.

December 1941 and January 1942. Few new separate battalions were created thereafter, however, and from 100 such units in early 1942 the number slowly declined to twenty-eight by the end of 1943 and then to five by the end of 1944.

In its place was the separate tank regiment. A few such units, never more than one or two, had existed during the first year of the war, but it was not until September 1942 that activation of these units for the close support of the infantry began in earnest. These units used the same TO&E as the tank regiments of the mechanized brigades, consisting of 339 men in a HQ (1 T-34), one light tank company (16 T-70s) and two medium companies (each with 11 T-34s). Thereafter the separate tank regiments developed in parallel with those in the mechanized brigades, and in January 1943 adopted the new TO&E that featured three 10-tank companies of T-34s and one 7-tank company of T-70s (plus two more T-34s and three armoured cars in regiment HQ), along with a new 94-man sub-machine gun company and an AT rifle platoon with 18 weapons. These elements brought regiment strength up to 572 men. In February 1944 the light tanks were dropped completely from the organization along with the AT rifles and

strength dropped to 401 men with thirty-five T-34s. Starting in April 1944 some of the regiments were reconfigured into four 10-tank companies of T-34s and one sub-machine gun company for a total of 401 men with 41 tanks and three armoured cars.

With the decision to strip the heavy tanks out of the tank brigades in late 1942 a new type of formation was created, the guards heavy breakthrough tank regiment. These began forming in October of that year, each consisting of four tank companies and a maintenance company. With only four tanks in each company, plus one in the regimental headquarters, these were little better than Western tank companies, totalling 215 men with twenty-one KV heavy tanks and one light armoured car. In February 1944 a 94-man sub-machine gun company, a pioneer platoon and a trains platoon were added, bringing strength up to 374 men. At the same time the process of replacing the KVs with new IS-2 tanks was begun, and the term 'breakthrough' was dropped from the title.

By the end of 1942 no fewer than seventy-seven separate tank regiments had been formed, including fifteen guards heavy breakthrough regiments. By the end of 1943 the number of separate regiments on strength had risen to 115, of which thirty-four were the heavy variety (two of which had been initially equipped with Churchills in lieu of KVs). From this point the number of separate tank regiments declined (to sixty-three at the end of 1944), in part reflecting conversions to assault guns.

In February 1945 one (medium) separate tank brigade was converted to a guards heavy tank brigade, to consist of three guards heavy tank regiments (each with twenty-one IS-2s) and a 403-man motorized sub-machine gun battalion. These gave the brigade a total of 1,666 men with 65 heavy tanks, 3 armoured cars (in the brigade scout platoon), 19 armoured trucks and 3 SU-76s.

Seven tank regiments were reconfigured as engineer tank regiments during 1943–4. Four were assigned to the same four engineer assault brigades as also received flame tank battalions, while the other three served as separate *RVGK* assets. They were identical to the regular tank regiments except that sixteen sets of tank-mounted mine-rollers were added to the establishment to clear mine paths.

ASSAULT GUN UNITS

The initial group of thirty assault gun regiments was ordered activated in late December 1942 and was completed the following March. Most of these regiments consisted of four batteries of SU-76s and two of SU-122s, with four vehicles in each battery and a further SU-76 for the regimental commander. A few units had two batteries of SU-76s and three of SU-122s. Complementing these for the heavy assault role was an initial batch of sixteen heavy assault gun regiments formed in March. Each of these consisted of six batteries (each with two SU-152s) plus a KV in the regimental HQ.

The burden of maintaining two completely different vehicles in the same small regiment

quickly proved too much and in April new TO&Es were issued for subsequently raised units that created homogenous light and medium assault gun regiments. An assault gun regiment (sometimes called a medium assault gun regiment) would now have four batteries each of four SU-122s, with a T-34 tank in the regiment HQ for a command vehicle, totalling 248 men. A light assault gun regiment would have four batteries each of five SU-76s, with another SU-76 for the regiment commander, totalling twenty-one SU-76s and 259 men in the regiment. The heavy regiment retained its earlier organization with 273 men. Indicative of its support role, the SU-152 regiment usually carried a basic load of 180 rounds of high explosives and sixty rounds of armour-piercing ammunition for its assault guns.

In August 1943 the SU-85 with greater tank killing power replaced the SU-122 on the production lines and the (medium) assault gun regiments were gradually converted to this new equipment. In September the howitzer-armed ISU-152 replaced the SU-152 and in December the ISU-122, with its gun armament, was also accepted for service. These two began replacing the SU-152s in the heavy assault gun regiments. Finally, the SU-100, a dedicated tank-killer, began production in September, and production of the SU-85 ended that December. Thus, the light regiments continued to be armed with SU-76s, the medium regiments started with SU-122s, then adopted the SU-85 and then the SU-100; while the heavy regiments started with the SU-152 then switched to the ISU-152 and ISU-122.

In October all assault gun regiments were reorganized on to a 4-battery basis, while keeping the same number of combat vehicles (21 SU-76s for a light regiment, 16 SU-122s or SU-85s plus a T-34 for a medium regiment, and 12 SU-152s or ISU-152s plus a KV or IS-2

	Officers	Political Officers	Warrant Officers	NCOs	Other Ranks	Pistols	Carbines	Submachine Guns	BA-64 Armored Cars	T-34 Tanks	SU-122 Assault Guns	Motorcycles	Cars	Trucks	Tractors
Regiment Headquarters	15	3	2	13	26	20	11	28	1	1	0	5	1	0	0
Four Batteries, each	6	0	0	10	12	8	0	20	0	0	4	0	0	0	0
Medical Section	2	0	0	2	3	4	3	0	0	0	0	0	0	1	0
trains elements	8	0	0	19	43	9	30	31	0	0	0	0	0	36	2

Table 2.23 Medium assault gun regiment (TO 10/192), from April 1943.

in a heavy regiment). This was an interim organization and in February 1944 all regiments were ordered to a uniform organization of four batteries each of five assault guns (plus a twenty-first vehicle in the regiment HQ), although it seems likely that the actual reorganization was not completed until the end of the year. Supporting the batteries in a regiment were also a sub-machine gun company, a pioneer platoon and trains elements for a total of 318 men, 21 assault guns, a BA-64 armoured car, 43 trucks and 2 tractors in, for instance, an SU-85 regiment.

The formation of larger units came in February 1944, with the raising of the first assault gun brigade. A total of seven light assault gun brigades were formed in the next four months, six of them for inclusion in tank armies. Each brigade consisted of three assault gun battalions, a sub-machine gun battalion, an AA machine gun company and trains elements for a total of 1,112 men. Each assault gun battalion had five batteries (each of four SU-76s) and a headquarters (one T-70 tank).

In January–March 1945 four (medium) assault gun brigades were formed, each consisting of three assault gun regiments, a reconnaissance company and an AA machine gun company, as well as trains elements. The brigade thus had sixty-five SU-100 and three SU-76 assault guns. Finally, in March 1945 a heavy assault gun brigade was formed, identical to the medium brigade but with heavy regiments instead of medium, thus giving sixty-five ISU-122s and three SU-76s.

By the end of the war the *RKKA* included 12 assault gun brigades (7 light, 4 medium and 1 heavy) and 241 separate assault gun regiments (119 light, 69 medium and 53 heavy), along with 70 battalions raised to support guards rifle divisions. Of these regiments, 105 were allocated as organic parts of tank, mechanized and cavalry corps, and the rest were independent units in the *VGK* reserve.

RECONNAISSANCE UNITS

The Soviet Army raised surprisingly few reconnaissance units for a force its size. Armoured cars were incorporated into rifle and mechanized divisions, but no separate units had been formed by the outbreak of the war except for three special units in the Transbaikal Military District. The vast distances and plains of that area made it ideal for wheeled combat vehicles and between 1936 and 1938 three armoured car brigades (7th–9th) were formed, each with about 190 heavy (BA-6/10) armoured cars.

One sign of the growing operational proficiency of the Soviet tank force was the recognition of the need for specialized equipment to assist in offensive breaching operations. Mines posed a serious threat to tanks attempting to break through prepared defences, and mine-rollers were a Soviet approach to counter the mine threat. The rollers detonated mines in front of the tank and could be replaced if they became too damaged. (Janusz Magnuski)

Soviet tankers prepare a meal in the early morning chill in the spring of 1945. Their tank is an *emcha*, a Lend-Lease M4A2 Sherman medium tank. Several Soviet tank corps operating in central Europe in 1945 were entirely equipped with this type in lieu of the more common T-34.

Little of the internal organization of these brigades is known but Japanese Army intelligence (unfortunately not known for its accuracy) assessed them in 1941 as being built around three armoured car battalions and a motorized rifle battalion. Although all three brigades still figured in the May 1940 force structure plans, by the time of the German invasion only one, the 9th, remained. It served in the Transbaikal until it too was disbanded in mid-1943.

Although motorcycles were the preferred reconnaissance platform for the Soviets, probably due to their low cost, armoured car battalions were formed for use with the Leningrad and Karelian fronts, which were simply too cold for much of the year for open vehicles. Three battalions were formed in May–June 1942 and twenty-one more during September–October. The bulk of these were diverted to the various corps organizations, so that by the end of 1943 only six remained as separate units. These six remained on strength to the end of the war.

The only large motorcycle units in the *RKKA* at the start of Operation Barbarossa were the motorcycle regiments found in each of the mechanized corps. The dissolution of the corps brought twelve of these regiments into the *RVGK* pool, although by the end of the year only seven remained. Each of these consisted of three motorcycle rifle companies, one mortar company (60 men with 18 × 50mm), an anti-tank battery (4 × 45mm), an armoured company (four armoured cars and four T-27As) and service elements for a total of about 900 men. Each rifle company consisted of three rifle platoons and a machine gun platoon for a total of 180 men, 54 sub-machine guns, and 9 light and 4 medium machine guns.

A new series of three motorcycle regiments was raised starting in March 1943 and a new TO&E was issued at the same time. The three rifle companies were grouped together under a battalion headquarters and the anti-tank component expanded to a battalion with three 4-gun batteries (two of 45mm and one 76mm). The armoured company was reconfigured as a tank company (initially sixteen T-70s, later ten T-34s), and a pioneer company and an armoured personnel carrier company added, the latter equipped with Lend-Lease M3A1 scout cars.

A smaller version was also authorized as the motorcycle battalion. A series of nineteen battalions was raised during March–September 1942. The bulk of these were diverted to the mechanized and tank corps during 1943, so that from October 1943 onward, only four to six battalions were held in the *RVGK* reserve. Initially such a battalion consisted of two rifle companies and an armoured car company for a total of 287 men. In mid-1943 they were reorganized to include a tank company of ten T-34s and an armoured personnel carrier company (replacing a motorcycle rifle company), increasing strength to 451. One motorcycle brigade was formed by the Western Front in May 1942, consisting of three motorcycle battalions, but it was disbanded in February 1943.

AEROSLED UNITS

A unique Soviet formation was the aerosled battalion equipped with the unique powered snow vehicles that the Russians called *aerosan*. An initial group of sixty-two battalions was raised starting in January 1942 but as warm weather approached they were disbanded, the last seventeen in June. A second group of seventy began forming in October but this time they were kept on duty through the summer of 1943, although their numbers slowly declined to fifty-seven at the end of the year. In May 1944 reduction began anew and in June all the remaining aerosled battalions

Clattering across another cobblestone street, Soviet armour enters another German town in the final campaigns of the war in 1945. The associated motor rifle troops ride on board this T-34-85 tank, an expedient method of infantry mechanization. By 1945, the Red Army had become an adept practitioner in the art of mechanized warfare, even if its tactics still remained stereotyped and costly.

were disbanded and no further examples were formed.

The battalions were exceptionally small, even by Soviet standards. The basic unit, the platoon, consisted of three NKL-26 armoured aerosleds, each with a 2-man crew and armed with a light machine gun. Three such platoons, plus a tenth aerosled for the commander, made up a company. The battalion consisted of three such companies plus a headquarters and a supply company, the latter with ten cargo/utility aerosleds. These elements gave the battalion a total strength of about 100 men.

SPECIAL MOTORIZED BATTALIONS

In May 1944 the Red Army formed nine 'independent special purpose motorized battalions' under the armour branch to take advantage of Lend-Lease American amphibious trucks. Such a battalion consisted of a headquarters company, two line companies, a mortar company, a pioneer company and a maintenance company. A line company had three platoons each of three sections, with each section having three amphibious trucks. The mortar company was similar to the line company but the pioneer company had only five amphibious trucks, complemented by four regular trucks. These battalions served to the end of the war, providing useful river-crossing capabilities and one was transferred to the Far East for use against the Japanese in Manchuria.

Notes

1. The data, which is taken from Magnuski and Kolomijec, seemingly does not show all the T-37 tanks.

2. Zaloga, 1984, p. 126

3. This change apparently did not apply to the tank brigades that were operating with older tanks. On 10 November 1941 the 54th Tank Brigade reported itself using the old (August) TO&E and at full strength in tanks, but all ninety-three tanks being T-26 models.

CHAPTER 3

RED ARMY CAVALRY

Although probably not as important in the Czarist Army as it was in the western European states, the cavalry had risen to importance rapidly during the Russian Civil War where the large spaces and relatively small number of combatants created situations well suited for the employment of mounted troops. The first major reorganization following the conclusion of the civil war occurred in 1925 and resulted in the reduction of the number of cavalry regiments per division from six to four, while simultaneously increasing the number of line squadrons in the regiments from four to six. In addition, a machine gun squadron with sixteen pieces on 2-wheel carts and a regimental battery were added. In the fall of 1931 an artillery regiment was added to each cavalry division, this consisting of one battalion of 76mm guns and one of 122mm howitzers each of two 4-gun batteries, substantially increasing the divisions' firepower.

The cavalry arm was again reorganized in April 1936. In addition to the four cavalry regiments, a cavalry division was now to include a regiment of thirty-four (later sixty-four) fast BT-5 tanks in three squadrons, eighteen armoured cars in one squadron, and amphibious tanks in one squadron. The cavalry regiment was reduced back to its former complement of four line squadrons, but retained its machine gun squadron and artillery battery, plus an anti-aircraft machine gun platoon attached to its regimental HQ.

THE PRE-WAR CAVALRY

The smallest unit was the squad, which came in two varieties: a 6-man light machine gun squad and a 6-man grenadier squad. One of each type of squad was incorporated into each mounted section, with one of the squad leaders functioning as the section leader. In addition, one of the two sections in each platoon also nominally included a headquarters (officially 'sabre') squad, this consisting of the platoon leader, a messenger, an observer/signaler, a corporal in charge of horses and two horse-holders.

These elements gave the platoon a total strength of one officer and twenty-nine enlisted men, although it should be noted that in dismounted combat the horse corporal and ten men were left back with the horses. When such a platoon dismounted for combat it formed a headquarters (platoon leader, observer and messenger), and two 8-man sections (each with a light machine gun and a rifle grenade launcher). In 1940 a 50mm mortar team was added to each platoon headquarters to provide limited fire against targets in defilade. A mounted squadron consisted of a small headquarters, a trains group and four (two or three in peace) mounted platoons.

The regimental machine gun squadron consisted of four or five platoons, each with two sections. A section was made up of a section leader and two 7-man gun squads each with four riding horses and a 4-horse wagon for the Maxim machine gun.

Urraaa! A cavalry charge might seem out of place in an age of tanks and machine guns, but in the vastness of the Eastern Front, a mounted charge against unprepared German infantry could prove effective. Nevertheless, most Soviet cavalry operations of the war employed the horse for mobility – combat was conducted dismounted. But sabre charges were still part of training.

The regimental artillery battery was composed of one platoon with four 76mm regimental guns and two platoons each with two 45mm AT guns. A regimental gun section consisted of a mounted section leader, four draft horses pulling a caisson and gun in tandem, and four more pulling two caissons in tandem, with each caisson carrying twelve rounds. In the late 1930s the anti-tank weapons were split off to form their own anti-tank battery of four weapons. Reportedly, the horse artillery battery was reduced to three guns at the same time, although this is not certain.

For a mobile force the cavalry regiment was not well provided with communications. The signal half-squadron included three 7-man wire sections (of doubtful utility for a mobile force), a 12-man radio section (with three radios), a 5-man optical signalling squad, a 6-man motorcycle squad and a 5-man mounted messenger squad. The only other radios in the regiment were three units in the horse battery.

The other maneouvre element of the cavalry division was the mechanized regiment. Several organizational patterns were tried for this unit. The earliest simply consisted of a headquarters (four BT tanks) and four 10 or 16-tank squadrons (three with the BT fast tanks, and one with T-37 light amphibious tanks). In August 1938 an armoured car squadron with BA-10 vehicles was added to the regiment but in at least some of the divisions this appears to have replaced, rather than supplemented, an existing armoured squadron. The armoured cars, with their high road speed, provided a useful reconnaissance capability in more developed areas.

By 1939 the cavalry division mechanized regiment had evolved into a comprehensive, if slightly unbalanced, combined-arms formation. In addition to the four armoured squadrons (with tanks, light tanks and armoured cars in varying mixes), it also included a motorized rifle company, an artillery battery and other units. The armoured squadrons each consisted of three platoons of either three or five vehicles each, with one further vehicle in the squadron HQ. A notable feature was the complete absence from these squadrons of any support elements, such as transportation or maintenance. The rifle company consisted of two rifle platoons (each of three 10-man squads) and a machine gun platoon (with two 4-man squads). Communications here were somewhat better than in the mounted regiments. Four of the armoured vehicles in each armoured squadron were provided with radios, one each for the squadron and platoon commanders; and the two tanks in the regimental HQ were also radio-equipped. In addition, the regimental HQ platoon and the signal platoons of the two battalions also each included an 8-man section with two radios. A further three radios were held by the artillery battery.

A large horse artillery battalion provided divisional fire support with four batteries of 76mm field guns. Such a battery had four 14-man gun teams (each with one gun and caisson, pulled in tandem by eight draft horses and ten riding horses), four 4-man ammunition teams (each with two caissons pulled in tandem by six draft horses) and one 16-man headquarters. By 1939 this had been expanded slightly to a regiment of two battalions by adding two intermediate HQs and two 122mm howitzer batteries.

The cavalry arm reached its pre-war peak strength in early 1938 with an establishment of thirty-two divisions and two independent brigades organized into seven cavalry corps. By this time, however, the drive to provide large-scale mechanized formations was starting to eat into cavalry strength, and in 1938 two corps were converted to mechanized units.

A scene reminiscent of the civil war, a horsedrawn *tachanka* moves to the front. The *tachanka* was invented by the anarchist leader Makhno during the civil war to permit the cavalry to move the heavy and cumbersome Maxim machine gun into combat. The *tachanka* could still be seen in action during the first years of the war, as here on the Western Front in 1942.

Cavalry played a major role in the Soviet invasion of Poland in September 1939. The major mounted units involved were the II, III, IV, V and VI cavalry corps. Available evidence suggests that each of the divisions included 30–45 older model BT-2 and BT-5 tanks and, in some cases, 10–15 armoured cars. The cavalry played no part in the Winter War against Finland, and thereafter the reduction in cavalry branch strength continued. By the outbreak of the war with Germany the cavalry arm had been reduced to four corps HQs and thirteen divisions.

During 1940 a few changes were made to the divisional organization. The anti-aircraft battery was expanded to a battalion, and it seems likely that the mechanized regiment lost many of its supporting elements to become a tank regiment. Economies in manpower appear to have been enforced at the same time. Thus, by the time of the German invasion a cavalry division had an authorized strength of 9,240 men with 64 light tanks, 18 armoured cars, 32 artillery pieces, 16 anti-tank guns, 20 anti-aircraft guns and 64 50mm mortars. A cavalry corps consisted of two or three cavalry divisions plus HQ and logistics elements, but no additional combat support such as artillery. A mountain cavalry division was substantially

Unit	Personnel	Pistols	Semi-Automatic Rifles	Rifles	Light Machine Guns	Medium Machine Guns	AA Machine Guns	45mm Anti-Tank Guns	76mm Infantry Guns	76mm Field Guns	122mm Howitzers	BT Tanks	T-37 Tanks	Armored Cars	Motorcycles	Trucks	Tractors	Riding Horses	Draft Horses	Wagons & Carts
Division Headquarters	82	43		39	0	0	0	0	0	0	0	0	0	0	0	0	0	82	0	
Headquarters Squadron	176	92		73	0	6	2	0	0	0	0	0	0	0	14	0	0	60	10	
HQ Transport Group	72	1		71	0	0	0	0	0	0	0	0	0	0	0	11	0	20	29	19
Anti-Aircraft Platoon	32	14		18	0	0	3	0	0	0	0	0	0	0	3	3	0	0	0	
Signal Squadron	98	23		69	5	0	0	0	0	0	0	0	0	0	6	0	0	80	10	8
Four Cavalry Regiments, each																				
Regiment HQ	22	17		5	0	0	0	0	0	0	0	0	0	0	0	0	0	22	0	0
HQ Platoon	45	7		34	4	0	0	0	0	0	0	0	0	0	0	1	0	37	8	4
Signal Half-Squadron	51	10		41	0	0	0	0	0	0	0	0	0	0	6	0	0	30	3	3
Five Line Squadrons, each	153	79		103	8	0	0	0	0	0	0	0	0	0	0	0	0	146	15	5
Machine Gun Squadron	210	100		179	0	20	0	0	0	0	0	0	0	0	0	0	0	180	30	29
Horse Battery	100	20		75	0	3	1	0	0	3	0	0	0	0	0	0	0	74	23	6
Anti-Tank Battery	50	6		44	0	0	0	4	0	0	0	0	0	0	0	0	0	22	38	4
Anti-Aircraft Platoon	20	4		16	0	0	3	0	0	0	0	0	0	0	0	3	0	0	0	0
Pioneer Platoon	26	4		24	0	0	0	0	0	0	0	0	0	0	0	0	0	17	18	9
Chemical Platoon	67	2		65	0	0	0	0	0	0	0	0	0	0	0	0	0	39	28	14
Band	15	?		?	0	0	0	0	0	0	0	0	0	0	0	0	0	15	0	0
Trains Group	130	19		133	0	4	0	0	0	0	0	0	0	0	0	5	0	48	174	72
Mechanized Regiment																				
Regiment HQ	24	19		5	0	0	0	0	0	0	0	2	0	0	0	0	0			
HQ Platoon	60	5		50	5	0	0	0	0	0	0	0	0	0	6	7	0	0	0	0
1st (Tank) Battalion																				
Battalion HQ	19	17		2	0	0	0	0	0	0	0	2	0	0	0	0	0	0	0	0
Signal Platoon	19	1		18	0	0	0	0	0	0	0	0	0	0	0	3	0	0	0	0
Two Tank Squadrons, each[a]	31	31		0	0	0	0	0	0	0	0	10	0	0	0	0	0	0	0	0
Light Tank Squadron[a]	33	33		0	0	0	0	0	0	0	0	0	16	0	0	0	0	0	0	0
Motorcycle Platoon	11	1		0	9	1	0	0	0	0	0	0	0	0	11	0	0	0	0	0
Trains Group	47	4		43	0	0	0	0	0	0	0	0	0	0	0	14	0	0	0	0
2nd (Mechanized) Battalion																				
Battalion HQ	27	18		9	0	0	0	0	0	0	0	0	0	0	0	2	1	0	0	0
Signal Platoon	23	5		18	0	0	0	0	0	0	0	0	0	0	0	3	0	0	0	0
Armored Car Squadron	72	66		6	0	0	0	0	0	0	0	0	0	16	1	1	0	0	0	0
Motorised Rifle Company	91	9		70	9	6	2	0	0	0	0	0	0	0	2	8	0	0	0	0
Artillery Battery	142	20		114	0	4	0	0	0	4	0	0	0	0	0	22	1	0	0	0
Anti-Tank Platoon	33	6		27	0	0	0	4	0	0	0	0	0	0	0	4	0	0	0	0
Anti-Aircraft Platoon	20	5		15	0	0	3	0	0	0	0	0	0	0	0	3	0	0	0	0
Pioneer Platoon	41	5		36	0	0	0	0	0	0	0	0	0	0	0	4	0	0	0	0
	160	20		140	0	0	0	0	0	0	0	0	0	0	0	32	2	0	0	0
Horse Artillery Regiment																				
Regiment HQ & Battery	125	?		?	0	0	0	0	0	0	0	0	0	0	0	?	0	141		16
AA Platoon	20	?		?	0	0	3	0	0	0	0	0	0	0	0	3	0	0	0	0
Two Battalions, each																				
Battalion HQ & Platoon	31	?		?	0	0	0	0	0	0	0	0	0	0	0	1	0	27		3
Signal Platoon	50	?		?	0	0	0	0	0	0	0	0	0	0	0	1	0	55		5
Two Gun Batteries, each	117	?		?	0	0	0	0	0	4	0	0	0	0	0	0	0	120		4
Howitzer Battery	121	?		?	0	0	0	0	0	0	4	0	0	0	0	0	0	125		4
Ammunition Column	87	?		?	0	0	0	0	0	0	0	0	0	0	0	0	0	70		33
Trains Group	14	?		?	0	0	0	0	0	0	0	0	0	0	0	0	0	12		6
Regimental Trains Group	262	?		?	0	0	0	0	0	0	0	0	0	0	?	?	?	210		103
Anti-Tank Battery	50	8		42	0	0	0	4	0	0	0	0	0	0	0	?	?	?	?	?
Anti-Aircraft Squadron	83	32		51	0	0	12	0	0	0	0	0	0	0	0	16	0	0	0	0
Pioneer Squadron	138	21		117	0	0	0	0	0	0	0	0	0	0	0	0	0	95	40	20
Chemical Squadron	150	50		100	0	0	0	0	0	0	0	0	0	0	?	?	?	?	?	?
Trains Elements	1750	?		750	0	0	0	0	0	0	0	0	0	0	9	215	5	100	1530	328

[a] may be replaced by three squadrons of BT-tanks

Table 3.1 Cavalry division, 1939.

smaller, consisting of three cavalry regiments, an artillery battalion with three batteries of 76mm guns, a tank squadron and supporting elements.

THE MOUNTAIN CAVALRY DIVISION

Four of the thirteen cavalry divisions existing in June 1941 were denominated mountain cavalry divisions. Little is known of their organization, for they saw little combat before being either destroyed or converted to the standard configuration. Smaller than their regular brethren, they had only three mounted regiments and only a single light tank squadron in lieu of the mechanized regiment. Although three more mountain

cavalry divisions were formed in the summer of 1941, by the end of the year only one such division remained, the 39th, which stayed in the Central Asia Military District until January 1944, when it too was converted to a normal cavalry division.

THE JULY 1941 CAVALRY DIVISION

The débâcles of the first five months of the war essentially destroyed the Soviet mobile reserves. Until the mechanized forces could be rebuilt the cavalry branch underwent a massive expansion to form an interim mobile force.

Expansion was facilitated by the hasty issuance of a new set of TO&Es on 6 July

	Officers	Political Officers	Warrant Officers	NCOs	Other Ranks	Light Machine Guns	Medium Machine Guns	Heavy Machine Guns	50mm Mortars	45mm AT Guns	76mm Infantry Guns	Trucks	Riding Horses	Draft Horses	Wagons	Carts
Regiment Headquarters	7	4	5	0	0	0	0	0	0	0	0	0	16			
Radio (Signal) Platoon	0	0	0	7	13	0	0	0	0	0	0	0	22	4	0	1
Medical Section	0	0	2	0	2	0	0	0	0	0	0	0	3	2	1	0
Veterinary Section	0	0	3	0	1	0	0	0	0	0	0	0	3	2	1	0
Transportation Platoon	1	0	0	4	17	0	0	0	0	0	0	5	11	0	0	0
Pioneer Platoon	1	0	0	5	24	0	0	0	0	0	0	0	34	0	0	
Anti-Aircraft Platoon	1	0	0	3	12	0	0	3	0	0	0	3	0	0	0	0
Four Mounted Squadrons, each																
Squadron Headquarters	1	1	1	2	1	0	0	0	0	0	0	0	6	0	0	0
Four Line Platoons, each	1	0	0	3	28	2	0	0	1	0	0	0	34	0	0	0
Machine Gun Squadron																
Squadron Headquarters	1	1	1	2	2	0	0	0	0	0	0	0	7	0	0	0
Four MG Platoons, each	1	0	0	5	25	0	4	0	0	0	0	0	19	16	0	4
Regimental Battery																
Battery Headquarters	1	1	2	1	2	0	0	0	0	0	0	0	7	0	0	0
HQ Platoon	1	0	0	2	16	0	0	0	0	0	0	0	18	2	0	1
Two Gun Platoons, each	1	0	0	3	31	0	0	0	0	0	2	0	23	24	2	0
Anti-Tank Platoon	1	0	0	5	41	0	0	0	0	4	0	0	31	32	0	0
Ammunition Column	0	0	0	2	16	0	0	0	0	0	0	0	1	24	12	0

note: caissons not shown.

Table 3.2 Cavalry regiment (TO 07/4), from 6 July 1941.

1941 that ruthlessly stripped the cavalry formations of all non-combat elements not strictly necessary for immediate operations. At the same time, the mechanized regiment was dropped from the cavalry division in order to concentrate what tanks were available into the new tank brigades.

In the new cavalry regiment (TO&E 07/4) the basic unit remained the mounted squadron with four platoons, each of two sections. Close-in firepower was provided in the form of 128 sub-machine guns per regiment. Communications were carried out by six mounted radio teams that formed the regimental signal platoon.

The cavalry division was drastically reduced in size. Not only was the mechanized regiment deleted but so was one of the four cavalry regiments, the anti-aircraft battalion, about half the artillery component and a large portion of the service support. These changes served to reduce division strength to the elements shown in Table 3.3.

The new artillery battalion was smaller than its predecessor, consisting of a 23-man headquarters, an 85-man HQ battery, two 119-man 76mm gun batteries, two 109-man mortar batteries, and a 69-man trains group. Each battery was provided with one light machine gun for close-in defence and four primary weapons: 76mm guns in two batteries and 120mm mortars in the other two. For communications the battalion held a total of thirteen radio transceivers.

The divisional signal squadron was provided with five radio transceivers, four trucks, four signal wagons and five carts. The chemical platoon (redesignated a squadron in August with no organizational change) held two cargo trucks, five decontamination trucks, and five 2-horse wagons, divided into a mounted chemical reconnaissance element and a motorized decontamination element.

Independent cavalry divisions, those not subordinated to cavalry corps, were each to have received an armoured squadron of thirty-four men with ten T-40 light tanks or

	Offs	Pol Offs	Warr Offs	NCOs	Other Ranks	Riding Horses	Draft Horses	Trucks
Division HQ	12	(8)	(15)	12	66	100	3	4
Signal Squadron	6	1	0	10	80	96	20	4
Three Cavalry Regiments, each	40	10	17	113	760	842	180	8
Horse Artillery Battalion	31	9	11	118	464	444	290	6
Artillery Ammunition Column	4	1	4	11	123	28	84	25
Tank Squadron	4	1	1	9	19	0	0	3
Pioneer Squadron	(4)	(1)	(0)	15	70	60	10	0
Chemical Squadron	3	(1)	(3)	12	45	36	10	7
Rations Supply Column	3	(1)	(3)	7	57	0	0	30
Medical Squadron	0	(1)	(22)	5	24	0	0	16

note: figures in parentheses are estimates

Table 3.3 Cavalry division, from July 1941.

The Red Army had an ambivalent attitude towards Russia's long tradition of Cossack cavalry. The Cossacks were widely associated with the anti-Bolshevik forces in the civil war, and in the Second World War many sided with the Wehrmacht if given the opportunity. Yet tales of Cossack bravery and élan were legendary, and the Red Army attempted to capitalize on these virtues by raising Cossack cavalry formations during the war. They often blended the old and the new: the traditional garb of the Kuban Cossacks but melded with *PPSh* sub-machine guns and Soviet steel helmets.

BA armoured cars plus one truck for fuel, one for ammunition and personnel, and one for a workshop. This diversion of armoured vehicles from the tank units, however, could not long be tolerated and only a few cavalry divisions appear to have actually received this element.

These new, smaller cavalry divisions considerably speeded up the mobilization process and also proved easier for the great mass of inexperienced new officers to command. The spectacular pace of the cavalry expansion is illustrated by the formation of no fewer than seventy-eight regular and three mountain cavalry divisions during July–December 1941.

THE LIGHT CAVALRY DIVISIONS

To quicken the process of mobilization even further six new divisions were activated with a new, even leaner, organization called the light cavalry division, seemingly a successor to the earlier mountain cavalry divisions.

	Officers	Enlisted	Notes
Division Headquarters	46	2	
Signal Squadron	5	99	Radio platoon (3 × 9-man squads) and wire platoon (3 × 15-man sections)
Three Mounted Regiments, each			
Regiment Headquarters	24	5	
Signal Platoon	1	22	Two 11-man sections, one radio and one wire
Reconnaissance Platoon	1	16	
Four Rifle Squadrons, each	7	165	Three platoons, each (1+48) with one light MG
Machine Gun Squadron	6	128	Two water-cooled MG platoons (each 2 MGs), one air-cooled MG platoon (2 light MGs)
Mortar Battery	6	81	Two platoons, each two 82mm mortars
Regimental Battery	6	126	Two platoons, each 2 × 76mm regimental guns, one platoon with 2 × 45mm AT guns
Anti-Tank Platoon	1	21	Seven AT rifles
Pioneer Platoon	1	42	
Medical & trains sections	5	33	
Artillery Battalion			
Battalion Headquarters	15	0	
Three Batteries, each	6	148	One battery with 76mm M27 guns, one with 76mm M39 guns, one with 82mm mortars
Chemical Squadron	5	61	
NKVD Group	11	36	
Ammunition Group	6	312	Ten 3-ton trucks & 50 horse-drawn wagons
Other trains elements	25	146	

Table 3.4 Light cavalry division, 1941.

Unlike the regular, square-type, mounted squadrons the rifle squadron in the light cavalry division was triangular, consisting of three platoons each of forty-nine men with a single light machine gun. The machine gun squadron consisted of three platoons, two of wagon-carried Maxim water-cooled machine guns and one with two light machine guns, presumably on pack horses to supplement the rather meagre firepower of the line squadrons. Other fire support for the regiment consisted of regimental gun and mortar batteries and an anti-tank platoon.

The divisional artillery battalion had three batteries with various different weapons. One battery was provided with four 76mm M27 regimental guns, one with four 76mm M39 field guns and one with four 82mm mortars. Apparently because of the widely disparate characteristics of the different weapons, no attempt was made at centralized control, the battalion HQ being primarily an administrative command.

Of the six light cavalry divisions none lasted more than six months. One was redesignated into a guards cavalry division, and presumably reorganized at the same time, but the others were disbanded. Their lack of firepower, particularly at the platoon and divisional levels, almost certainly limited their effectiveness in combat.

A MODEST RESTORATION: THE JANUARY 1942 REORGANIZATION

On 6 January 1942, however, the organization of the rest of the cavalry divisions was subjected to a thorough revision. A new table of organization (TO&E 06/233) was issued

	Officers	Political & Warrant Officers	NCOs	Other Ranks	Submachine Guns	Light Machine Guns	Medium Machine Guns	Heavy Machine Guns	Anti-Tank Rifles	50mm Mortars	82mm Mortars	45mm AT Guns	76mm Infantry Guns	Trucks	Horses	Wagons
Regiment Headquarters	9	12	1	0	1	0	0	0	0	0	0	0	0	0	17	0
Signal Platoon	0	0	12	22	0	0	0	0	0	0	0	0	0	0	44	4
Pioneer Platoon	1	0	3	16	3	0	0	0	0	0	0	0	0	0	22	0
Anti-Aircraft Platoon	1	0	3	9	0	0	0	3	0	0	0	0	0	3	0	0
Four Mounted Squadrons, each																
Squadron Headquarters	2	1	3	1	3	0	0	0	0	0	0	0	0	0	7	0
Four Line Platoons, each	1	0	3	24	3	2	0	0	0	0	0	0	0	0	30	0
Mortar Platoon	1	0	4	16	0	0	0	0	0	4	0	0	0	0	29	0
Anti-Tank Platoon	1	0	7	31	0	0	0	0	6	0	0	0	0	0	41	2
Trains Section	0	0	0	5	0	0	0	0	0	0	0	0	0	0	6	3
Machine Gun Squadron																
Squadron Headquarters	2	1	3	2	0	0	0	0	0	0	0	0	0	0	8	0
Four MG Platoons, each	1	0	5	13	0	0	4	0	0	0	0	0	0	0	23	4
Trains Section	0	0	0	5	0	0	0	0	0	0	0	0	0	0	6	3
Mortar Squadron																
Squadron Headquarters	2	1	3	2	0	0	0	0	0	0	0	0	0	0	8	0
Two Platoons, each	1	0	4	16	1	0	0	0	0	0	3	0	0	0	24	3
Supply Section	0	0	1	13	1	0	0	0	0	0	0	0	0	0	23	11
Regimental Battery																
Battery Headquarters	2	1	3	2	0	0	0	0	0	0	0	0	0	0	8	0
Headquarters Section	1	0	2	12	1	0	0	0	0	0	0	0	0	0	12	1
Two Gun Platoons, each	1	0	5	28	1	0	0	0	0	0	0	0	2	0	46	0
Anti-Tank Platoon	1	0	9	37	1	0	0	0	0	0	0	4	0	0	63	0
Supply Section	0	1	2	16	1	0	0	0	0	0	0	0	0	0	27	13
Trains Group	1	4	5	13	0	0	0	0	0	0	0	0	0	6	15	4

note: caissons not shown

Table 3.5 Cavalry regiment (TO 06/233), from 6 January 1942.

for the cavalry regiment that increased both its size and its firepower. The 50mm mortars were withdrawn from the platoons (as had happened in the infantry as well) and centralized under the squadron commander while an independent section of anti-tank rifles was added to the squadron. Further, trains elements were decentralized from regiment to squadron level in order to increase small-unit self-sufficiency.

Simultaneously, the machine gun squadron was drastically reduced in manpower, although its firepower remained the same. The other major change was the addition of an 82mm mortar battery to the regiment. The mortars could go places in pack form that were inaccessible to the 76mm guns and were capable of plunging fire that often proved useful. The January 1942 cavalry regiment showed an increase of almost 200 men as a result of these modifications, and came out as a powerful and balanced formation.

The divisional artillery battalion, on the other hand, was reduced in strength. It lost one battery, usually a 76mm gun battery but sometimes a 120mm mortar battery, reducing battalion strength to 496 men. These changes combined to increase division strength to 4,443 men with 4,754 horses.

In March 1942 an 80-man motorized anti-aircraft battery with six 37mm guns was added to the divisional establishment and in June a 14-man chemical platoon was added to each cavalry regiment. These and other detail changes brought division strength up to 4,619 men with 4,770 horses. A pioneer squadron was also nominally added to each cavalry division but in fact only the guards cavalry divisions received such a unit at this time.

About mid-year the cavalry corps establishment was strengthened by the addition of an artillery battalion (three batteries of 76mm guns) and a mortar regiment (five batteries of 120mm mortars) to complement the existing HQ, signal battalion and pioneer squadron. In late 1942 the capabilities of the cavalry divisions were further expanded through the addition of a 70-man pioneer squadron, although there

	Men	Horses	Trucks
Corps Headquarters	109	68	11
Signal Battalion	185	52	1
Three Cavalry Divisions, each			
Division Headquarters	84	68	3
Signal Squadron	53	46	3
Three Cavalry Regiments, each	1160	1303	9
Horse Artillery Battalion	496	563	6
Artillery Column	143	112	25
Chemical Squadron	64	46	7
Medical Squadron	50	0	10
Veterinary Hospital	25	10	3
Transport/Supply Group	48	0	30

Table 3.6 Cavalry corps, January 1942.

While still carrying sabres on their saddles, this view is a reflection of the more common style of cavalry warfare in 1941. The primary weapon is the carbine or *PPSh* sub-machine gun, and Cossack dress has given way to the ordinary drab khaki of the common infantryman.

	Personnel			Horses
	Officers	NCO	OR	
Corps Headquarters	78	12	52	74
Signal Battalion	33	30	124	52
Horse Artillery Battalion	40	73	381	585
Mortar Regiment	87	155	537	635
Anti-Tank Battalion	35	78	474	627
Supply Squadron	16	27	217	412
Medical Platoon	0	1	16	0
Field Hospital	18	21	37	0
Veterinary Hospital	10	4	51	25
NKVD Platoon	1	6	29	0
Training Battalion	38	76	58	159
Chemical Platoon	2	1	26	0
Other service elements	23	2	12	58

Table 3.7 Cavalry corps base, June 1942.

was apparently some delay in providing these squadrons to all divisions.

At the same time a reconnaissance battalion was added to each division, so as to conserve the line cavalry strength for combat duties. This battalion had a strength of 353 men in a HQ, pioneer platoon, mounted squadron and armoured squadron. The mounted squadron was similar to that in the cavalry regiments, while the armoured squadron had three platoons, each with three T-60 or T-70 light tanks, plus a tenth tank in squadron HQ.

THE DEFINITIVE ORGANIZATION: FEBRUARY 1943

Finally, in February 1943, a new table of organization was issued for the cavalry regiment. At the squadron level the cavalry

	Officers	Political & Warrant Officers	NCOs	Other Ranks	Submachine Guns	Light Machine Guns	Medium Machine Guns	Anti-Tank Rifles	50mm Mortars	82mm Mortars	45mm AT Guns	76mm Infantry Guns	Riding & Pack Horses	Draft Horses	Wagons	Carts	Trucks
Regiment Headquarters	12	11	2	0	1	0	0	0	0	0	0	0	21	0	0	0	0
Headquarters Section	0	0	1	8	3	0	0	0	0	0	0	0	9	0	0	0	0
Signal Platoon	1	0	11	25	4	0	0	0	0	0	0	0	38	10	3	1	0
Pioneer Platoon	1	0	4	18	8	0	0	0	0	0	0	0	26				
Chemical Platoon	1	0	3	11	0	1	0	0	0	0	0	0	12	4	2	0	0
Four Mounted Squadrons, each																	
Squadron Headquarters	3	0	2	3	3	0	0	0	0	0	0	0	8	0	0	0	0
Four Line Platoons, each	1	0	3	23	8	2	0	0	0	0	0	0	29	0	0	0	0
Machine Gun Platoon	1	0	9	17	6	0	4	0	0	0	0	0	23	8	0	4	0
Anti-Tank Platoon	1	0	2	19	9	0	0	6	0	0	0	0	7	12	3	0	0
Trains Section	0	0	1	4	0	0	0	0	0	0	0	0	0	8	3	0	0
Mortar Squadron																	
Squadron Headquarters	3	0	3	1	1	0	0	0	0	0	0	0	7	0	0	0	0
Three Mortar Platoons, each	1	0	9	27	15	0	0	0	0	4	0	0	27	8	4	0	0
Ammunition, Supply & Trains	0	0	3	10	0	0	0	0	0	0	0	0	1	22	11	0	0
Regimental Battery																	
Battery Headquarters	3	0	2	1	0	0	0	0	0	0	0	0	6	0	0	0	0
Headquarters Platoon	1	0	2	13	7	0	0	0	0	0	0	0	15	2	0	1	0
Two Gun Platoons, each	1	0	5	24	7	0	0	0	0	0	0	2	24	12	0	0	0
Ammunition, Supply & Trains Group	0	0	2	13	0	0	0	0	0	0	0	0	15	26	13	0	0
Anti-Tank Battery																	
Battery Headquarters	3	0	2	1	1	0	0	0	0	0	0	0	6	0	0	0	0
Headquarters Platoon	1	0	2	11	5	0	0	0	0	0	0	0	14	2	0	1	0
Two AT Platoons, each	1	0	5	19	6	0	0	0	0	0	2	0	19	12	0	0	0
Ammunition, Supply & Trains Group	0	0	2	11	0	0	0	0	0	0	0	0	1	20	10	0	0
Medical Section	0	2	1	2	0	0	0	0	0	0	0	0	1	4	2	0	0
Veterinary Section	0	2	1	2	0	0	0	0	0	0	0	0	1	2	1	0	0
Supply Section	1	0	3	31	0	0	0	0	0	0	0	0	11	20	10	0	10
Workshop	0	0	5	1	0	0	0	0	0	0	0	0	0	0	0	0	1

note: caissons not shown

Table 3.8 Cavalry regiment (TO 06/313), from 8 February 1943.

followed the infantry pattern in the deletion of the 50mm mortar and increased use of the sub-machine gun as a personal weapon for combat troops, this latter by re-equipping one of the rifle platoons in each mounted squadron almost entirely with sub-machine guns. The mortar squadron was increased from two 3-piece platoons to three 4-piece platoons, doubling the firepower of the squadron. In a slight loss of flexibility, the regimental machine gun squadron was broken up and a platoon assigned directly to each of the line squadrons. At the same time the regimental battery was split into two along functional lines. The 45mm anti-tank guns, the function of which was entirely separate from that of the infantry guns, were grouped into a new anti-tank battery with its own HQ and supply elements. The regimental trains were restored and the squadron trains retained, which contributed to the ability of the cavalry regiment to operate independently. However, its capacity in this respect, as in most other Soviet formations, remained below that of its European counterparts.

This regimental organization apparently served the Soviets well, for only detail changes were made through the rest of the war, including the addition of a 28-man reconnaissance platoon in July 1943 and a 12-man guard/bugler section in September.

One feature of interest is that despite the additional firepower that found its way into the regiment structure, the communications remained the same at the end of the war as they did at the start, six pack-carried radios (five *RB*-type and one 5TK-type). In some cases the machine gun platoons were withdrawn from the mounted squadrons and recentralized in a regimental machine gun squadron, but it is not clear if this reflected an amendment to the TO&E or simply a field expedient preferred by some commanders. The service support base of the regiment was also strengthened with the addition of an ammunition column with thirty horse-drawn wagons.

Two changes were made at the divisional level. The first was the addition of a small tank regiment with two medium companies, one light company and one support unit with a total of 29 T-34 tanks and 16 T-70 tanks. The second was the enlargement of the artillery component to an 'artillery-mortar regiment' with two 4-gun batteries of 76mm

	Men	Notes
Division Headquarters	?	
Signal Squadron	117	
Reconnaissance Squadron	88	
Three Cavalry Regiments, each	1,138	As in text above
Tank Regiment	352	2 medium companies, 1 light company
Artillery-Mortar Regiment	700	10 AAMGs, 8 × 76mm guns, 18 × 120mm mortars
AA Machine Gun Battery	?	18 AAMGs
Engineer Squadron	50	
Division Services	?	
Total	6,000	

Table 3.9 Cavalry division strength, mid-1943.

field guns and three 6-gun batteries of 120mm mortars, with each battery also including two 12.7mm *DShK* anti-aircraft machine guns. Also included was an anti-aircraft machine gun battery with three platoons of *DShKs* and a reconnaissance squadron. Later in 1944, the artillery-mortar regiment was restructured into two full battalions, one of field guns and one of heavy mortars.

The corps structure was also considerably modified by the February 1943 reorganization. The corps mortar regiments were reorganized into mortar battalions and the horse artillery battalions into anti-tank regiments. In April–May 1943 an anti-aircraft regiment was added to each corps. In June rocket-launcher regiments began being added to the corps structure. In August the first assault gun regiments began showing up in the corps structure and by the end of the year all the corps in the west would have such a unit. These elements brought corps strength up to 21,000 men (including 18,000 in the cavalry divisions). The only corps not to benefit from these additions were the XVIII Corps in the Far East and the XV Corps in the Transcaucasus.

By 1944 the Soviets had arrived at the definitive cavalry organization, at least in terms of their needs. The powerful cavalry regiments were assigned to a much-

In the later years of the war, cavalry formations were often teamed with mechanized formations during the exploitation phase of deep operations. They were particularly successful in wooded regions such as Belorussia, which were less accessible to tanks and mechanized formations.

strengthened cavalry division, with a full complement of artillery and a fairly large trains component. The division lacked the anti-tank battalion normally found in Soviet units of comparable size, and this can probably be ascribed to their doctrine of using cavalry formations in areas such as the Pripet Marshes that were inaccessible to tanks. The trains elements were expanded somewhat, but in spite of this additional cargo capacity the division was capable of independent action for only one to two days in moderate combat.

The corps elements were also progressively strengthened. An apparent plan to add three tank regiments to each cavalry corps was only partially implemented. The II Guards Cavalry Corps received such an increment in the spring of 1944 but it was removed again in December. The IV Guards Corps also had three regiments during March–September 1944 and the VII Guards Corps during May–December 1944. Thus, by January 1945 the corps had settled on a standardized organization of three cavalry divisions, an SP artillery regiment, a rocket-launcher regiment, a mortar battalion, an anti-tank regiment and an anti-tank battalion, an anti-aircraft regiment, a reconnaissance unit and service support elements.

The 1944–5 cavalry corps was by far the most powerful cavalry division (for that was what it, in fact, was) ever in the world. It combined firepower with mobility to a degree never before seen in horsed units. During 1944 the cavalry corps rendered useful service in the so-called 'cavalry/mechanized groups'. Consisting of a cavalry corps and a mechanized or tank corps under a single HQ, the cavalry/mechanized group proved very efficient in terrain that was marginal for tanks, with each corps complementing the efforts of the other.

Unfortunately, horsed cavalry was still vulnerable to tanks, aircraft and massed artillery to a degree not suffered by other branches. By the start of 1945 the Soviet Army had advanced past all the marginal terrain of eastern Europe and the cavalry corps were relegated to second-line security duties. Even the campaign in Manchuria, with its rough, desolate terrain, found little use for the horsed cavalry elements. A cavalry/mechanized group was formed under the Transbaikal Front but this included only one Soviet cavalry division, the 59th, and appears to have been formed mainly to take advantage of the existing Mongolian 5th, 6th, 7th and 8th cavalry divisions rather than out of any specified military requirement for horsed units. The other cavalry division in the Far East, the 84th, played no major role in the operation.

Nevertheless, horsed cavalry formations remained in the Soviet order of battle until 1955, when the last was finally deactivated. The Soviets had clearly pushed an obsolete organizational form to its absolute limits.

CHAPTER 4
RED ARMY ARTILLERY

ANTI-TANK ARTILLERY

Until 1941 there had been no non-divisional anti-tank (AT) units in the Red Army. The lightning German victories of 1940 forced a re-evaluation of this policy and on 26 April 1941 the *NKO*, in something of an overreaction, ordered the creation of ten AT brigades. (One additional brigade was formed after the German invasion.) An AT brigade was a large formation of 5,309 men and was fully motorized with scarce vehicles, comprising 180 tractors (60 towing trailers), 10 motorcycles and no fewer than 706 cars and trucks. It consisted of two AT artillery regiments, a minelaying engineer battalion, a motor transport battalion and service elements. With a total of 120 guns it was expected to defend a front 5–6 km long with a density of 20–25 guns per kilometre.

Each of the brigade's artillery regiments consisted of five 12-gun AT battalions and an AA battalion. An AT battalion was made up of three 4-gun batteries. Two of the battalions were equipped with 76mm guns, two with 85mm AA guns used in the AT role, and one with 107mm guns (a weapon that never left the drawing board and was replaced in practice with more 76mm guns). The AA battalion had two 4-gun 37mm batteries and a 6-gun heavy machine gun company.

The brigades suffered grievously in the opening stages of the war. A prerequisite for the effective use of such massive units was a warning of where the German tanks were going to strike next. This the Soviets did not

have during the first year of the war. The bulk of the brigades were disbanded in the autumn of 1941 and reformed into separate AT regiments. The last of these brigades was finally disbanded in March 1942.

In late June and early July the *Stavka* ordered the formation of twenty additional AT regiments, but these large formations proved difficult to raise quickly. In response, fifteen more regiments were ordered activated in July, these consisting of five 4-gun batteries with no intermediate battalion HQs – a pattern that was to remain characteristic of Soviet AT regiments throughout the war. Because of the shortage of 76mm guns, these units were armed with 85mm AA guns, powerful if clumsy and vulnerable for this application. All these regiments were lost in October 1941 in the battles outside Moscow.

To speed mobilization the next group of AT regiments was even smaller, with only four 4-gun batteries. Two of these batteries had 85mm AA guns and the other two either 45mm AT guns or 37mm AA guns, depending on availability. Thirty-six such regiments were raised in this configuration during August–October 1941.

By October 1941 sufficient 76mm guns had become available to permit the raising of small numbers of AT units with this weapon. A new TO&E was published that provided for six 4-gun batteries, five of them with 76mm guns and one with 25mm or 37mm AA guns for air defence. Only one regiment was formed with this TO&E but nine other

In the years preceding the war, the Red Army made a determined effort to mechanize their heavy artillery. Here, a Komintern artillery tractor tows a 76mm Model 1931 anti-aircraft gun in front of the GUM department store in Moscow's Red Square during one of the annual armed forces parades. Most of these specialized artillery tractors were lost during the summer 1941 fighting.

regiments were converted to this organization from the older AT brigades.

Finally, on 19 April 1942, orders were issued to standardize the organization of all separate AT regiments on a new TO&E. Under this new structure a regiment was to consist of a headquarters, five gun batteries and trains elements. Each of the batteries consisted of a headquarters and two 21-man platoons. A platoon was provided with one light machine gun, two AT rifles, two 76mm guns and two gun tractors. Provision was also made for the addition of a sixth battery, bringing regimental strength to 564 men. Production of 76mm guns was apparently still insufficient, for on 15 May a new structure was authorized, organizationally

similar to the April regiment, but with fewer men and equipped with 45mm guns. At the same time the bulk of the 76mm AT regiments were redesignated as light artillery regiments but on 1 July they were redesignated again as tank-destroyer artillery regiments.

At this point also the infantry branch began raising its own AT units in the form of tank-destroyer brigades. The most obvious change from the pre-war AT brigades was the replacement of the AT gun as the primary weapon by the AT rifle. Also, notably, the brigade was provided with a tank battalion for the counter-attack role, although this component appears to have been present only rarely. Similarly, the mortar battalion

Date	TO&E No.	Personnel	Light MGs	AT Rifles	37mm AA guns	45mm AT Guns	76mm AT Guns	85mm AA Guns	107mm Guns	Tractors	Trucks
Apr-41	08/133	n/a	n/a	0	8	0	36	24	0	n/a	n/a
Jul-41	08/56	550	10	0	0	0	0	20	0	30	66
Jul-41	08/70	364	4	0	0	8	0	8	0	12	46
Oct-41	08/55	545	10	0	4	0	20	0	0	30	57
Apr-42	08/107	462	10	20	0	0	20	0	0	0	74
May-42	08/100	260	10	20	0	20	0	0	0	0	39
Jun-42	08/135	551	10	50	0	0	0	0	15	20	52
Aug-42	08/148	585	3	27	0	0	12	0	0	3	48

Table 4.1 Separate anti-tank regiments and battalions, 1941–2.

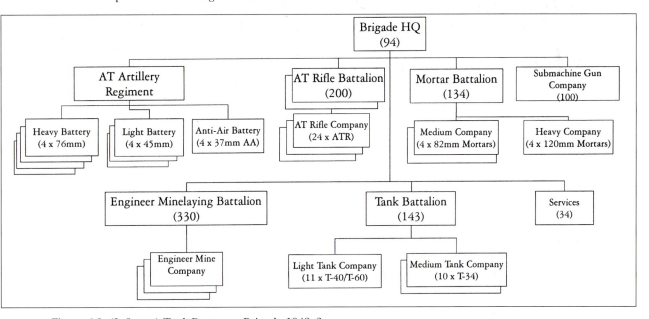

Figure 4.1 (Infantry) Tank Destroyer Brigade 1942–3.

was initially equipped only with 82mm weapons, the 120mm mortars being added in the late summer and autumn. A total of twenty-five tank-destroyer brigades were raised during April–May 1942, along with five division HQs that controlled varying numbers of brigades (see Figure 4.1). One further brigade was formed in 1942 but losses were so high that by the end of the year only thirteen remained, and by mid-1943 only six. The last of the tank-destroyer brigades was disbanded at the end of 1943.

One of the most common artillery pieces in service in the Red Army during the war was the 45mm Model 1937 anti-tank gun, a derivative of the German 37mm *PaK* 36 anti-tank gun. Although obsolete by late 1942, it remained in widespread use in Soviet infantry formations as a general purpose infantry gun, since it was capable of firing high-explosive as well as anti-tank projectiles.

The attempt at standardization within the artillery branch did not last long. In the summer the Leningrad Front organized eleven regiments on its own local TO&E; this provided a large formation of 964 men in four battalions each of three batteries, with three of the battalions having twelve 76mm guns apiece and the fourth eighteen 45mm guns. In November 1942 the Transcaucasus Front raised two regiments on its own TO&E; each consisted of four gun batteries, an AT rifle company and a sub-machine gun company for a total of 484 men. The gun batteries were unique in comprising one gun platoon (three 45mm guns), two heavy machine gun platoons (each with four *DShK*) and one AT rifle platoon (16 AT rifles).

Even the *Stavka* could not resist the urge to fine-tune the organization. In June they ordered the activation of three heavy tank-destroyer AT regiments, each of 551 men with fifteen 107mm guns in five batteries. They also ordered raised four tank-destroyer artillery battalions, each with three 4-gun batteries of 76mm guns, a mortar company (nine 82mm mortars), one AT rifle company (27 AT rifles) and one sub-machine gun company for a total of 585 men.

Nevertheless a great deal of uniformity was generated. By 1 November 1942 of 238 tank

Substantial modernization of Soviet artillery designs took place immediately before the war, leaving the Red Army with an inventory of excellent designs. The 152mm ML-20 gun-howitzer was the member of a new family, the related A-19 122mm gun being identical but for the gun tube. Here, the troops prepare their weapon for action having towed it into position with one of the STZ-3 tractors in the background.

	Officers	Political Officers	Warrant Officers	NCOs	Other Ranks	Light MGs	AT Rifles	76mm AT Guns	Field Cars	Trucks, GAZ-AA (1.5 ton)	Trucks, ZIL-5 (3-ton)	Special Trucks	Tractors
Anti-Tank Artillery Regiment (TO&E 08/246) from 13 April 1943													
Regiment Headquarters	7	3	7	2	4	0	0	0	1	1	0	0	0
Headquarters Platoon	1	0	0	6	28	0	0	0	0	2	0	0	0
Five Anti-Tank Batteries, each													
Battery Headquarters	2	1	0	2	0	0	0	0	0	0	0	0	0
Headquarters Platoon	1	0	0	5	14	0	1	0	0	1	0	0	0
Firing Battery													
Firing Battery Group	0	0	0	2	1	0	0	0	0	0	0	0	1
Two Platoons, each	1	0	0	6	11	1	1	2	0	0	1	0	2
Ammunition Platoon	1	0	0	2	18	0	0	0	0	0	12	0	0
Logistics Section	0	0	2	5	13	0	0	0	0	4	2	2	0
other trains elements	0	0	4	9	15	0	0	0	0	2	3	3	0
Total	34	8	13	129	263	10	10	20	1	14	27	5	25
Anti-Tank Artillery Regiment (TO&E 08/531) from 15 July 1943													
Regiment Headquarters	10	3	5	4	4	0	0	0	1	1	0	0	0
Headquarters Platoon	1	0	0	6	27	0	0	0	0	1	0	0	0
Five Anti-Tank Batteries, each													
Battery Headquarters	1	0	0	3	0	0	0	0	0	0	0	0	0
Headquarters Platoon	1	0	0	4	13	0	0	0	0	1	0	0	0
Firing Battery													
Firing Battery Group	0	0	0	2	4	0	0	0	0	0	1	0	1
Two Platoons, each	1	0	0	6	10	1	2	2	0	0	0	0	2
Logistics Section	0	0	1	4	10	0	0	0	0	1	1	3	0
other trains elements	0	0	4	10	13	0	0	0	0	4	1	2	0
TOTAL	31	3	10	129	239	10	20	20	1	12	10	5	25
Separate Anti-Tank Artillery Regiment (TO&E 08/539) from 7 July 1943													
Regiment Headquarters	10	3	5	4	3	0	0	0	1	1	0	0	0
Headquarters Platoon	1	0	0	6	28	0	0	0	0	3	0	0	0
Six Anti-Tank Batteries, each													
Battery Headquarters	1	0	0	3	0	0	0	0	0	0	0	0	0
Headquarters Platoon	1	0	0	4	13	0	0	0	0	1	0	0	0
Firing Battery													
Firing Battery Group	0	0	0	2	4	0	0	0	0	0	1	0	1
Two Platoons, each	1	0	0	6	10	1	2	2	0	0	0	0	2
Ammunition Platoon	1	0	1	5	15	0	0	0	0	0	9	0	0
Logistics Section	0	0	1	4	10	0	0	0	0	1	3	3	0
other trains elements	0	0	4	10	13	0	0	0	0	2	2	2	0
TOTAL	36	3	11	155	291	12	24	24	1	13	20	5	30

Table 4.2 Anti-tank artillery regiments, 1943.

destroyer artillery regiments, 160 were on the April 1942 TO&E for 76mm guns (evenly split between 5-gun and 6-gun regiments), 65 were on the May TO&E for 45mm guns, 3 were heavy regiments and the remaining 13 the local variants. These efforts also paid off in the ease of activation of large numbers of units. No fewer than 111 separate tank-destroyer artillery regiments were activated in the second half of 1942, followed by thirty-seven more in January–March 1943.

Also activated during April to September 1943 were forty-nine AT rifle battalions. The initial TO&E, adopted by 33 of the battalions, provided for 193 men and 72 AT rifles in three companies, while a later version had 332 men and 108 AT rifles in four companies.

By early 1943 supply of AT guns had reached a level where artillery branch brigades could again be formed. Such a brigade consisted of three tank-destroyer artillery regiments and in April 1943 two TO&Es were issued: one for the regiment in a brigade and one for a separate regiment, the difference being the addition of a sixth gun battery to the separate regiment. Powerful formations, these units were somewhat lavish in their use of manpower and vehicles, by Soviet standards, and in July two new TO&Es replaced them, again one for a brigaded regiment and one for a separate regiment. During April–July 1943 thirty-four tank-destroyer artillery brigades were formed (along with fifty-one separate regiments), the first twenty or so by aggregating existing separate regiments, thereafter being formed *ex novo*.

Generally, these brigades consisted of a 42-man headquarters, two heavy regiments (each with 412 men and 20 76mm guns), one similar smaller-calibre regiment (250 men with 20 45mm or 57mm guns) and a 77-man transport platoon. In September 1943 a new TO&E replaced the 45mm regiment with a 57mm regiment, with the new 57mm regiment adopting the TO&E of the 76mm regiment. Separate TO&Es were issued that expanded the 57/76mm regiment to a 6-battery (24-gun) configuration. This strengthening of the AT force was begun immediately and had begun to show up in the order of battle. The numbers of different types of *RVGK* anti-tank units at various dates are shown in Table 4.3.

Few changes were made after early 1944. On 2 August 1944 the *Stavka* directed the addition of a self-propelled regiment of twenty-one SU-85s to fifteen of the tank destroyer brigades, although this was not implemented fully until 1945. In contrast, a 25 December order to replace a 76mm regiment with a 100mm regiment in twelve brigades was implemented immediately.

ANTI-AIRCRAFT ARTILLERY

In June 1941 air defence of the field forces was entrusted to the divisional anti-aircraft (AA) battalions (usually two 37mm batteries and a 76mm battery) and independent AA battalions, each with three batteries of 76mm or 85mm guns. There were a total of forty such independent battalions at the start of the war, about one-third short of its goal of providing one battalion to each of the sixty-one rifle corps. Rapid mobilization improved this somewhat, and by 1 August 1941 there were sixty such battalions. In September the divisonal air defence component was reduced to a battery but the number of independent battalions continued to rise, so that by the end of the year there were 101.

The heavy guns (by mid-1942 there were 916 76mm guns in service with the field air defence forces and only twenty-eight 85mm guns) had not proven effective against marauding German low-level attack aircraft and in June a massive expansion of the light AA forces was begun. Over the next three months 118 AA regiments were raised, although many had short lives. Such a

TO&E	Men	Armament	1 Jan 42	1 Jan 43	1 Jan 44	1 Jan 45
Separate Battalions						
08/102	193	72 ATR	0	33	0	0
08/140	332	108 ATR	0	16	0	0
08/148	585	12 × 76mm guns	0	4	4	0
Separate Regiments						
08/55	545	4 × 37 AA, 20 × 76mm guns	9	0	0	0
08/56	n/a	20 × 85mm (AA) guns	17	0	0	0
08/70	364	8 × 45mm, 8 × 85mm (AA) guns	23	0	0	0
08/84	964	18 × 45mm, 36 × 76mm guns	0	11	0	0
08/100	260	20 × 45mm guns	0	64	0	0
08/107	489	20 × 76mm guns	0	91	0	0
08/135	551	15 × 107mm guns	0	3	0	0
08/166	484	12 × 45mm guns	0	2	0	0
08/547	n/a	20 × 45mm guns	0	0	11	2
08/548	n/a	15 × 107mm guns	0	0	2	0
08/549	n/a	18 × 45mm, 36 × 76mm guns	0	0	9	1
08/586	353	20 × 57mm guns	0	0	2	1
08/868	n/a	24 × 76mm guns	0	0	111	88
Brigades						
04/132	5,309	16 × 37mm AA, 48 × 76mm guns 48 × 85mm AA, 24 × 107mm guns	1	0	0	0
04/270	1,791	4 × 37mm AA, 12 × 45mm, 16 × 76mm guns	0	13	0	0
08/530	1,297	20 × 45/57mm, 40 × 76mm guns	0	0	37	11
08/595	1,492	24 × 57mm, 48 ×7 6mm guns	0	0	13	16
n/a	n/a	60 × 76mm guns	0	0	0	2
n/a	n/a	72 × 76mm guns	0	0	0	1
n/a	n/a	40 × 76mm, 16 × 100mm guns	0	0	0	7
n/a	n/a	48 × 57mm, 24 × 76mm guns	0	0	0	6
n/a	n/a	48 × 57mm, 24 × 76mm, 21 SU-85 guns	0	0	0	6
n/a	n/a	24 × 57mm, 48 × 76mm 21 SU-85 guns	0	0	0	2
n/a	n/a	24 × 57mm, 24 × 76mm, 16 × 100mm guns	0	0	0	5

Table 4.3 RVGK anti-tank units at various dates.

regiment, actually a small battalion in strength, consisted of 326 men divided into three gun batteries (each with four 37mm guns), an AA machine gun company (with three platoons each of four quad Maxim 7.92mm machine guns) and a second AA machine gun company (with two platoons each of four *DShK* 12.7mm machine guns). In August new TO&Es were issued for the independent AA battalion as well, providing for two types. Both types were built around three gun batteries (each with a single *DShK* machine gun and four 76/85mm

Another common Soviet artillery weapon was the 76mm Model 1927/39 regimental gun. This was a modernized version of the old Tsarist 3in gun, and provided the infantry with a handy source of direct-fire support. Here, one is being manhandled into position during streetfighting in Gleiwitz, Germany, in 1945.

guns), but one type included a searchlight battery (six lights) and the other did not. The larger battalion had a strength of 514 men, the smaller 380 men. In late August provision was also made for forming heavy AA regiments, each of 807 men with two of the smaller type AA battalions but only eight of these were actually raised.

In November 1942 orders went out to form forty-six AA artillery divisions, largely through the consolidation of the existing AA regiments. Each of these divisions consisted of a small headquarters element and four AA regiments, for a total of 1,345 men with 48 quad Maxim guns, 32 *DShK* guns and 48 37mm guns.

Although the new AA divisions concentrated a fair amount of low-level firepower, they were helpless against higher altitude threats, the reverse of the problem of a year before. In response a new TO&E for the AA division was issued in February 1943 to add heavier guns. One of the light regiments in each division was broken up and its batteries distributed to the remaining regiments to give them four gun batteries (sixteen guns) apiece. In its place a new heavy regiment was added consisting of four batteries each of four 76mm or 85mm guns. At the same time the Maxim machine gun companies of the light regiments were abolished and used to double the number of

A standard weapon of the Soviet divisional artillery was the 76mm divisional gun. This particular example is an F-22 *USV*, an interim design of the late 1930s which preceded the wartime ZiS-3 type. This category of weapon is frequently misunderstood in Western accounts as an anti-tank weapon, partly because the Germans used captured examples in this role. This weapon is seen in use during the Stalingrad fighting in 1942.

platoons in the *DShK* companies. Service support elements were also added to the division. In addition, a further fourteen AA divisions were formed during 1943, bringing the total by the end of the year to sixty.

A new type of unit was also ordered formed for the defence of forward airfields, the aerodrome AA regiment. They were organized identically to the 1942-style AA regiments (12 Maxims, 8 *DShK* and 12 37mm) but dispensed with most of the transport, which reduced strength to 270 men. Thirty-eight such regiments were formed during 1943.

In April 1943 a new table was issued for the independent AA regiment, similar to that in the AA divisions, with 420 men. However, of fifty-two regiments formed during 1943, only four used this configuration, the rest being raised on the old 12-gun TO&E. A new table was also issued for the independent AA battalion. Armed exclusively with 76/85mm guns, these had been the mainstay of high-altitude field air defence, but the new table provided a mixed unit of 320 men with two 4-gun batteries of 37mm and one of 85mm, along with a 4-gun platoon of *DShK*s. Only two battalions were activated with this new organization, however.

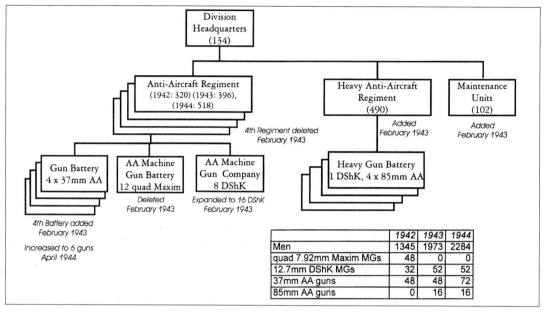

Figure 4.2 Anti-aircraft Division 1942-5.

The final major change in AA organization came in April 1944, when the light batteries in the AA divisions were ordered expanded to six guns apiece. This brought division strength up to 72 of these weapons, with 52 *DShK*s and 16 85mm guns.

MORTAR UNITS

The appearance of the 120mm heavy mortar in 1938 permitted the activation of separate mortar battalions and by June 1941 there were eight such battalions, each consisting of a 30-man HQ, three 90-man batteries (each with twelve 120mm mortars) and a 50-man transport company. The unit was entirely motorized, each mortar team being provided with a 5-ton Jaroslav truck. Eleven further battalions were raised during 1941. Although various fronts would raise expedient mortar battalions during 1942, the independent mortar battalion was an evolutionary dead-end.

In January 1942 a new type of unit entered

the order of battle: the mortar regiment. Under the initial TO&Es such a unit consisted of 800 men divided into a medium mortar battalion and a heavy mortar battalion. Each battalion had four batteries each of four mortars, giving the regiment a total of sixteen 82mm and sixteen 120mm mortars. In contrast to the earlier battalions, these were non-motorized formations, each regiment having 273 horses, 116 wagons and 14 motor vehicles.

The mixture of medium and heavy mortars was apparently not a success, for on 19 April two new TO&Es were issued for 120mm mortar regiments, one for a motorized version, the other for horse drawn. The 848-man motorized regiment was divided into three battalions, each of three 4-gun batteries, and was provided with 135 motor vehicles. The 477-man horsed regiment had no battalion HQs, commanding directly five 4-gun batteries, and had a total of 7 motor vehicles, 252 horses and 91 wagons. Mortars were cheap and easy to produce, so once

The heaviest artillery was placed in special *RVGK* Supreme Command Reserve formations which allowed the Red Army to concentrate its firepower and missions. Here, a pair of 203mm B-4 Model 1931 howitzers are towed by *Voroshilovets* artillery tractors. The BR-2 used an unusual tracked undercarriage to better distribute its heavy weight – the undercarriage was not powered.

infantry losses had been replaced, explosive growth in *RVGK* mortar assets became possible. During 1942 no fewer than 209 mortar regiments were formed: 52 mixed 82/120mm regiments, 126 horsed regiments and 31 motorized regiments.

During 1943 many of the mixed and horsed regiments were converted to the motorized configuration, while nine more horsed and twenty-two motorized regiments were raised. In mid-year the motorized regiments were converted to a new configuration that reduced manpower. One of the three battalions was eliminated, while increasing the number of mortars in a platoon from two to three. Firepower thus

remained the same, while manpower (in the form of headquarters overhead) was dramatically reduced to 597 men.

Mortar brigades had been formed in 1942 for inclusion in the artillery divisions, and some of these had existed briefly pending the formation of the division HQs, and some of the military districts had formed mortar brigades as temporary holding units for regiments in training, but the first regular independent mortar brigades were not formed until April 1943. Such a brigade, nearly identical to that in the artillery divisions, consisted of a small HQ and four motorized mortar regiments for a total of 144 heavy mortars. By the end of the year there were eleven such brigades, although that number had fallen to six by the end of 1944 with the diversion of some units into new artillery divisions.

A variant of this formation was the independent heavy mortar brigade, using the newly available 160mm mortar. Two of these were formed in 1944 and another two in early 1945. Such a brigade, identical to those in the later breakthrough artillery divisions, consisted of four battalions each with eight 160mm mortars.

Another variant of the mortar unit was the mountain mortar regiment. The first four were raised as new units in November/December 1942, and nine more added in 1943–4, mostly through conversion of existing horsed units. Such a unit had 540 men divided into a headquarters, five 86-man batteries and trains elements. Each battery was provided with four 107mm mountain mortars (each carried by four pack horses) and the regiment held twelve motor vehicles and about 300 horses. In mid-1944 the regiments were reorganized to consist of two battalions, each of three 4-gun batteries.

CORPS ARTILLERY

As a result of a 1937–8 reorganization each rifle corps was to receive two motorized artillery regiments for general support. One (Type A) had a mixture of guns and howitzers plus an observation battalion, and the second (Type B) had only 152mm howitzers or gun-howitzers. Due to the expansion of the Red Army in 1939 it proved impossible to provide each corps with two regiments, so a third variant (Type C) was authorized, to include an observation battalion, for corps for which only one regiment would be available. In all cases the regiments were divided into battalions with a single type of weapon in three 4-gun batteries. The strengths of the three types of regiments were:

Type	Men	107/122mm guns	152mm Howitzers or Gun-Howitzers	Tractors	Cars & Trucks
A	2,173	24	12	84	250
B	1,861	0	36	84	212
C	2,565	24	24	112	308

By June 1941 the Red Army had corps artillery regiments to provide forty corps with a 2-regiment structure and thirteen corps with a single Type C regiment, as against sixty-one rifle corps actually on strength. The corps regiments appear to have been at or near strength in personnel, weapons and STS and TTS tractors at the outbreak of the war, but with only about half of the trucks authorized.

In September the rifle corps structure was abolished and the surviving corps artillery regiments reverted to the *RVGK* pool where they were allowed to attrite away. In January 1942 rifle corps were reintroduced but on a much smaller scale, consisting of the new small rifle brigades. Being about the size of Western infantry divisions the corps did not need the massive formations used earlier and eleven corps artillery regiments raised in the first half of 1942 were armed with only sixteen 76mm guns and twelve 122mm howitzers each.

By late 1942 *Stavka* had been integrating rifle divisions into the rifle corps so that by the end of the year only seven of twenty-five corps were still composed exclusively of rifle brigades. The larger corps needed more firepower than that provided by the current corps artillery regiment. As an interim measure about ten new corps regiments were raised, each with one or two battalions of 122mm guns and one of 152mm gun-howitzers. In June 1943 a new TO&E was published for the corps artillery regiment that scaled this effort back to a battalion-size formation of a headquarters and four 4-gun batteries of 122mm guns (sometimes replaced

The Red Army considered its 120mm mortars to be artillery weapons. Its wartime designs were successful and one of the few Soviet weapons directly copied by the Germans.

in two batteries by 152mm gun-howitzers) with 512 men. By the end of 1943 there were forty corps artillery battalions on strength, about one-quarter of them representing conversions from *RVKG* gun regiments. In April 1944 a number of these were redesignated as corps gun artillery regiments, although without any apparent change in organization.

In April 1944 four corps artillery regiments were ordered reorganized to a new format: the corps artillery brigade. Such a unit consisted of an observation battalion and two regiments, each of five 4-gun batteries, one regiment with 100mm guns the other with 152mm howitzers. Their title was clearly a misnomer, for they were treated as *RVGK* assets, being moved frequently from one corps

to another as needed. Seven additional corps artillery brigades were formed in the Far East in May 1945 for operations against Japan.

FIELD AND HEAVY FIELD ARTILLERY

By 1939 the *RVGK* included twenty-four artillery regiments, as well as several battalions of extra-heavy artillery. One of the lessons learned from the Finnish débâcle of 1939–40 was the need for more heavy artillery. The 122mm howitzers of the *RVGK* regiments were deemed too light for such a role and were handed out to the rifle divisions as an additional battery per division. The former *RVGK* regiments were redesignated howitzer regiments and

The Red Army's artillery was never known for its sophisticated tactics, but its heavy application, particularly in the final year of the war, was legendary. Here, a battery of ML-20 152mm gun-howitzers prepare to fire.

Type	Quantity	Men	Tractors	Trucks	Weapons
Howitzer	29	2,318	108	202	48 × 152mm howitzers
Gun	13	2,565	112	308	24 × 122mm guns
					24 × 152mm gun-howitzers

expanded to four battalions each with three 4-gun batteries of 152mm howitzers. Some were also converted to extra-heavy (*BM*) howitzer regiments equipped with 203mm weapons. Complementing these were new gun regiments, identical to the Type C corps artillery regiments. The quantity of these units present on 22 June 1941 and their strengths were as shown above.

On 4 September 1941 new TO&Es were issued, halving the howitzer and gun regiments in size by the simple expedient of reducing batteries from four guns to two. Since this did not reduce the HQ overhead, overall strength was not halved, falling to 1,669 for the howitzer regiment and 1,980 for the gun regiment. At the same time a new structure was created, called simply 'artillery

Regiment	Men	Tractors	Weapons
Howitzer (Type A)	947	36	24 × 122–152mm howitzers
Howitzer (Type B)	864	30	20 × 122–152mm howitzers
Gun (Type A)	1120	35	18 × 107–122mm guns or 152mm gun-howitzers
Gun (Type B)	758	24	12 × 107–122mm guns or 152mm gun-howitzers

Table 4.4

regiment *RVGK* (sometimes also called the army artillery regiment), in two types: one with an observation battalion, two battalions of 122mm guns and one of 152mm gun-howitzers; and the second with simply three battalions of 152mm gun-howitzers, all using 2-gun batteries. The first type had 1,622 men and the second 1,330. During the second half of 1941 two howitzer regiments, twenty-four army regiments (all of the 152mm type) and twelve gun regiments were formed, and the former corps artillery regiments redesignated as army or gun regiments.

To reduce personnel overhead new TO&Es were issued for the RVGK artillery on 19 April 1942. The howitzer regiment was restructured as two battalions each of three 4-gun batteries. A variant also permitted the elimination of one of the batteries. Although the 152mm howitzer was the preferred weapon, the 122mm howitzer could be substituted. Of 38 howitzer regiments activated in 1942 (excluding those destined for artillery divisions), 23 had 24 × 152mm, 9 had 24 × 122mm and 6 had 20 × 122mm each. The gun regiments were reorganized as two or three battalions each of three 2-gun batteries. Of the 79 non-divisional gun regiments raised in 1942, 25 were armed with 18 × 152mm gun-howitzers, 27 with 12 × 152mm gun-howitzers and 12 with 12 × 107mm or 122mm guns. The strengths of the 1942 *RVGK* regiments are shown in Table 4.4.

These regimental TO&Es apparently proved satisfactory, for they remained in force with only detail changes for the rest of the war. Activations of separate regiments during 1943 comprised 16 howitzer regiments (6 with 20 × 122mm and 10 with 24 × 122mm) and 20 gun regiments (19 with 18 × 152mm gun-howitzers and one unique unit with 12 × 122mm guns and 12 × 152mm gun-howitzers).

The major change was the increasing concentration of the *RVGK* artillery, even outside the formation of the artillery divisions. In February 1943 the howitzer regiments armed with 152mm weapons were ordered, combined and reformed into independent heavy howitzer brigades. Such a brigade consisted of four battalions, each with four 2-gun batteries of 152mm howitzers. Their existence was short, for they were promptly incorporated into the artillery divisions. Longer lasting were the gun and extra-heavy howitzer brigades, formed by combining separate regiments. Eleven gun brigades were formed, each with two 18-gun regiments. These brigades, however, also eventually disappeared to form artillery divisions, so that by the end of 1944 only one such brigade remained, a gun brigade.

On 10 April 1943 the *Stavka* ordered the artillery component of a field army (excluding tank armies) standardized as one gun regiment, one AT regiment, one mortar regiment and one AA regiment. Each of these had the word 'army' placed in front of their former title, so the bulk of the gun regiments were retitled army gun artillery

Type	Quantity	Men	Artillery Pieces	Tractors	Trucks
203mm Howitzer Regiment (*BM*)	32	2,304	24 Model B-4	112	252
152mm Gun Regiment (heavy)	2	2,598	24 Model BR-2	104	287
280mm Howitzer Battalion	8	740	6 Model BR-5	54	86
305mm Howitzer Battalion (*OM*)	5	747	6 Model 1915	0	44
210mm Gun Battalion (*OM*)	1	858	6 Model BR-17	78	32
305mm Gun Battalion (*OM*)	1	912	6 Model BR-18	95	32
152mm Gun Battery (heavy)	2	n/a	2 Model BR-2	n/a	n/a

Table 4.5

regiments, although this new appellation was only intermittently used.

On 16 May 1944 orders went out to convert the army gun regiments to a new configuration called the army gun artillery brigade. Each such brigade would consist of one observation battalion, two battalions each with 12 × 152mm gun-howitzers and one battalion with 12 × 122mm guns. Fifty-five such brigades were formed (at the cost of 86 of the 106 gun regiments), one for each field army, although those in the Karelian and Transcaucasus fronts had theirs diverted to the reserve pool.

Further centralization came in 1945, with the formation of two howitzer brigades and two extra-heavy howitzer brigades, along with seven more army gun brigades. Thus, by the end of the war, the *RVGK* field artillery pool consisted of 63 gun brigades, 2 howitzer brigades and 57 separate regiments (33 gun/army gun and 24 howitzer), in addition to the artillery divisions and the corps artillery units.

HEAVY ARTILLERY

What Westerners would call heavy artillery the Soviets designated with an often confusing variety of names. Initially the term 'heavy' (*tyazheliy*) was applied only to gun regiments equipped with 152mm BR-2 guns.

The next heavier category, abbreviated *BM*, was given to howitzer regiments equipped with 203mm B-4 howitzers. The final category, *OM*, was given to artillery units with guns 210mm and larger, or howitzers 280mm and larger.

The Force Structure Plan of May 1940 provided for one heavy gun regiment, 20 *BM* howitzer regiments, 10 super-heavy (*OM*) battalions and 2 independent heavy gun battalions. This force structure was generally met and with mobilization the Red Army was able to field the heavy artillery shown in Table 4.5 at the start of Operation Barbarossa.

The heavy gun regiment and the *BM* howitzer regiment each consisted of four firing battalions, each with three 2-gun batteries. In addition, the heavy gun regiment also included an observation battalion. Each of the super-heavy battalions was made up of three batteries, each of two guns.

Because of the cost and complexity of heavy artillery little effort was devoted to modernizing this portion of the *RVGK* pool. The sole significant exception was the *BM* howitzer force, which expanded from twenty-three surviving regiments at the end of 1941 to fifty-two a year later. Even this, however, was mostly due to halving the size of the regiments on 2 April 1942 from four battalions to two, reducing it to 904 men with 12 B-4 howitzers, 26 tractors and 36 trucks.

Soviet tactics in the later war years placed greater emphasis on firepower and armoured shock tactics due to the declining manpower reserves. Here, a battery of the heavy 203mm B-4 Model 1931 howitzers prepare to fire.

The bulk of the *BM* howitzer regiments was incorporated into the artillery divisions and separate *BM* howitzer brigades during 1943, leaving only eight at the end of that year as separate units. Seven such brigades were formed in 1943, and a few others in 1944, but these too were gradually incorporated into the artillery divisions. They were supplemented in June 1944 by the raising of four more battalions using captured German 210mm howitzers.

In January 1943 the separate gun batteries were expanded to form four separate battalions of 152mm BR-2 guns, and on 25 November 1944 these battalions were further expanded to

OM regiments. Each of these regiments consisted of four 2-gun batteries, three with 152mm BR-2 guns and one with 210mm guns.

At the end of the European war the *RVGK* heavy artillery park, not including units in artillery divisions, consisted of two *BM* howitzer brigades, four *OM* gun regiments, one *BM* howitzer regiment, and seventeen *OM* battalions of various types.

ARTILLERY DIVISIONS

The creation of that uniquely Soviet formation, the artillery division, dates to 31 October 1942 when the *Stavka* ordered

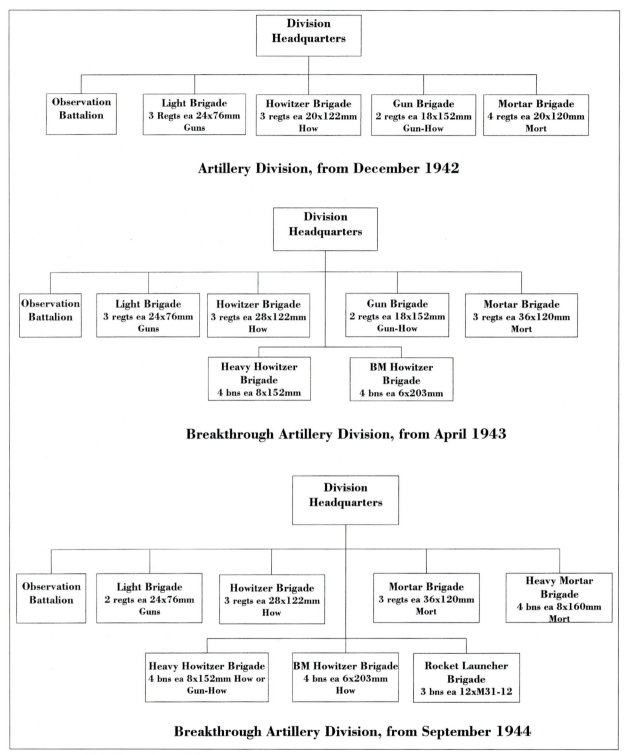

Figure 4.3 Main artillery division types.

The heavy losses of 1941 forced many Red Army artillery units to rely on civilian tractors for motorized towing during the middle war years. By the last year of the war, Lend-Lease trucks provided a welcome addition, greatly increasing artillery mobility during the offensive drives through central Europe. Here, a pair of American Studebaker US-6 trucks are used to tow *ZiS-3* 76mm divisional guns during river-crossing operations over the Dnepr river in 1944.

the raising of twenty-six such units. Under this original order a division would consist of 3 howitzer regiments (each with 20 122mm howitzers), 2 gun regiments (each with 18 122mm guns or 152mm gun-howitzers), 3 tank-destroyer artillery regiments (each with 24 76mm guns) and an observation battalion. The placing of eight firing units directly under the division HQ quickly proved impractical and on 6 December a new organization table was promulgated that both strengthened the division through the addition of mortars and provided intermediate HQs in the form of four

brigade headquarters. The artillery divisions had converted to the new organization by the end of January 1943.

One additional anomalous division was formed at Stalingrad in late 1942. This unit, the 19th Artillery Division, was sometimes referred to as a heavy artillery division for it consisted of five gun regiments, one *BM* howitzer regiment, one *OM* gun battalion and an observation battalion. It converted to the December 1942 standard in April 1943.

Further strengthening and centralization of the artillery came in April 1943. One element was the creation of five artillery corps headquarters to control groupings of artillery divisions. At the same time a new divisional format was created: the breakthrough artillery division. This was a standard artillery division reinforced with two additional brigades: one of 152mm howitzers and one of 203mm howitzers. Seven artillery divisions were converted to the breakthrough configuration in April. Further conversions followed, so that by the end of 1943 no fewer than seventeen of the twenty-six artillery divisions were of the breakthrough type.

Indeed, only six of the divisions were still on the December 1942 TO&E, three others being on yet other TO&Es as gun divisions used for the counter-battery role. In June 1943 an organization table for a heavy gun artillery division was issued, consisting of an observation battalion and four gun brigades, each of three 4-battery battalions. Since the batteries in this division had four weapons each the division had the staggering total of 144 152mm gun-howitzers. One division (4th Guards) was converted to this organization and one (6th Guards) was raised with it from existing gun units. In October another TO&E was issued, this time for a gun artillery

division. This was similar to the heavy gun division but replaced one battalion in each gun brigade with a 4-battery battalion of 76mm guns. One division (a second incarnation of the 8th) was raised with this organization, although it never seems to have received its fourth regiment.

The next major change came in September 1944 when ten new breakthrough artillery divisions were raised. These used a different organization that deleted the gun brigade in favour of a heavy mortar brigade (with the new 160mm mortar) and a rocket-launcher brigade (with twelve-rail 310mm truck-mounted launchers). At the same time three of the regular artillery divisions and one heavy gun division (6th Guards) were converted to the 1943 breakthrough division configuration. To accommodate these new divisions five additional artillery corps HQs were formed.

The structure at the end of 1944, which remained in effect to the end of the war in Europe, provided for 10 corps HQs, ten 1944-style breakthrough artillery divisions, twenty-two 1943-style breakthrough artillery divisions, two gun artillery divisions and three basic 1942-style artillery divisions.

Type	Date	Men	76mm Guns	122mm Howitzers	152mm Howitzers	152mm Gun-Howitzers	203mm Howitzers	120mm Mortars	160mm Mortars	M31-12 Rocket Launchers	Tractors	Trucks
Artillery Division	Dec-42	9,214	72	60	0	36	0	80	0	0	221	1,156
Breakthrough Artillery Division	Apr-43	10,869	72	84	32	36	24	108	0	0	175	1,101
Heavy Gun Artillery Division	Jun-43	5,063	0	0	0	144	0	0	0	0	n/a	n/a
Gun Artillery Division	Oct-43	5,249	48	0	0	108	0	0	0	0	n/a	n/a
Breakthrough Artillery Division	Oct-44	n/a	48	84	32*	0	24	108	32	36	n/a	n/a

* may be replaced by 152mm gun-howitzers

Table 4.6 Artillery division totals.

ROCKET ARTILLERY

Officially known as 'guards mortar breakthrough' units the rocket forces saw the most explosive growth of any component of the Red Army during the war.[1] The first three batteries were fitted out with *BM*-13s in June and July 1941 and in early August *Stavka* ordered the formation of eight rocket regiments, each to consist of three battalions each of three 4-vehicle batteries. This goal was exceeded, with fourteen regiments being raised in September–October, along with nineteen separate battalions. With Germans advancing everywhere and crises erupting constantly the rocket units were hastily deployed in small units, and indeed in November–December nine of the regiments were dissolved and broken up into independent battalions, and twenty-eight new battalions formed.

This proved a mistake, however, for with their short range, long reload time and prominent launch signatures the rocket units had to fire massive concentrations quickly and then move to avoid deadly counter-

Artillery mechanization had very low priority during the war and the Red Army showed little interest in self-propelled field artillery. By the final year of the war, pressures on industry lightened and new designs were introduced for the first time since 1941, including the Ya-12 artillery tractor seen here towing an ML-20 152mm gun-howitzer belonging to a formation of the Allied Polish People's Army. (Janusz Magnuski)

battery fire. Thus, in January 1942, *Stavka* ordered the bulk of the independent battalions consolidated back into regiments, at the same time ordering the formation of twenty more regiments.

In early June 1942 twenty independent battalions were raised with the new M-30 rocket launcher, each consisting of three batteries with thirty-two 4-round launch frames each. Since considerable work must have been involved in setting these units up and reloading them with the 72kg rockets, they were presumably intended more for the set-piece offensive than the more mobile *BM*-8 and *BM*-13 units. By the end of August more than seventy M-30 battalions had been activated and in November the Army began forming ten heavy brigades, each of five M-30 battalions, through consolidation of existing units. A month later orders went out to continue centralization of rocket units with the creation of four rocket divisions, each consisting of four regiments of M-13 and two brigades of M-30.

The basic organizational unit for the *BM*-8 and *BM*-13 was the regiment, consisting initially of fifty-eight men in the HQ elements and three 250-man battalions. A battalion included two AA platoons (one with two *DShK* machine guns and the other with two 37mm guns) and two rocket batteries each with four rocket-launcher systems. In mid-1942 battalion strength was reduced to 191 men and the 37mm AA guns centralized as a regimental battery.

A rocket-launcher division consisted of two heavy brigades and three light regiments. A heavy brigade had five battalions of M-30s, each of three batteries with thirty-two M-30 launch units each. A light regiment had three battalions, each of three batteries with four *BM*-13 launchers. Such a division could launch a crushing volley of firepower but

were apparently regarded as cumbersome because of the disparate characteristics of the two types of weapons. When the 5th and 6th rocket divisions were formed in January 1943 they retained the earlier organization, but in February the 7th Division was formed with a new structure. It consisted simply of three heavy brigades, each of four battalions. These battalions had three batteries, each with twenty-four M-30 launch systems. This division thus had 864 launch systems for a total salvo of 3,456 rockets.

The other divisions began converting to this organization in the spring of 1943, so that by the end of the year only one still retained its original structure. The *BM*-13 units made surplus by this were distributed to the tank and mechanized corps. Thus, by the end of 1943, the Army included 7 divisions (20 brigades) and 13 independent brigades of M-30s, 96 regiments and 30 battalions of M-13s, and 19 regiments and 8 battalions of M-8s. This force structure remained relatively intact through the rest of the war, although the replacement of the M-30 by the improved M-31 gave the rocket divisions considerably greater power and flexibility.

Note

1. Many Western (and even some Soviet) sources shorten this to 'guards mortar'. This creates some difficulty since normal mortar units could, and did, receive the guards honorific. The official order of battle distinguishes between the two in their abbreviations by referring to, for instance, *gr. minp.* (mortar regiments with a guards honorific) and *gr. mp.* (rocket launcher regiments). Unfortunately, this usage is not always followed, even in Russian/Soviet sources. To avoid confusion the text here uses the terms rocket and rocket launcher to refer to the guards mortar breakthrough units.

CHAPTER 5

RED ARMY AIRBORNE AND CHEMICAL UNITS

Pioneers in the development of airborne troops and tactics, the Soviets began parachuting squad-size units in 1930 on a trials basis. Further successful trials led to an 11 December 1932 order creating the 3rd Airborne Brigade (*aviatsionnyyu brigadu*). In addition, non-permanent air-landing battalions would be set up in various rifle corps and divisions throughout the Soviet Union for use as needed. By 1 January 1934 the airborne force comprised the 3rd Brigade, four regular air-landing detachments, twenty-nine ad-hoc air-landing battalions and some company and platoon-size units for a total strength of 10,000 men.

The airborne brigade consisted of a parachute battalion, a motorized battalion and an air group of three squadrons of aircraft (two heavy TB-3 units and one light). In 1934–6 two additional airborne brigades were formed, the 13th in the Kiev Military District (MD) and the 47th in the Belorussian MD. At the same time, three separate non-permanent airborne regiments (1st, 2nd and 5th) were formed by the Moscow MD and sent to the Far East.

This proliferation of airborne units was getting difficult to control and in 1938 the airborne elements were combined into six airborne brigades and three airborne regiments:

201st Airborne Brigade	Leningrad MD
202nd Airborne Brigade	Far East
204th Airborne Brigade	Kiev MD
211th Airborne Brigade	Kiev MD
212th Airborne Brigade	Far East
214th Airborne Brigade	Belorussian MD
1st 'Rostov' Regiment	Moscow MD
2nd 'Gorokhovets' Regiment	Moscow MD
3rd 'Voronezh' Regiment	Moscow MD

The 212th Brigade participated in the battles at Khalkin-Gol, while the 201st, 214th and at least one of the Kiev brigades participated in the Russo-Finnish War of 1939–40. In all these cases, however, the brigades fought as regular foot infantry. The first operational use of the airborne brigades came in June 1940 when the 201st and 204th made air-landings to seize important points from the Romanians during the unopposed Soviet occupation of Bessarabia. They were carried into action by four regiments (170 aircraft) of TB-3 heavy bombers.

Apparently the usefulness of the airborne brigades impressed the Soviet High Command for, in November 1940, the *Stavka* issued new TO&Es for the airborne brigades that doubled their size to about 3,000 men. The new brigade structure was triangular, consisting of a parachute group, a glider group, and an air-landing group.

The Red Army of the 1930s was in the forefront of tactical innovations and was one of the pioneers of airborne forces. Some of their equipment was unique as well, including these double-canopy parachutes. Soviet airborne operations during the early years of the war were hampered by the lack of transport aircraft, and these élite troops were often expended as ordinary infantry.

HQ, Airborne Brigade
Parachute Group
   Signal company
   Motorcycle-bicycle reconnaissance company
   Two parachute battalions (546 men each)
      Signal platoon
      Reconnaissance platoon (37 men each)
      Three parachute rifle companies (141 men each)
      Pioneer demolition platoon
      Combat rations and supply platoon
      Medical platoon
Glider Group
   same organization as parachute group
Airlanding Group
   Mortar company (9 × 82mm mortars)
   Air defence company (12 heavy anti-aircraft machine guns)
   Tank company (11 T-38 or T-40 light tanks)
   Artillery battalion
      Mountain battery (4 × 76mm mountain guns)
      Anti-tank battery (4 × 45mm AT guns)

A rifle company consisted of a 12-man HQ squad, three 38-man rifle platoons and a mortar platoon with 50mm mortars.

In March–April 1941 the airborne arm was again strengthened. Five of the airborne brigades, all except the 202nd in the Far East, were ordered expanded into airborne corps, each of three brigades. At the same time the distinction between parachute and glider troops within the airborne brigades was abolished and the group HQs dissolved. The new structure for the brigade was

Brigade HQ
Signal Company
Reconnaissance Company (113 bicycles)
Four Parachute Infantry Battalions, (458 men each)
   Signal platoon
   Reconnaissance platoon
   Three rifle companies
   Pioneer demolition platoons
   Combat rations & supply platoon
   Medical platoon
Mortar Company (6 × 82mm mortars)
Anti-Aircraft Machine Gun Company (6 × 12.7mm machine guns)
Brigade Artillery (6 × 76mm M27 guns and 12 × 45mm AT guns)

A notable feature of the new organization was the issuance of twenty-four backpack flamethrowers to the third platoon of each rifle company to assist in the assault role. Overall battalion strength, however, dropped somewhat.

In addition to the three airborne brigades each corps also included a three-company air-landed light tank battalion with fifty light tanks and a long-range radio platoon. Shortly thereafter the number of tanks in the battalion was reduced to thirty-two (ten per company) and the radio platoon expanded to a signal company with a long-range radio platoon, a dispatch rider platoon (fifteen motorcycles) and a light aircraft flight.

In June 1941 the five airborne corps were allocated as follows:

Kiev Special MD	1st Airborne Corps	1st, 204th and 211th Airborne Brigades
Kharkov	2nd Airborne Corps	2nd, 3rd and 4th Airborne Brigades
Odessa	3rd Airborne Corps	5th, 6th and 212th Airborne Brigades
Western Special MD	4th Airborne Corps	7th, 8th and 214th Airborne Brigades
Pre-Baltic Special MD	5th Airborne Corps	9th, 10th and 201st Airborne Brigades

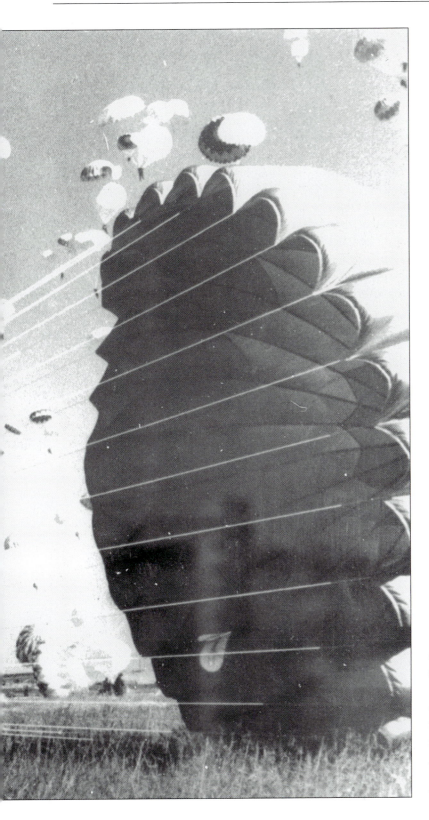

Soviet airborne operations were singularly unsuccessful during the war. The last major drop, during the Dnepr river crossing in October 1943, was such a fiasco that it dissuaded the Red Army from any further massed airborne operations during the war.

The airborne corps suffered grievously in the opening campaigns of the war, fighting as regular infantry in desperate defensive actions and breaking out of encirclements. By September 1941 the corps were clearly no longer capable of conducting combat airdrops and orders went out to raise five more airborne corps (6th–10th) on new TO&Es and to rehabilitate the existing corps.

The main change made by the new TO&Es was the strengthening of the parachute infantry battalion to 678 men and its reorganization into three rifle companies, a mortar company, a machine gun platoon, a pioneer demolition platoon, a flamethrower platoon and a signal platoon.

Little more detailed information on the organization of these crucial early airborne brigades is available. In mid-1942 the Germans reported that an interrogated Soviet airborne captain gave the strength of the airborne brigade as shown in Table 5.1.

According to this account each infantry battalion was also provided with 18 light machine guns, 6 medium machine guns, 9 anti-tank rifles, 18 50mm mortars and 6 82mm mortars, along with 7 radios. The artillery battalion consisted of a mortar battery (identical to the mortar company in the infantry battalion, with six 82mm weapons) and two 4-gun batteries of 45mm AT guns.[1]

By December 1941 the airborne forces were up to full strength and were finally used in their intended role in the defence of Moscow. On 14–15 December one battalion of the 214th Brigade was dropped in a diversionary raid, followed by a battalion of the 201st Brigade on 2–4 January 1942 and two more battalions of the 201st on 18–22 January. Finally, an operational-level mission was planned that called for the dropping of the entire 4th Airborne Corps in late January, although due to lack of planning and poor initial results only the 8th Brigade actually landed – on 27–31 January. A second operational-level mission was launched with the dropping of the 4th Airborne Corps (less part of 8th Brigade) on 13–23 February. Although this last-mentioned group survived in the German rear for six months, the longest airborne operation in history, it did not accomplish its original objectives.

When the scene of heavy fighting shifted

	Officers	Political Officers	NCO	Other Ranks	Pistol	Rifle	Sub-Machine Guns
Brigade HQ	43	16	30	58	73	74	15
Signal Company	4	1	10	21	12	15	9
Bicycle Reconnaissance Company	4	1	12	99	8	4	54
Four Infantry Battalions, each	34	8	86	544	67	394	142
Artillery Battalion	22	6	30	114	35	121	16
Pioneer Company	5	1	12	64	12	39	31
AA Machine Gun Company	5	1	8	25	11	19	6
Total	219	58	446	2,557	419	1,888	699

Table 5.1

With the Soviet Baltic Fleet and much of the Black Sea Fleet bottled up in harbour, many Soviet sailors were pressed into service as infantry. Although there were a number of specialized naval infantry units formed during the war, many others were formed out of desperation in the dark days of 1941–2.

south in the summer of 1942, so too did the airborne forces. Desperately needed in front of Stalingrad the ten airborne corps (less three brigades) were converted to regular infantry units and redesignated the 32nd–41st guards rifle divisions in June 1942.

To replace these units the *Stavka* ordered the formation of eight new airborne corps (1st and 4th–10th) in the autumn of 1942. Once again, however, the pressing need for ground combat troops forced them to convert these in December 1942, and the three existing airborne brigades, to ten of a new type of unit: the guards airborne division

(*gvarddeiskaya vozdushno-desantnaya diviziya*). Although filled out with trained parachutists and retaining the airborne designation, these units converted to the regular guards infantry division TO&Es and fought as regular infantry.

Once again the *Stavka* had to start almost from scratch to build up an airborne arm and in April–May 1943 formed twenty new airborne brigades. By September, however, all but three had been used to form six more (11th–16th) guards airborne divisions for regular ground operations. The new brigades had the strength shown in Table 5.2.

	Officers	NCOs	Other Ranks	Total
Brigade HQ	61	35	71	167
Signal Company	6	24	32	62
Bicycle Reconnaissance Company	6	26	86	118
Four Infantry Battalions, each	55	172	488	715
Anti-Tank Battalion	26	52	117	195
AA Machine Gun Company	7	26	37	70
Pioneer Company	6	12	63	81
Total	332	863	2,358	3,553

Table 5.2

By October 1943 the strength figures had been reduced slightly to give the organization shown in Table 5.3.

The brigade signal company was provided with ten radios (including six backpack RB models and two longer-ranged RSB models), four bicycles, four motorcycles and three light trucks. The reconnaissance company was mounted entirely on bicycles and was provided with 91 sub-machine guns, 11 rifles and 9 light machine guns.

The parachute infantry battalion consisted of three rifle companies (each with nine light machine guns and three 50mm mortars), a machine gun company (twelve Maxim guns), a mortar company (six 82mm mortars), an anti-tank company (twenty-seven AT rifles), a signal platoon and a medical platoon. The anti-tank battalion replaced the former artillery battalion. It was made up of two anti-tank batteries, each with four 45mm guns, and an AT rifle company with eighteen weapons. The AA machine gun company was considerably strengthened, probably in reaction to the pounding the earlier airborne brigades had taken at the hands of the Luftwaffe, to man twelve 12.7mm *DShK* machine guns. The brigade pioneer company consisted of a 6-man HQ and three 25-man platoons. Each of these platoons was made up of a platoon leader and three 8-man squads armed with two sub-machine guns, one carbine and five automatic rifles.

Although some changes had been introduced by the new TO&Es, such as the centralization of the anti-tank rifles in a new battalion AT company and the expansion of

	Officers	NCOs	Other Ranks	Total
Brigade HQ	60	38	71	169
Signal Company	4	24	32	60
Bicycle Reconnaissance Company	4	27	85	116
Four Infantry Battalions, each	44	172	483	699
Anti-Tank Battalion	21	58	117	190
AA-Machine Gun Company	5	26	37	68
Pioneer Company	4	12	63	79
Total	274	867	2,337	3,478

Table 5.3

the anti-aircraft machine gun company, few substantive alterations had been made. Indeed, one of the primary failings of the earlier organization, the lack of heavy weapons, was not addressed at all.

On 24 September 1943 the 3rd and 5th airborne brigades were dropped on the west bank of the Dnepr[2] to seize a bridgehead for the advancing Soviet forces. Poor planning and abysmal drop procedures condemned the operation to failure from the beginning.

Organizational problems were to be remedied by a profound reorganization of the brigade structure undertaken in late October 1943. Two batteries were added to the anti-tank battalion to bring total strength up to slightly over 200 and armament to sixteen 45mm guns and eighteen anti-tank rifles. An artillery battalion of about 250 was added to the brigade, this consisting of two gun batteries (each four 76mm M43 regimental guns) and a mortar battery (with four 120mm mortars). The anti-aircraft machine gun company was further expanded to an anti-aircraft battalion of about 170 men consisting of two anti-aircraft machine gun companies (each with twelve *DShK* machine guns) and a light anti-aircraft battery (with four 37mm guns). At the same time the rifles were deleted from the rifle companies (except for sniper personnel) and the companies rearmed almost entirely with *PPSh* sub-machine guns.

Once again, efforts were made to reform a major airborne arm and in August 1944 the *Stavka* formed the 37th, 38th and 39th guards airborne corps as a separate Airborne Army.

A notable feature of this reorganization was that while six of the nine airborne divisions were originally airborne units, the other three (98th, 99th and 100th) were conversions of normal guards infantry divisions of the same numbers. In this incarnation the nine divisions were actual airborne units, each consisting of three

HQ, Airborne Army
37th Guards Airborne Corps
    13th, 98th and 99th guards airborne divisions
38th Guards Airborne Corps
    11th, 12th and 16th guards airborne divisions
39th Guards Airborne Corps
    8th, 14th and 100th guards airborne divisions

Order of Battle

airborne brigades. In the process of conversion the divisions lost their artillery regiments and other divisional base elements and were thus actually the old airborne corps with a new designation. As before, however, this could not last and in December 1944 the Airborne Army was redesignated the 9th Guards Army and its constituent units redesignated as guards rifle units.

The Dnepr operation of mid-1943 was the last significant airborne mission by the Soviet Army. Its failure apparently meant the end of such attempts, although the 1st Guards Airborne Division did participate in the liberation of Manchuria and two independent airborne battalions undertook air-landing operations there against no opposition.

Despite having by far the largest and most experienced airborne force in the world in the 1930s and through the early part of the war, the Soviets experienced little but failure in their operational employment. Although the paratroopers fought bravely, they rarely achieved the goals set for them. The most conspicuous reason for their failure was what one knowledgeable analyst has called 'higher command planning failures of criminal proportions'.[3] Higher HQs launched airborne operations with no understanding of their limitations, requiring night-time drops with no pathfinder support on drop zones held by undefined enemy forces.

Soviet naval infantry formations were best known for their traditional sailor's garb. But as the war dragged on, Soviet naval infantry formations gradually adopted the uniform and equipment of the Army which proved more practical in harsh weather conditions – as here in the barren landscape of northern Russia with a Baltic Fleet unit. The sailor in the foreground is armed with a captured German Schmeisser submachine gun, while two others are armed with the *SVT*-40 automatic rifle.

Organizationally, the airborne brigades suffered from a lack of heavy weapons. This is partially explainable by the lack of suitable transport for dropping them. During the 1930s the Soviets had always assumed that a light parachute force would seize a landing zone and cargo aircraft (usually TB-3 bombers, in fact) would then ferry in the heavier forces needed to accomplish the mission. In fact, this technique was never used and the parachute forces wound up bearing the weight of the whole mission with machine guns, anti-tank rifles, light and medium mortars and backpack flame-throwers. Gliders were allocated to carry the 45mm guns of the airborne forces in the Dnepr operation but, due to poor planning, do not seem to have actually been used. It was not until late 1943 that cargo parachutes were developed that enabled the dropping of 76mm infantry guns and 120mm mortars, weapons desperately needed by the parachute forces on the ground. By this time, however, it had become academic.

CHEMICAL (FLAME) UNITS

Flamethrower units were under the direction of the Chemical Branch. At least one such unit, the 201st Separate Tank Battalion (Chemical), saw service in the Winter War. Such a unit was built around three companies each of three platoons and was armed almost exclusively with the OT-26 or OT-130 flamethrower tank, the only gun-armed tanks being allocated to the battalion and company commanders. Platoon, company and battalion HQ tanks all had radios, as did the armoured cars or amphibious tankettes in the scout platoon, but the line tanks did not.

With the decision to form tank divisions in 1940 and the expansion of the force in 1941 almost all the flame tank battalions were apparently incorporated into the new

divisions at one battalion per tank regiment. At the time of the German invasion the offensive elements of the chemical branch were found in a few flame tank battalions, a small number of armoured car flame battalions (three companies each of fifteen vehicles), chemical mortar battalions (three companies each of twelve mortars) and conventional flamethrower battalions.

The remaining separate flame tank battalions were authorized variants of the new models of tanks, with each battalion to be configured as two 10-tank companies of KV-8s and two 16-tank companies of OT-34s, although it seems likely that few of these vehicles were actually available at the time. In mid-1942 the size of the flame tank battalions was reduced, to two 5-tank companies of KV-8s and one 11-tank company of OT-34s. For large operations some of the battalions were grouped into 3-battalion brigades. In May 1944 some of the flame tank battalions were redesignated as regiments (with twenty tanks apiece) and assigned to engineer assault brigades, and the rest of the flame tank units were disbanded.

The backpack flamethrower battalions did not survive long into the war. In July 1941 they were disbanded and the assets distributed to the infantry, first as regimental and then as divisional assets. The July 1942 infantry TO&Es deleted the flamethrowers from subsequent divisions and in mid-year the first eleven separate flamethrower companies of the *VGK* reserve were formed, each of three platoons and each platoon with forty ROKS-2 flamethrowers. The standardized infantry TO&Es of December of that year finally removed all flamethrowers from infantry forces, permitting the activation of eight more separate companies, with the total of nineteen remaining constant for the rest of the war. In May 1944 a few additional companies were raised to form small flamethrower battalions for some of the

	Men	BA-20 Armoured Cars	OT-26 (flame) Tanks	T-26 (45mm) Tanks	Motorcycles	Cars	Trucks
Battalion HQ	30	0	0	1	0	0	0
Signal Platoon	20	0	0	0	6	0	2
Scout Platoon	9	3	0	0	0	0	0
Three Tank Companies, each	51	0	15	1	0	0	0
trains elements	80	0	0	0	0	1	41

Table 5.4 Flamethrower tank battalion, 1939.

assault engineer brigades. Such a battalion had 390 men mainly in two 161-man companies, each of which consisted of three platoons, each of four squads for a total of 120 ROKS-2 per company.

The second type of flamethrower was the FOG-1, a static defensive weapon placed in a pit in the ground and remotely fired. The first fifty separate fougasse flamethrower companies were formed in August 1941, each consisting of three platoons, each of three squads, with twenty FOG-1 per squad. Additional companies for the fortified regions, with 300 FOG-1 per company, were also formed. The field companies proved successful in the battles outside Moscow and in January 1942 a further ninety-three smaller companies were formed, these with 135 FOG-1. The companies were consolidated into flamethrower battalions (sometimes called anti-tank flamethrower battalions) in 1943, starting with five motorized battalions in April. Such a battalion consisted of three flame companies and a motor transport company and had a total of 540 FOG-1. In August semi-motorized and horsed battalions were formed with the remaining companies. A semi-motorized battalion had

401 men in three 114-man companies, each of three 4-squad platoons for a total of 576 FOG-1 and twenty-seven trucks. A horsed battalion had a similar structure, but totalled 648 FOG-1. In December 1943 a machine gun company with nine medium machine guns was added to each fougasse flamethrower battalion to supply covering fire for the weapons. The initial twenty-eight battalions were supplemented by sixteen more in May 1944, although the number had dropped back down to twenty-nine by the end of the year, before rising again to forty-one in early 1945.

Notes

1. Another German source gave the brigade a total strength of 203 officers, 45 political officers, 49 warrant officers, 453 NCOs and 2,311 other ranks. Although the overall structure of the brigade in this report was identical to that described above, the battalions here were smaller (each 614 men) and the artillery battalion was armed exclusively with 45mm guns.

2. The 1st Airborne Brigade was also scheduled to participate but could not assemble in time and never made it into combat.

3. Glantz, 1994, p. 109.

CHAPTER 6

WEAPONS OF THE RED ARMY: ARMOURED VEHICLES

The Soviet tank pool at the beginning of the Great Patriotic War was as large as the rest of the world combined, totalling 23,106 vehicles. Yet by the end of the first year, about 90 per cent of this force was destroyed by the German onslaught. Few of the pre-war tank types survived beyond 1941 except in isolated areas, such as in besieged Leningrad or in the Far East.

Most of the Soviet tank arsenal in 1941 was made up of two types: the T-26 infantry tank, of which over 12,000 had been built, and the BT cavalry tanks, of which over 8,300 had been built. The T-26 was a licence-built version of the British Vickers 6-ton tank. The original T-26 Model 1931 was fitted with two machine gun turrets but this was superseded by the more common T-26 Model 1933, equipped with a more conventional single turret and armed with a dual-purpose 45mm anti-tank gun. This design underwent continual modernization through the 1930s, there being two later versions which used improved turrets with better armour layout; otherwise, the combat characteristics were similar to the earlier model. For its day, the T-26 was an excellent light tank. It was used in significant numbers during the Spanish Civil War and dominated the smaller German *PzKpfw* I light tank and Italian L.3 tankettes. Its primary advantage was its excellent 45mm gun, which could fire both a high-explosive and an armour-piercing round (see Table 6.1).

The BT tank was a licence-built derivative of the American Christie tank, fitted with a locally designed turret and gun. After small-scale production of the BT-2 with a 37mm tank gun, the series production BT-5 introduced a 45mm gun, mounted in the same turret as used on the T-26 Model 1933. The difference between the BT and T-26 was in their roles: the T-26 was a much slower tank than the BT and intended for infantry support, while the BT tank was a high-speed design, similar in concept to British cruiser tanks, and intended for exploitation and deep attacks. The BT-5 underwent modernization in the late 1930s, resulting in the BT-7. This introduced a new turret and hull front with sloped armour for better protection, but retained the same 45mm gun. A small number of BT-5 tanks saw combat use in Spain in 1937–8 with Republican forces.

The Soviet 45mm tank gun that armed these two types was the best general-purpose tank gun in common service in the mid-1930s, firing an excellent anti-tank projectile that could defeat nearly any existing tank, and also firing a useful high-explosive round for defeating enemy infantry or anti-tank guns. Many tank guns of the period did not show such versatility and could either fire a good anti-tank projectile or a good high-explosive projectile, but not both; for example, contemporary French infantry tanks were armed with a short 37mm gun with little anti-armour capability, and the British 2pdr gun lacked a useful high-explosive round. The contemporary German *PzKpfw* I was armed only with two 7.62mm machine guns, and the *PzKpfw* II only with a 20mm gun.

By the time of the 1941 campaign, the T-26 and BT tank designs were somewhat outdated. They were comparable in performance to the German light tanks, including the *Pz.Kpfw* I, *PzKpfw* II and *PzKpfw* 38(t), in terms of armour and mobility but with somewhat better main guns. Their most serious shortcoming was not their design but their poor state of repair. Over 65 per cent of the light tank force required major or capital rebuilding. When the war broke out, many Soviet tank units ground to a halt during road marches to the front; the older light tanks broke down and there were neither the spare parts nor facilities to repair them. Far more Soviet tanks fell victim to mechanical problems than to German guns.

Besides the T-26 infantry tank and BT cavalry tank, there were several other significant types in service. The standard medium tank of the Red Army in the 1930s was the T-28. This was a relatively large tank, inspired by the multi-turreted design fad of the 1930s. It had a single 76mm howitzer in the main turret and two subsidiary machine gun turrets. This design was obsolete in 1941, and a generation behind its closest German counterpart, the *PzKpfw* IV. In addition, it suffered the same mechanical problems as Soviet light tanks of the period. The Red Army had two battalions of T-35 heavy tanks in service in 1941. This multi-turreted tank was fitted with the same main gun and machine gun turrets of the T-28 but in addition had a pair of 45mm gun turrets. Nearly all of these tanks fell victim to

mechanical breakdown within a few days of the start of the war.

The Red Army also possessed a number of specialized light armoured vehicles in 1941. The T-37 and T-38 were small, amphibious light tanks used for scouting; they were armed only with a 7.62mm machine gun, though there was some limited production of an uparmed T-38 with a 20mm gun. The T-20 *Komsomolyets* was a light armoured tractor similar in concept to the French Army's Renault UE that was used to tow 45mm anti-tank guns and 76mm regimental guns. It was fitted with a single machine gun in an armoured mount and so in desperation was sometimes used as a light tank. The Red Army also had an extensive array of armoured cars. The most important light armoured car was the BA-20, fitted with a small machine gun turret and intended for scouting. The standard medium armoured car was the BA-10, armed with the usual 45mm tank gun and based on the local copy of the Ford AAA truck, the *GAZ-AAA*.

During the Spanish Civil War, the Red Army sent more than 300 tanks and more than 300 tank crewmen to support the Republican forces. The Spanish experience convinced Soviet tank designers that existing levels of tank armour, which had not changed since the First World War, were not adequate in the face of contemporary anti-tank guns such as the German 37mm *PaK* 36 or the Soviet 45mm gun. As a result, a new generation of tanks were designed in the late 1930s to correct these deficits. While designing these tanks with significantly thicker armour, the designers realized that the firepower of the tanks would have to be improved as well; it was assumed that a tank should be equipped with a gun adequate to defeat enemy tanks protected by levels of armour similar to its own.

A column of T-37 amphibious tanks on the move. These small, machine gun-armed vehicles were designed for scouting. Few survived the devastating battles of the summer of 1941 and the Red Army gave up on the luxury of amphibious scout tanks until after the war.

The Red Army's standard medium tank at the outbreak of the war was the T-28, a multi-turreted type with a 76mm gun in the main turret and two subsidiary machine gun turrets. These tanks were poorly armoured compared to new designs such as the T-34, and few survived the 1941 fighting. This tank from the 5th Tank Division was knocked out near Alitus, Lithuania, on the first day of the war.

The BT-7 fast tank was intended for use by the large mechanized formations to conduct deep operations, and was comparable to British cruiser tanks. Although well armed for its day, its thin armour proved a liability and thousands were lost in 1941, such as this example destroyed in combat with the Finnish Army on the Karelian peninsula in 1941. (Esa Muikku)

As was the fashion in the 1930s, the Red Army adopted thousands of T-20 Komsomolyets light artillery tractors which were used by infantry formations to tow anti-tank guns, similar to the French UE tractor or the British Universal Carrier. It was armed with a single machine gun, and so could be used as an improvised tankette. However, the concept never proved entirely viable and the high casualties of the 1941 campaign put an end to its use.

The most common Soviet tank in 1941 was the T-26 Model 1933 light tank, a derivative of the British Vickers 6-ton export tank. It was intended primarily for infantry support and had a distinguished combat record during the Spanish Civil War. But by 1941 its poor mechanical state and thin armour doomed it to extinction.

Four major new types were designed: the T-40 light amphibious tank to replace the T-37 and T-38, the T-50 infantry tank to replace the T-26, the T-34 cavalry tank to replace the BT, and the KV heavy tank to replace the T-28 and T-35. Development of the T-50 was the most protracted and none were in service when the war broke out in 1941. The T-34 cavalry tank proved to be such a well-balanced and revolutionary design that it took over both the infantry tank and cavalry tank roles, becoming the standard medium tank of the Red Army through the war. The KV-1 was the most thickly armoured tank of its day and proved to be a great shock to the Wehrmacht when first encountered in June 1941. Besides the standard tank version, a small number of KVs were built in the KV-2 configuration with a 152mm howitzer, a design inspired by the Finnish campaign and intended for bunker-busting. The new T-34 and KV tanks were available in significant numbers in June 1941 with some 508 KVs and 967 T-34s in service. Besides their excellent armour, both the T-34 and KV were fitted with good 76mm guns that could defeat any German tank of the time.

The best German tanks available in 1941 were the *PzKpfw* III, armed with a 37mm gun, and the *PzKpfw* IV, armed with a short 75mm gun with poor anti-armour performance. There were 1,449 *PzKpfw* IIIs and 517 *PzKpfw* IVs in service in June 1941. They were inferior to the new Soviet tanks in armour, firepower and mobility; indeed, the revolutionary combination of armour, firepower and mobility of the T-34 tank established it as the technological pace-setter of Second World War tank design. The locus of tank technology shifted from its traditional centre in England and France, eastwards to Germany and the Soviet Union. The technological arms race between Germany and the USSR, prompted by the

revolutionary T-34 and the need to match it, set the pace for worldwide tank development throughout the war.

In spite of significant technical advantages, neither the T-34 nor KV tank designs had a substantial impact on the summer 1941 fighting. There were many local successes for the new tanks, especially when opposing German infantry units which were only protected by the obsolete 37mm *PaK* 36 anti-tank gun; there were few successes in large scale engagements, however, and the Soviet tank divisions were obliterated along with the rest of the Red Army in a month of fighting. The reasons for this unimpressive performance can be traced to the general inadequacies of the Red Army of the time, such as the poor level of training at nearly all levels, the lack of experience with large mechanized formations and the lack of preparedness prior to the German invasion. As was the case with French armour in 1940, most of the new tanks arrived in Soviet units only months before the outbreak of the war, leading to little or no time for training the new conscript tank crews; there was a general shortage of 76mm gun ammunition, particularly armour-piercing ammunition; and the new tanks were plagued by technical problems, notably the poor transmission and clutch of the KV that led to frequent breakdowns.

In the wake of the defeat of the Red Army in the border battles of the summer of 1941, the Soviet tank force was plunged into a second crisis in the autumn when it became apparent that the two main centres of Soviet tank production, at Kharkov in Ukraine and in Leningrad, were about to be overrun or surrounded. At the cost of short-term production, these and other key war plants were transferred to the Urals. As a result, tank production plummeted for the remainder of 1941 and did not begin to recover until early in 1942 when the plants had been re-established. The decline in production and the demand for new tanks to equip the new independent tank brigades and infantry support tank regiments led to hard choices for the Soviet tank industry. In early 1942 decisions were made to freeze tank designs to the greatest extent possible so as to ensure maximum production; the only changes permitted were those which helped increase production or drive down cost. For example, the T-34 hull design was simplified in the T-34 Model 1942, and a new easily manufactured hexagonal cast turret was introduced in the spring of 1942 as the T-34 Model 1943. As a result of these decisions, Soviet tank design stagnated for nearly a year until the summer of 1943. But the decision paid off as the industry was able to turn out tanks in increasing numbers. Production was also rationalized in early 1942: the T-50 infantry tank proved to be almost as expensive as the T-34 medium tank and, as a result, further production was halted; the T-40 amphibious tank, likewise, was deemed too expensive and in its place, a non-amphibious and cheaper derivative, the T-60 was introduced. Plans to deploy improved versions of the T-34 and KV such as the T-34M and KV-3 were cancelled.

The superior technical quality of the T-34 and KV were made even more evident in the winter of 1941 due to the contrasting poor performance of German tanks in the harsh winter conditions with the excellent mobility of the Soviet tanks in snow. The tank panic which afflicted the German infantry after encounters with the KV and T-34 led to cries for a better anti-tank gun; the new 50mm *PaK* 38 was quickly deemed inadequate and a new 75mm *PaK* 40 anti-tank gun developed. The encounters had been equally shocking to the hitherto invincible panzer force and they led to two parallel efforts: on the one hand, existing designs were uparmoured and received better guns, a long 50mm on the *PzKpfw* III and a long 75mm on the *PzKpfw* IV; at the same time, two new tanks were developed, the Panther medium tank with a long 75mm gun and the Tiger heavy tank with a tank version of the legendary 88mm anti-aircraft gun.

By the summer of 1942 both sides were nearly equal in the technical sense. The upgunned German tanks could finally defeat the Soviet tanks, while the Soviet tanks still had adequate firepower to deal with German tank armour. Soviet tanks continued to enjoy some mobility advantages but German tanks enjoyed better turret layouts, better radios and better fire controls. The crew layout of Soviet tanks was poor: the T-34 had a turret crew of only two, which meant that the commander could not execute his command functions and had to double as a gunner; nor was the commander provided with adequate vision devices and the poor hatch design made it impossible for him to ride with his head outside the tank as was the German practice. Soviet tank commanders, already hampered by inadequate training, were overwhelmed with the simple mechanics of operating the tank, their problems then compounded further by a lack of radios which made it impossible to coordinate tank units on the battlefield. The combination of all these features, plus very limited training, led to abysmal tank tactics that made the Soviet tank units increasingly vulnerable to their more experienced German opponents. Total Soviet tank losses from June to December 1941 were 20,500; German losses from 22 June 1941 through to the end of February 1942 were only 3,402, a 6:1 exchange ratio.

By the summer of 1942, greater confidence in tank warfare led the Red

The Red Army built large numbers of armoured cars before the war, primarily for reconnaissance roles. The BA-20 was the latest model in the light armoured car category and was based on a standard civilian automobile chassis. Here, a captured example is examined by German troops in 1941.

No weapon terrorized German infantry in 1941 more than the KV-1 heavy tank. Impervious to the standard German 37mm anti-tank gun, there were several recorded instances of the KV simply running over and crushing Wehrmacht guns. Numerous hits can be seen on this KV-1 of the 6th Mechanized Corps, knocked out finally by an 88mm gun near Zelva, Lithuania, in July 1941. The Achilles heel of the design was a balky transmission and powertrain, exacerbated by poor crew training.

The Finnish campaign of 1940 convinced Red Army leaders of the need for a heavy tank capable of destroying heavily reinforced bunkers, hence the production of the KV-2 'Dreadnought' armed with a 152mm howitzer. Only 334 were built and nearly all were lost in the 1941 battles, like this example abandoned in Lvov in June 1941.

Army to introduce tank corps, which were roughly comparable to Western tank divisions. However, these new units were very roughly handled by the Germans in the summer 1942 campaign. Recriminations followed in the wake of the heavy tank losses. Soviet tank officers were especially critical of the KV heavy tank. Although it had been popular through the spring of 1942 due to its virtual invulnerability to German guns, the advent of the 75mm German tank and anti-tank guns removed this advantage; its vices became more readily apparent, especially its poor mobility compared to the T-34, the difficulty of moving it across typical bridges due to its weight, and lingering automotive problems. Many urged that KV production cease in favour of the T-34. The T-34 emerged as a solid, reliable performer; its main disadvantage was its thinner armour, even more vulnerable than the KV to the new German guns. In addition, the 2-man turret configuration was widely recognized to be a tactical problem. The little T-60 light tank was dismissed as being nearly useless; its small 20mm gun and its thin armour made it a toothless death trap.

As a result of these harsh criticisms, the tank industry was permitted a modest

The T-34 was the most formidable tank of its day when introduced in combat in the summer of 1941. But its actual impact on fighting in June and July 1941 was negligible due to the inexperience of its crews and the chaotic state of many of the Soviet mechanized formations on the eve of war. Mechanical teething pains also contributed to its poor showing, evident from the spare transmission lashed to the back deck of this T-34 of the 4th Mechanized Corps, also abandoned in Lvov in June 1941.

amount of leeway in developing new designs. In the short term, the KV heavy tanks were taken out of the tank brigades and relegated to the separate tank regiments used for infantry support. In addition, a lighter version was developed, the KV-1S, to cure its mobility problems. Although light tanks were not popular, the automotive plants manufacturing them could not produce medium tanks, so the T-60 was replaced by the slightly larger T-70 which was armed with an inadequate, but better, 45mm gun. T-34 tanks produced

later in 1942 had a commander's vision cupola added as a quick fix for its turret layout problems. In the long run, the Red Army decided that it needed a 'universal tank' to replace the light, medium and heavy tanks. This was basically intended to meld the better features of the T-34 and KV, namely to increase the armour to the level of the KV to protect against the new German 75mm guns and to introduce better turret layouts in the hope of improving tactical performance. Two competitive designs were developed, the

Medium armoured cars such as the BA-10 were successfully used by the Red Army on the dry steppes of the Far East against Japanese forces in the 1938–9 border fighting. They were less successful in the softer soil of northern Europe, and no replacements were forthcoming as the pre-war BA-10s suffered from attrition in 1941.

Aerosans were a unique Soviet innovation for winter warfare and were a type of ski vehicle propelled by surplus aircraft motors. An armoured version, the NKL-26, was produced during the war for raiding operations in northern regions. They could only be operated on relatively flat, open terrain.

The intended replacement for the T-26 light tank was the T-50 infantry tank. Production was only beginning when the war broke out and only a few dozen reached service. It was almost as costly to produce as the T-34 cavalry tank and more poorly armed and armoured. As a result, the Red Army wisely chose to standardize on the T-34 tank to fulfil the needs of both an infantry tank and a cavalry tank.

Soviet automotive factories could not produce designs as large and heavy as the T-34 and so instead were diverted to manufacture light tanks such as the T-60. Armed only with a 20mm gun, the T-60 proved inadequate in combat. In 1942 it was replaced by the slightly larger T-70 light tank, armed with a better 45mm gun.

T-43, based on the T-34, and the KV-13, based on the KV-1S.

The *Wehrmacht* made its first significant deployment of the new Tiger I heavy tank near Leningrad in January 1943 and the Red Army soon captured an example. Although it was clear that such a heavily armoured and well-armed tank would represent a formidable opponent, the Red Army did not believe that the Tiger would appear in anything more than token numbers. This was not a particularly unique view, as the US Army reacted with similar complacency after engaging the Tiger I in Tunisia in 1943. The Soviets were convinced that it made more sense to concentrate on the production of large numbers of dependable tanks than to switch to the production of small numbers of superior tanks. Indeed, only 1,354 Tiger I tanks were produced during the entire war, equal to less than a month of T-34 production. The Soviet concentration on production paid off. The Soviet tank inventory rose from 7,700 tanks in January 1942 to 20,600 tanks at the beginning of 1943, in spite of massive combat losses in 1942 caused by the inept tactical use of the new tank corps. German tank inventories also rose during the same period from 4,896 in January 1942 to 5,648 in January 1943. But discounting obsolete types, the combat-ready inventory actually fell slightly, from 4,084 at the end of 1941 to 3,939 at the end of 1942. Soviet tank losses in 1942 were 15,000, while German losses (on all fronts) were 2,648 – an exchange ratio of more than 6:1, nearly as bad as the 1941 disaster.

Technically, the Soviet tank force in the summer of 1943 was much the same as a year before. The bulk of the force was made up of T-34 Model 1943 tanks, armed with the same 76mm gun. The new KV-1S had appeared and although it was more mobile and more reliable automotively its tactical characteristics were much the same. One of the few technical improvements was the addition of radio receivers in most medium and heavy tanks. The great tank battles around the Kursk-Orel salient in the summer of 1943 were won largely due to the growing skill of Red Army commanders in the use of large mechanized formations and the growing tactical skill of the average Soviet tanker. However, by the summer of 1943 the Red Army no longer enjoyed any technological advantage over German panzer units due to the advent of the Tiger I heavy tank and the new Panther medium tank. This is very evident in terms of tank losses: through September 1942, on average, only 46 per cent of T-34 tanks hit by German guns were penetrated; by Stalingrad, 55 per cent of the tanks hit were penetrated; and by Kursk, in 1943, 88 per cent of those hit were penetrated.

The Panther had little impact on the summer 1943 fighting due to lingering technical problems. But as its bugs were cured it became a scourge of the Soviet tank force because it was manufactured in larger numbers than the Tiger. The Panther was nearly half as heavy again as the T-34 and its greater complexity meant that few were produced – only 5,976 during the entire war. There were seldom more than 500 Panthers in service on the Eastern Front at any given time. While the Wehrmacht may have enjoyed a technological edge in tank design in late 1943, it did not translate into useful combat power. By 1943 the Red Army was on the offensive and the role of the tank and mechanized corps was to exploit breaches in German lines after they had been won by rifle divisions supported by separate heavy tank regiments. As a result, the Soviet tank units more often than not faced German infantry units weakly protected by small numbers of towed 75mm

In late 1941 the design of the T-34 was frozen, even though improvements had been planned. The only changes tolerated were those that made it cheaper and easier to manufacture. This concentration on simplicity helped the Red Army build up its tank forces after the savage losses of 1941. But by 1943 the T-34 was losing in the technological arms race with the Wehrmacht.

By the autumn of 1942, the KV heavy tank's days of glory had passed. Its armour was now vulnerable to the new German tank guns and its heavy weight and lingering automotive problems caused serious tactical problems when used alongside the fleet T-34. Although many Red Army tankers wanted to end its production in favour of the T-34, a decision was made instead to remove it from the tank corps and segregate it into separate tank regiments used for infantry support.

Instead of tanks, the Wehrmacht used turretless assault guns, called *Sturmgeschutz*, for infantry support. The Red Army decided to follow suit in 1942, mounting the 122mm M-30 howitzer on the T-34 tank chassis. Medium assault guns such as these were never popular but light and heavy assault guns became a staple of the Red Army in 1944–5.

The SU-152 was an assault gun version of the KV-1S heavy tank, mounting the ML-20 152mm gun-howitzer in a fixed casemate. This was one of the few Soviet armoured vehicles available at the time of the Kursk armour battles that could defeat the new German heavy armoured vehicles such as the Tiger tank and the *Elefant* tank destroyer.

One of the less popular Lend-Lease designs provided to the USSR was the M3 Lee medium tank, the ancestor of the better known and more successful M4 Sherman. Its archaic design, with a hull-mounted 75mm gun and turreted 37mm gun, and its thin armour led to its caustic Russian nickname, which translates as 'a grave for seven brothers'.

One of the few heavy tanks supplied to the Red Army through Lend-Lease was Britain's Churchill tank. This example was knocked out during the fighting at Kursk in the summer of 1943.

The most numerous Soviet armoured vehicle of the war after the T-34 tank was the SU-76M assault gun. This was an attempt to employ the production plants previously committed to manufacturing the unsatisfactory T-60 and T-70 light tanks. The SU-76M mated a lengthened T-70 light tank hull with the ZiS-3 76mm divisional gun. The SU-76M assault gun was used much like the German *StuG* III assault gun, as a direct-fire, infantry support weapon, not as indirect-fire field artillery.

The only Soviet armoured car manufactured during the war years was the light BA-64, based on the *GAZ*-67 jeep. It was armed only with a 7.62mm light machine gun in an open turret, and so its use was confined to scouting and liaison work. (Janusz Magnuski)

anti-tank guns and *StuG* III assault guns. Even if inadequate against the Panther or Tiger, the T-34 Model 1943 was more than adequate when facing its usual infantry opponents.

The summer 1943 fighting also saw the first large-scale use of assault guns by the Red Army. Assault guns were patterned after the German *StuG* III *Sturmgeschutz*. Although often misidentified as self-propelled artillery, they were in reality direct-fire weapons manned by tank troops. The main attraction of assault guns was that they could carry a heavier weapon than their tank counterpart and were cheaper to manufacture. The most common of these in the Red Army was the SU-76M light assault gun, nicknamed *Suka* (bitch) by its crews with little fondness. The SU-76M consisted of a lengthened T-70 light tank chassis armed with the 76mm ZiS-3 divisional gun in an open-topped fixed casemate at the rear of the hull. It was much more poorly armoured than its German equivalent, the *StuG* III, but was used in the same role for direct-fire infantry support. It was not popular with its crews because of its open roof and thin armour, but it was a cheap and effective method of providing mobile firepower for the infantry during offensive operations. It was produced in larger numbers than any other Soviet armoured vehicle during the war except for the T-34 tank. A medium assault gun was produced on the T-34 chassis, the SU-122, and armed with a version of the ubiquitous M-30 122mm howitzer. Unlike the SU-76M, it was fully armoured but was never produced in the same numbers. Finally, a heavy assault gun was built on the KV-1S tank chassis as the SU-152, armed with a massive 152mm howitzer. Of the trio of new assault guns, this was certainly the most popular. During the Kursk fighting it was the only Soviet

armoured vehicle capable of defeating the new German Tiger and Panther, so earning the nickname *Zvierboi* or 'animal hunter'.

The Red Army also used a number of British and American Lend-Lease tanks, few of which were popular. The Red Army was shipped 1,683 light tanks and 5,488 medium tanks from the United States and 5,218 tanks from Britain and Canada. This amounted to 16 per cent of Soviet wartime tank production. The American M3 Lee medium tank was in particular disfavour due to its archaic layout and was dubbed the 'grave for seven brothers'. The British Matilda infantry tank and American M3 Stuart light tank were disliked for their puny guns. The only British tank to win any favour in 1943 was the Valentine. It became the standard Soviet scout tank by late 1943 due to the influx of most of the Canadian production run and the conversion of the T-70 light tank plants over to the SU-76M assault gun. Lend-Lease tanks were widely used in Soviet units and in 1943 about 20 per cent of Soviet tank brigades were of mixed Soviet/Lend-Lease composition, while about 15 per cent were equipped exclusively with Lend-Lease types.

The advent of the new Panther tank forced the Red Army to relax its freeze on tank innovation. By 1943 the inventory situation was not as desperate as in 1942, and Soviet tank crews were clamouring for a tank with a 'long arm' to deal with the Tiger and Panther. As a temporary expedient, a tank-destroyer version of the T-34 tank was rushed into service as the SU-85, with an 85mm gun mounted in a fixed casemate like the SU-122 assault gun. In addition, the final production run of KV-1S tanks were completed with a larger turret and 85mm gun as the KV-85. In December 1943 the Red Army approved a new derivative of the T-34 tank, the T-34-85.

Kursk was a painful reminder of how far Soviet tank technology had slipped behind German due to its concentration on quantity over quality. As a result of the appearance of the German Panther tank, Soviet tank designers were forced rapidly to develop a better armed version of the T-34, fitted with an 85mm gun. The resulting T-34-85 tank entered combat in the spring 1944 offensives and is seen here during the liberation of Minsk at the conclusion of Operation Bagration in Belorussia in the summer of 1944.

Another of the outcomes of the Kursk fighting was the decision to abandon the KV heavy tanks for a completely redesigned type, the IS-2 Stalin heavy tank. The IS-2 was an evolutionary development of the KV, using a related chassis and engine, but with a radically improved armour layout and new 122mm gun. Unlike the German Tiger I which was optimized for tank-versus-tank fighting, the IS-2 was intended to assist in offensive operations, in both the breakthrough and exploitation phases.

As in the case of the KV series with its related SU-152 assault gun version, the IS tank had its assault gun relatives. Two types were developed, the ISU-122, as seen here, armed with the 122mm A-19 gun, and the ISU-152, with the ML-20 152mm gun-howitzer. As on the towed field artillery versions, the two guns shared a common mounting and were nearly interchangeable.

This substituted a new 3-man turret armed with an 85mm gun, solving both the firepower problem and the longstanding tactical problem. However, these did not begin to enter service until April 1944. Although its new gun was not as effective as either the Panther's long 75mm gun or the Tiger I's 88mm gun, it could defeat either tank under the right circumstances. Given its low cost, it was produced in far larger numbers than all of its German opponents combined.

By 1944, the Red Army had begun to receive significant numbers of American M4A2 Sherman tanks. The versions available in the summer of 1944 were armed with a 75mm gun, while a 76mm gun version became available late in 1944. By this time in the war, these tanks were usually used to equip entire regiments or brigades and were generally not used in mixed formations.

The KV-1S was replaced on the assembly lines by the new IS heavy tank, named after Joseph Stalin (Iosef Stalin). Originally, the IS-1 was armed with the same 85mm gun as the T-34-85; however, given its greater size and weight, the Red Army decided to arm it with a better gun. Two weapons were considered: the 100mm D-10 gun had better anti-armour performance but it was in a new calibre and ammunition was still scarce; a 122mm gun derived from the towed A-19 gun was selected instead. Although its anti-tank performance was not as good as the D-10, the A-19 had a better high-explosive round that would be more useful due to the tank's role in breakthrough operations. As a result, the IS-1 was upgunned and series production in 1944 consisted entirely of the IS-2 heavy tanks equipped from the outset with the 122mm gun. These were first deployed in significant numbers in the spring of 1944.

The new generation of tanks was accompanied by a new generation of assault guns. The SU-76M remained in production and the SU-122 was largely replaced by the SU-85 tank destroyer. The most important of the new assault guns were based on the IS heavy tank chassis and designated ISU-122 and ISU-152. Both these vehicles were identical except for the gun tube. The ISU-122 was armed with a version of the A-19 122mm gun and the ISU-152 with a version of the ML-20 152mm gun-howitzer; these proved so successful in combat that more of the assault gun version of the IS heavy tanks were produced than the IS-2 tanks themselves.

In 1943 the Germans had been able to maintain a combat equilibrium on the Eastern Front by offsetting their numerical weakness with modest technological advantages and superior crew and unit performance. In 1943 they were still destroying about four Soviet tanks for every one of their own lost, thereby dulling the impact of Soviet numerical advantages. In 1944, however, the Germans were not able to maintain the equilibrium because of the revival in Soviet tank design, substantial German armour transfers to western Europe in the spring of 1944 to deal with the forthcoming Allied invasion, and a diminishing disparity in German versus Soviet tank crew tactical skills. It is worth pondering whether the German industrial policy of manufacturing small quantities of high-quality tanks was not one of the root causes for the German reverses in 1943-4. During the final year of the war the technological balance between the Wehrmacht and the Red Army was fairly level but the Red Army enjoyed an enormous superiority in numbers – this was due to a far more prudent Soviet industrial policy and the remarkably inept management of the German war industries.

Combat Ranges of Armoured Vehicle Engagements 1943–4

(Percentage of Soviet tanks and assault guns knocked out by range)

Distance in metres	75mm gun	88mm gun
100–200	10.0	4.0
200–400	26.1	14.0
400–600	33.5	18.0
800–1,000	7.0	13.5
1,000–1,200	4.5	8.5
1,200–1,400	3.6	7.6
1,400–1,600	0.4	2.0
1,600–1,800	0.4	0.7
1,800–2,000	0	0.5

The style of fighting that took place in early 1945 had changed considerably from the fighting on the Russian steppes in the summer of 1943. Much of the combat now took place in urban areas and German infantry anti-tank rockets, such as the *Panzerfaust*, became a much more lethal threat to Soviet armour than in open terrain. Table 6.1, reproduced from a wartime Soviet study of the cause of T-34 tank losses, gives a good idea of the changing nature of tank fighting during the war. The chart clearly shows the escalating calibres of tank and anti-tank guns during the war, as well as the increasing casualties caused by *Panzerfaust* anti-tank rockets in the final months of the fighting.

In the final months of the war, there were few major changes in the Soviet armoured force. The new SU-100 tank destroyer, armed with a 100mm gun, began to replace the SU-85 tank destroyer in order to deal with heavier German tank armour, such as on the King Tiger. Two new tanks were on the verge of production: the T-44 was the culmination of Soviet wartime tank design but it was not mature enough in the spring of 1945 to enter service; the IS-3 heavy tank was the most thickly armoured Soviet tank of the war with an armour basis of 200mm. It entered production in May 1945, too late to see action in Europe, though small numbers did serve with the Red Army in Manchuria against Japan.

	20mm	37mm	short 50mm	long 50mm	75mm	88mm	105mm	128mm	AT rocket	Unknown
Up to September 1942	4.7	10.0	7.5	54.3	10.1	3.4	2.9	0	0	7.1
Stalingrad operation	0	0	25.6	26.5	12.1	7.8	0	0	0	28.0
Central Front, Orel operation 1943	0	0	10.5	23.0	40.5	26.0	0	0	0	0
First Belorussian Front, June–September 1944	0	0	0	0	39.0	38.0	–	–	9.0	14.0
First Belorussian Front, January–March 1945	0	0	0	0	29.0	64.0	0	1.0	5.5	0.5
First Ukrainian Front, January–March 1945	0	0	0	0.5	19.0	71.0	0.6	0	8.9	0
Fourth Ukrainian Front, January–March 1945	0	0	0	0	25.3	51.5	0.9	–	9.0	13.3
First Belorussian Front, Oder–Berlin 1945	0	0	0	1.4	69.2	16.7	–	–	10.5	2.2
2nd Guards Tank Army, Berlin 1945	0	5.4	0	0	36.0	29.0	6.6	0	22.8	0

Table 6.1 Causes of T-34 tank losses during the Second World War (per cent).

	1941	1942	1943	1944	1945	Total
Light Tanks						
T-40	41	181				222
T-50	48	15				63
T-60	1,818	4,474				6,292
T-70		4,883	3,343			8,226
T-80			120			120
Sub-total	1,907	9,553	3,463			14,923
Medium Tanks						
T-34	3,014	12,553	15,529	2,995		34,091
T-34-85			283	11,778	7,230	23,661
T-44					200	200
Sub-total	3,014	12,553	15,812	14,773	7,430	53,582
Heavy Tanks						
KV-1	1,121	1,753				2,874
KV-2	232					232
KV-1S		780	452			1,232
KV-85			130			130
IS-2			102	2,252	1,500	3,854
Sub-total	1,353	2,533	684	2,252	1,500	8,322
Total Tanks	6,274	24,639	19,959	17,025	8,930	76,827
Assault Guns						
SU-76		26	1,928	7,155	3,562	12,671
SU-122		25	630	493		1,148
SU-85			750	1,300		2,050
SU-100				500	1,175	1,675
SU-152			704			704
ISU-122/ISU-152			35	2,510	1,530	4,075
Sub-total		51	4,047	11,958	6,267	22,323
Total AFVs	6,274	24,690	24,006	28,983	15,197	99,150

Table 6.2 Soviet wartime tank production.

Note

1941 figures are for the last six months of the war; 1945 figures are for the first six months. There are some discrepancies in published totals, probably due to the inclusion of prototypes in some figures and their omission in others.

The ISU-152 assault gun bears a close resemblance to the ISU-122, and can be distinguished by its shorter barrel and slatted muzzle brake. These heavy assault guns were so successful that they were produced in larger numbers than the IS-2 tank on which they were based. They were primarily used to provide direct-fire support for infantry and armour units, and were especially useful in overcoming German bunkers and in urban warfare.

	1941	1942	1943	1944	1945	
Soviet Tank strength*	22,600	7,700	20,600	21,100	25,400	
German Tank strength*	5,262	4,896	5,648	5,266	6,284	
	1941	**1942**	**1943**	**1944**	**1945**	**Total**
Soviet Tank production	6,274	24,639	19,959	16,975	4,384	72,231
German Tank production	3,256	4,278	5,966	9,161	1,098	23,759
Production ratio	1:2	1:5.6	1:3.3	1:1.85	1:4	1:3
	1941	**1942**	**1943**	**1944**	**1945**	**Total**
Soviet Tank losses	20,500	15,000	22,400	16,900	8,700	83,500
German Tank losses	2,758	2,648	6,362	6,434	7,382	25,584
Tank exchange ratio** (German:Soviet)	1:7	1:6	1:4	1:4	1:1.2	1:4.4

*As of January each year, except for 1941 which is as of 22 June 1941. German strength is entire strength, not only the Eastern Front. In July 1944 the Germans had over 1,500 tanks in Normandy and several hundred in other theatres such as Italy and the Balkans. Likewise, the Soviets kept about 3,000 tanks in the Far East through much of the war.
**German tank losses here include all fronts; the tank exchange ratio deletes estimated German losses to Anglo-American forces and so reflects only the Soviet-German loss ratio.

Table 6.3 The Eastern Front tank balance 1941–5: critical indices.

Although assault gun versions of the T-34 had not proven particularly useful, tank-destroyer versions were more successful. The SU-85 was developed as a quick method to rearm the T-34 with a more potent 85mm anti-tank weapon. The SU-85, like the one seen here, was used in special anti-tank units. When the T-34 tank itself was armed with the 85mm gun in late 1943, the tank-destroyer version was redesigned to accommodate a larger 100mm anti-tank gun, resulting in the SU-100. (Janusz Magnuski)

Type Variant	T-60 Model 42	T-70 Model 42	T-34 Model 41	T-34 Model 43	T-34-85 Model 44	KV-1 Model 42	KV-1S Model 43	IS-2M Model 45
Crew	2	2	4	4	5	5	5	4
Weight (tonnes)	6.4	9.2	26.5	30.9	32	47	42.5	46
Length (m)	4.1	4.29	6.68	6.75	8.15	6.8	6.8	9.9
Width (m)	2.3	2.32	3	3	3	3.32	3.25	3.1
Height (m)	1.74	2.04	2.45	2.45	2.6	2.71	2.64	2.73
Gun type	TNSh	Model 38	F-34	F-34	ZiS-S-53	ZiS-5	ZiS-5	D-25T
Gun calibre (mm)	20	45	76.2	76.2	85	76.2	76.2	122
Ammo stowed	780	94	77	100	60	114	114	28
Engine type	GAZ-202	GAZ-203	V-2	V-2	V-2	V-2	V-2	V-2-IS
Horsepower	85	140	500	500	500	600	600	600
Fuel (litres)	320	440	460	790	810	600	975	820
Max. road speed (km/h)	45	45	53	55	55	28	45	37(cont.)

| Type | T-60 | T-70 | T-34 | T-34 | T-34-85 | KV-1 | KV-1S | IS-2M |
Variant	Model 42	Model 42	Model 41	Model 43	Model 44	Model 42	Model 43	Model 45
Road range (km)	450	360	400	465	360	250	250	240
Terrain range (km)	250	180	260	365	310	180	160	210
Armour (mm)								
turret front	25	60	52	70	90	120	82	160
turret side	15	35	52	52	75	120	82	110
turret rear	15	35	45	52	60	90	82	100
turret roof	7	10	20	20	20	40	30	30
hull glacis	35	45	45	47	47	110	75	120
hull side	25	45	45	60	60	90–130	60	95
hull rear	25	35	47	47	47	60–75	40–75	60
hull top	13	10	20	20	20	30	30	30
hull floor	13	10	20	20	20	30	30	30

Table 6.4 Soviet tank technical characteristics.

Soviet wartime support vehicles were derived from pre-war designs, often licensed copies of American designs. The ZiS-5 was a copy of a 1931 Autocar design. The example here, in service with the Allied Polish People's Army, is the wartime ZiS-5V version, which had simpler mudguards and a simplified wooden cab to reduce costs. Such trucks had limited off-road capability. (Janusz Magnuski)

The Studebaker US-6 2½-ton truck was synonymous with US Lend-Lease shipments. Vehicles such as these helped provide the Red Army with vital tactical mobility during the offensive drives of 1944–5. In the background is an older ZiS-5V truck.

Type	SU-76M	SU-85	SU-100	SU-122	SU-152	ISU-122	ISU-152
Crew	4	4	4	5	5	5	5
Weight (tonnes)	10.2	29.2	31.6	30.9	45.5	45.5	46
Length (m)	5	8.15	9.45	6.95	8.95	9.85	9.18
Width (m)	2.7	3	3	3	3.25	3.07	3.07
Height (m)	2.1	2.45	2.25	2.32	2.45	2.48	2.48
Armament	ZiS-3	D-5S	D-10S	M-30S	ML-20S	A-19S	ML-20S
Calibre (9mm)	76.2	85	100	122	152	122	152
Ammo stowed	60	48	34	40	20	30	20
Engine	GAZ-203	V-2	V-2	V-2	V-2	V-2	V-2
Horsepower	170	500	500	500	500	600	600
Fuel (litres)	420	810	770	810	975	860	860
Max. road speed (km/h)	45	47	48	55	43	37	37
Road range (km)	320	400	320	300	330	220	220
Terrain range (km)	190	200	180	150	120	80	80
Armour (mm)							
hull front	35	45	45	45	60	90	90
hull side	16	45	45	45	60	90	90
hull rear	16	45	45	45	60	60	60
hull roof	0–10	20	20	20	30	30	30
hull floor	10	20	20	20	30	30	30

Table 6.5 Soviet assault gun and tank destroyer technical characteristics.

SOVIET TRANSPORT VEHICLES

Due to the militarized nature of the Stalinist economy, the distinction between civil and military transport before and during the Second World War was not significant. Much as with the Tsarist policy towards horses, the large civil motor pool was viewed as a potential war reserve and so there was a high degree of commonality between civil and military types. The Red Army motor pool on the eve of the Second World War was heavily dependent on two families of trucks. The twin-axle GAZ-AA and the triple-axle GAZ-AAA light trucks were licence-produced copies of the Ford-AA and Ford-AAA, built at Gorkiy since 1934. The GAZ-AA made up 58.5 per cent of the Red Army motor pool at the outbreak of the war. The ZiS-5 twin-axle and the ZiS-6 triple-axle medium trucks were licence-built copies of the American Autocar-2 series. A smaller number of indigenous Soviet designs were also in service, namely the YaG-10 and YaG-12 heavy trucks. The standard staff car was the GAZ-61, derived again from US Ford designs. At the outset of the war the Red Army had 272,600 vehicles in service.

The German invasion caused massive losses in the Red Army's motor pool and also severely disrupted the automotive industry. In late 1941 a decision was made to divert large segments of the automotive industry to higher priority efforts, especially the production of light armoured vehicles. As a result, Soviet wartime automotive production fell to only about one-third of pre-war levels. This was cushioned by the large number of vehicles in the civil economy, which were pressed into military service as needed.

Wartime production focused on pre-war designs, modified to meet wartime needs. For example, the ZiS-5 was redesigned into the ZiS-5V, substituting an inexpensive wooden cab for the pre-war sheet metal cab. Likewise, the *GAZ*-AA gave way to a simplified derivative, the *GAZ*-MM. A larger percentage of production was shifted to military requirements; for example, to specialized types such as the *GAZ*-55 ambulance on the *GAZ*-AA chassis, and the ZiS-42M half-track truck on the ZiS-5 chassis. One of the few new military vehicles to emerge from the war was the *GAZ*-67B, a Soviet counterpart to the US Army jeep, of which about 5,300 were built in 1942–5.

The wartime diversion of the automotive industry to other products forced the Red Army to depend more heavily on Lend-Lease supplies than in nearly any other major sector of the war economy. In total, the United States, Britain and Canada provided the Red Army with about 401,000 vehicles during the war, nearly twice the Soviet wartime production. The Lend-Lease supplies were vital not only because of their quantity but also due to the quality of material provided. Most Soviet trucks were civilian types with poor cross-country performance; in contrast, the Lend-Lease supply contained large numbers of specialized military trucks with superior cross-country capabilities. The American supplies included 77,972 Willys jeeps, 24,902 Dodge ¾-ton trucks, and 351,715 medium trucks, mainly the Studebaker US-6 2 ½-ton truck. The majority of these arrived from late 1942 onwards. The Lend-Lease trucks were essential to the motorization of the Red Army in the final two years of the war, and central to its ability to supply large-scale offensive operations.

	1941	1942	1943	1944	1945	Total
Automobiles	3,980	2,567	2,546	5,382	4,995	19,470
Trucks	116,169	30,947	45,545	53,467	68,548	314,676
Buses	4,027	1,462	1,175	1,700	1,114	9,478
Total	124,176	34,976	49,266	60,549	74,657	343,624

Note: These figures cover the immediate pre-war and post-war months. Actual wartime production totalled about 205,000 vehicles.

Table 6.6 Soviet automotive production 1941–5.

CHAPTER 7

WEAPONS OF THE RED ARMY: INFANTRY WEAPONS

PISTOLS

The Red Army used a large number of pistol types during the war but two types predominated: the Nagant Model 1895 7.62mm revolver was a dependable, if somewhat heavy design; the preferred type was the Tokarev Model 1930 or Model 1930/33 7.62mm automatic, built in large numbers before and during the war. At the outset of the war, production of both pistols and revolvers was on a similar scale: 120,903 automatic pistols and 118,453 revolvers in 1941 for example; however, there was a marked preference shown for the Tokarev automatic, so wartime production shifted in that direction, totalling 161,485 automatics and 15,485 revolvers in 1942.

SUB-MACHINE GUNS

Probably no weapon is so closely associated with the Red Army soldier as the *PPSh* sub-machine gun. As early as 1925 the Armament Committee had expressed the belief that a sub-machine gun was required for 'junior and middle-rank commanders'. There followed about ten years of efforts by a variety of designers, the most promising of whom was Vasiliy Degtyarev. His work culminated in the M1934 Degtyarev sub-machine gun, or *PPD*, which was accepted for service in June 1935. Modifications to strengthen the magazine attachment yielded the *PPD* M1934/38. These

two models used a 35-round box magazine. Acceptance for service did not guarantee a substantial production, however. Indeed, some of Stalin's non-military inner circle, including Molotov, Zhdanov and Malenkov, were adamantly opposed to sub-machine guns, considering them suitable only for police duties. Thus, in January 1939 the order was given not only to cease production of the *PPD* after only 4,173 had been built, but also to withdraw the weapons already issued and place them in storage.

That sub-machine guns could be effective military weapons was demonstrated almost immediately by the Finns on the outbreak of the Winter War. As a result, in late December 1939 the previous order was rescinded and directives issued to hurriedly develop a version of the *PPD* suitable for mass production, and in January distribution of sub-machine guns was again authorized. Degtyarev had already developed a 73-round drum magazine that could be used with the M1934/38 and by April 1940 he had modified the gun design to simplify production somewhat. This was accepted for service as the *PPD* M1940 and 81,118 were built in 1940, followed by 5,868 when production ceased.

The termination of PPD production was not due to any tactical shortcomings, but because another designer, Georgiy Shpagin, had turned his efforts to the simplification of production. In 1940, while at the Kovrov

As the war went on, the proportion of automatic weapons in the rifle section continued to increase. Two of the soldiers here are armed with the *PPSh* sub-machine gun, while the soldier to the right is armed with the *DP* 'record player' light machine gun, the standard support weapon in the section and the Soviet equivalent of the British Bren gun or the US Army BAR. It received its nickname from its large circular magazine. The wrecked armoured vehicle is a Soviet T-20 Komsomolyets light artillery tractor.

works, he developed a sub-machine gun that reduced the number of machine hours needed for production from 13.7 for the *PPD* to 5.6, through the use of stamping and welding rather than machining. The simplification led not only to reduced manufacturing time and cost, but also to an exceptionally reliable weapon that used the same 71-round drum magazine as the earlier *PPDs*. In December 1940 the new weapon was accepted for service as the *PPSh* M1941 sub-machine gun. Due to the simplicity of the weapon it proved possible to assign production to firms with no prior experience in gun making and production rapidly soared. Not only did this add close-in firepower to the infantry, but it reduced the number of rifles required, thus reducing shortages of that weapon and the burden on rifle-producers as well. Small changes were incorporated into *PPSh* during its production run, the most notable being the replacement of the 71-round drum magazine with a curved 35-round box magazine with a directive of February 1942. The drum magazine had proven hard to carry and subject to stoppages, but more importantly turned out to be a bottleneck in gun

production due to their complexity. Thereafter box magazines, made sturdier in 1943, were the standard sub-machine gun magazine, although the drum magazne remained popular and was never completely supplanted.

That there was still room for simplification was demonstrated by Aleksey Sudaev, who designed a new sub-machine gun that further reduced the number of machine hours needed for production to only 2.7. Like the *PPSh*, the Sudaev design was a blowback-operated weapon. It fired only the full-automatic mode, fed from a staggered-row 35-round magazine. It was accepted for production in July 1942 as the *PPS* sub-machine gun, although mass production did not start until 1943. Detail improvements led to the *PPS-43*. Since it was considered inadvisable to interrupt facilities already building the *PPSh*, production of the *PPS* was handed over to shops with no prior experience. As a result, production of the *PPS* never caught up with that of the *PPSh*, although the former was favoured by the troops for its collapsible stock, light weight and reliability.

The importance attached to sub-machine guns by the Soviets is shown by the fact that of 18.3 million rifles and sub-machine guns

The Red Army made some use of automatic rifles such as the Tokarev *SVT*-40 seen here in the foreground. However, many troops found them to be unreliable, too complex and inaccurate. Their production largely ceased after 1942. The remainder of the troops here are armed with the popular *PPSh* sub-machine gun.

produced during the war, 6.3 million (34 per cent) were sub-machine guns, while Germany's 11.6 million weapons included only 1.2 million sub-machine guns (11 per cent).

Although few small arms were provided to the Red Army via Lend-Lease, the US shipped 137,729 Thompson .45cal sub-machine guns.

RIFLES

The Red Army had inherited and, in 1922, standardized on the most numerous of the Tsarist rifles, the M1891 Mosin-Nagant magazine-fed, bolt-action weapon. Detail changes, including a new bayonet mount, new sights and an improved cartridge clip design, were incorporated in 1930 to yield the M1891/30. Production of the new rifle ramped up slowly in the early 1930s, but had reached 560,000 in 1937 and averaged 1.3 million per year in 1938–40 at two factories, Tula and Izhevsk. Production of the basic M1891/30 was completed at Tula in mid-1942 and at Izhevsk in 1944. Two variants of the M1891/30 were produced. A sniper version was built that differed mainly in the closer tolerances employed by the factory (in

the form of a manual rework of rifles selected from the production line) and the down-turned bolt handle needed to clear the 4x VP (later replaced by the shorter 3.5x PU) optical sight. Production started in 1937 and did not end until 1963 (excepting a break in 1941–2 for the ill-fated SVT sniper rifle), reflecting its popularity. The second was a carbine version known as the M1938 with a shorter barrel and no bayonet attachment that was approved for use with cavalry, artillery and signal troops in February 1939. It was produced solely at the Izhevsk Arsenal.

Although reliable and powerful, the M1891/30 with its archaic design was simply too long and cumbersome for close-quarters fighting. The M1938 carbine was better, but lacked a bayonet. The Izhevsk works took the M1938 and modified it slightly, particularly the stock, fitted a permanent integral folding bayonet and produced 50,000 for field trials in 1943. The sturdy and dependable weapon was an instant success with the troops and it was standardized as the M1944 carbine. Production of the two types of carbines overlapped, with the last M1938 not coming off the line until 1945. The M1944 carbine

One of the failures of the Soviet weapons industry was the lack of an effective infantry anti-armour weapon during the war. The Degtaryev 14.5mm *PTRD* anti-tank rifle was in widespread service from 1941 but the arms race on the Eastern Front rendered it increasingly ineffective as tank armour continued to increase. By the middle of the war, it could penetrate only the thinner side armour of many German tanks and the German addition of stand-off, side-skirt armour deprived it of any real anti-armour effectiveness. Yet it served on through 1945, cumbersome and of little combat use.

was issued to infantry troops as a replacement for the M1891/30 basic rifle starting in February 1944, although it never completely supplanted it.

Soviet small-arms designers had developed semi-automatic rifles before the war but production was quite limited. In 1936, the Red Army adopted the Simonov *AVS*-36 7.62mm semi-automatic rifle, but only 65,800 had been built when production ended at the Izhevsk works in 1940. The weapon was not reliable and its maintenance was beyond the capabilities of most conscripts. A competitive trial was held in 1938 to select a cheaper and more reliable weapon. It came down to the heavy but well-tested Tokarev against a lighter and simpler (but untried) Simonov. The Tokarev was selected in February 1939 as the *SVT*-38. The Tula Small Arms Factory was directed to cease production of the Mosin-Nagant models and revamp itself for large-scale production of the new rifle. Deliveries of small batches began in July 1939 and mass production began in October, which was introduced into combat during the Russo-Finnish War in 1939–40. War lessons learned led to the adoption of a slightly improved type, the *SVT*-40, adopted in April 1940. Major

problems with the rifle, however, were ignored in the interests of speeding production. The troops regarded them as complex, unreliable and inaccurate. As a result, although production had skyrocketed to 1,031,861 in 1941 as a result of the Tula works' impressive efforts, it was cut back to 264,148 in 1942 and a mere trickle after that. A sniper version of the *SVT*-40 was also fielded that differed from the basic version only in the addition of a bracket for an optical sight. It suffered the same problems as the basic rifle and production totalled only 34,782 in 1941 and 14,210 in 1942.

Building on the questionable success of the *SVT* series, Tokarev embarked on the design of a selective-fire version. The result was the *AVT*-40, in which the trigger mechanism was modified to permit automatic firing, and the safety lever altered to also serve as a selector switch between full and semi-automatic firing. This was intended as an infantry rifle, as its components were not strong enough to stand up to sustained (or even frequent) automatic fire, so the semi-automatic mode was to be standard, with burst fire only for emergencies. Not surprisingly, the weapon proved a failure, so

The other anti-tank rifle adopted at the outset of
the war was the Simonov *PTRS*. It was more
complicated than the Degtaryev *PTRD*, being semi-
automatic with a magazine while the *PTRD* was a
single-shot, bolt-action type. Its anti-tank
performance was no better than the *PTRD* and
fewer were manufactured.

that although it was ordered into production
in May 1942, production only lasted a year.

MACHINE GUNS

The standard light machine gun of the Red
Army in the Second World War was the
7.62mm Degtaryev *DP* machine gun,
popularly called the 'record-player' by the
troops due to its large drum magazine. Hastily
adopted in 1927 for its simplicity and ease of
manufacture, the weapon suffered from a few
shortcomings, including a main spring that
lost its strength over time and a weak safety.
These defects became noticeable once the war
started and in August 1944 a revised model,
the DPM Model 1944 was approved that
corrected earlier problems and added a pistol
grip for better aiming stability. The shortage
of *DP* machine guns occasionally led to
improvised solutions, such as the use of the
related *DT* tank light machine gun in the
infantry role. Lend-Lease provided a further
2,487 Bren guns from Britain and 5,403 .30in
cal Browning light machine guns from the US.

As in the case of rifles, the standard Soviet
machine gun in the Second World War was

nearly the same as in Tsarist times, the old
Maxim Model 1910 water-cooled machine
gun. This was issued on various wheeled
mounts, including the older Sokolov mount
and the 1915 Koleshnikov mount, in an effort
to give the heavy and cumbersome weapon
some degree of mobility. The requirement for
a lighter and simpler medium machine gun
led to the air-cooled *DS* machine gun, which
was adopted in September 1939. Field service
soon showed it to be a seriously flawed and
unreliable weapon and production was
terminated in 1941 after 10,345 had been
built. Full production of the Maxim was
reinstated, and no fewer than 55,258 M1910s
were built in 1942, pending a second
replacement attempt. A relative unknown,
Mikhail Goryunov, was to provide the answer
and in May 1943 his weapon was adopted as
the *SG*-43 machine gun. It was never produced
in the quantities needed to replace the Maxim
but became more common in the final year of
the fighting. Like the Maxim, it was usually
deployed on a small wheeled carriage.

The standard Soviet heavy machine gun of
the war was the 12.7mm Degtaryev *DShK*.
This had begun life as the DK heavy machine

The Red Army used the same machine gun as the Tsarist Army, the Maxim water-cooled 7.62mm Model 1910. It was fitted to a wheeled carriage with a small armoured shield. Its heavy weight meant that it required a three-man crew for carriage, two for the gun itself and one for ammunition. It was eventually supplanted by the Goryunov SG-43, starting in 1943, but remained in widespread service until the end of the war.

gun in 1931, but few had been built because of its low rate of fire. This problem was solved by Georgiy Shpagin, who redesigned the feed mechanism, and in February 1939 the resultant weapon was adopted as the *DShK*, with deliveries to the troops beginning in 1940. Reliable and hard-hitting, the weapon was especially useful in the anti-aircraft role. Some were also issued on a wheeled mount for infantry use but its considerable weight made these impractical.

INFANTRY ANTI-TANK WEAPONS

The lack of a modern infantry anti-tank weapon was one of the singular failures of the wartime Soviet weapons industry. In late 1938 specifications had been drawn up for the ammunition needed for an anti-tank rifle and in 1939–40 trials were conducted of various models of 14.5mm armor-piercing rounds. In July 1941 the result was officially adopted as the B-32 AP-Incendiary round. In anticipation of this round, Nikolay Rukavishnikov began work on an AT rifle to fire it. The result, a single-shot weapon was officially adopted as

the *PTR* M1939 in October 1939, with plans to build up to 15,000 the following year. The September 1939 infantry TO&Es even provided for 18 such weapons per infantry regiment. In fact, the same fate befell them as had the sub-machine guns at the same time. Marshall Kulik, overestimating the armor thickness of German tanks, ordered production to be halted. Only a handful were actually made.

In July 1941 the Supreme Military Council hurriedly revisited the issue. The *PTR* M1939 worked fine, but was far too complicated for mass production. Instead, experienced designers Degtyarev and Simonov were ordered to develop simpler models and were given one month to do so. Degtyarev's first prototype was a semi-automatic magazine-fed weapon that proved unreliable. Given the pressing need for anti-tank weapons, he responded by eliminating all unnecessary parts to yield a bolt-action single-shot weapon. A muzzle brake and a spring-loaded butt plate were provided to reduce recoil on the firer. The Simonov model was a semi-authomatic weapon fed from a 5-round magazine and was also fitted with a muzzle brake.

Wartime shortages of the Degtaryev *DP* light machine gun sometimes forced the substitution of the Degtaryev *DT* tank machine gun. This weapon was fitted with a smaller drum magazine and had an adjustable metal stock instead of the wooden stock of the *DP*. The infantryman in the foreground is armed with the standard Moisin-Nagant Model 1891/30 rifle.

The standard light infantry mortar in the Red Army at the outbreak of the war was the 50mm Model 1938, sometimes called the 50-PM 38. It was a conventional design and was followed by the cheaper Model 1939, and quickly thereafter by the even simpler Model 1940. All three versions could be seen in service through much of the war.

195

The Simonov was, tactically speaking, a more useful weapon with its semi-automatic operation, but the Degtyarev was much easier to produce, so on 29 August 1941 the State Defense Committee adopted both, as the *PTRS* and *PTRD*, respectively. Not surprisingly, production of the *PTRD* ramped up quickly, from 17,688 in 1941 to 184,800 in 1942; well exceeding that of the *PTRS*, of which 77 and 63,308, respectively, were built in that period. They were both very large and cumbersome weapons, the *PTRS* weighing 44.7 lb, and the *PTRD* some 35.2 lb, requiring two soldiers to carry them. Their ammunition could penetrate 35mm of armour at 100 m, which made them a viable weapon for the first year of fighting. By the middle of 1942, German tanks were uparmoured to the point where the anti-tank rifles were useless in frontal engagements; however, they could still penetrate from the sides and rear, especially when used from close range. The anti-tank rifles remained the principal anti-tank weapon of the Soviet infantry through to the end of the war due to the lack of a more modern replacement; their

main advantage was the sheer number available. Although not powerful enough to destroy a tank, they were such a painful nuisance that in 1943 the Germans began to place armour skirts around the sides of the turret and hull of their tanks and assault guns to protect against this menace.

The Red Army also issued the infantry with the *RPG-40* Model 1940 anti-tank grenade but this was largely ineffective against a modern tank. Another widely used anti-tank weapon was the 'Molotov cocktail', a glass bottle filled with petrol. Although these 'cocktails' were often simple field improvisations, in 1940 a team under B. Ya. Kachugin and P. Solodovnikov had developed a more reliable version using an exterior chemical packet to ignite the weapon after it shattered on the tank. These were called 'KS bottles', after their inventors, and were mass-produced early in the war for the lack of any better anti-tank weapons.

During the desperate days of 1941, the Red Army trained special anti-tank mine dogs. The dogs were fitted with a saddle which included two packets of high-explosive on either side,

The 50-PM 41 (50mm infantry mortar Model 1941) was an attempt to simplify the production of light infantry mortars; it dispensed with the bipod, using a simple yoke instead, and could hurl a 1.8lb mortar bomb about 875 yd.

and a triggering mechanism on the top which set off the charges when the dog ran under the tank. The dogs were trained by feeding them only under tanks. A total of thirteen dog tank-destroyer units were formed and Russian accounts claim they destroyed 300 German armoured vehicles. German accounts dispute their effectiveness and the practice was quickly abandoned in favour of using dogs for more suitable roles, including mine detection.

The Red Army did not follow the course of most other major armies in Europe which deployed various forms of rocket grenade launchers by 1942–3. The Red Army had been one of the first developers of rocket weapons as early as 1931 but these proved ineffective against armour since they relied on a high-explosive blast warhead rather than a shaped-charge warhead and their development had halted before the outbreak of the war.

The Germans began introducing the *Raketen-panzerbüsche 42*, which fired an 88mm anti-tank rocket, in late 1942. This was a crew-served weapon, much like the American bazooka, and did not become common until the autumn 1943 campaigns. The Germans also deployed a less complicated rocket-propelled grenade, the *Panzerfaust*, in the autumn of 1943. Unlike the *RP 42* or bazooka, this weapon was disposable once fired. It was so inexpensive that it could be issued *en masse* to the infantry, a distinct departure in anti-tank tactics from previous weapons and a major threat to Soviet tanks after 1943. The Soviets began development of similar weapons, the *RPG*-1 and *RPG*-2, but none were ready during the war. The US provided the Red Army with 8,500 bazooka anti-tank rocket launchers although there is little information about how these were used in combat.

In the absence of novel anti-armour technologies, and especially the shaped charge, the Soviets made a number of attempts to develop improvised anti-tank weapons. The most unusual weapon deployed for the anti-armour role was the *ampulomet*, a crude mortar which fired a ball-shaped vial containing jellied gasoline to a range of 250 m. It weighed 28 kg and was crewed by three men. It could be fired at a rate of about eight rounds per minute, but was neither very accurate nor very lethal when fighting tanks. It was used during the desperate days of late 1941 and early 1942 but soon passed from the scene due to its ineffectiveness. Considerable attention was paid to the use of man-portable flame-throwers as an anti-tank weapon, and in 1943 the Red Army even formed separate motorized anti-tank flamethrower battalions to this end.

Small numbers of infantry anti-tank weapons were provided via Lend-Lease, including 1,000 PIAT grenade launchers and 3,200 Boys anti-tank rifles from Britain.

(units in millions)	1941	1942	1943	1944	1945	Total
Pistols & revolvers	.13	.17	.37	.57	.21	1.45
Rifles & carbines	1.57	4.04	3.85	2.06	.24	11.76
Sub-machine guns	.1	1.56	2.06	1.78	.03	5.53
Light machine guns	.0453	.1728	.2502	.1797	.0145	0.6625
Machine guns	.0084	.058	.0905	.0899	.0108	0.2576
Heavy machine guns	.0014	.0074	.0144	.0148	.0073	0.0453
Anti-tank rifles	.0177	.249	.1645	.0377	.0008	0.4697
Total	1.8728	6.2572	6.7996	4.7321	0.5134	20.1751

Table 7.1 Soviet small arms production June 1941–May 1945.

MORTARS

Development of a light mortar for use at the platoon level was officially launched in 1937 and the resultant weapon accepted for service the following year as the 50mm M1938 (or 50mm PM-38), although production did not begin until a year later. The weapon owed a lot to the Brandt designs of the time, with a small bipod, through which passed the vertical mounting bar. Two small recoil cylinders were fitted at the fore end of the barrel for attachment to the traverse rod, while an iron sight was carried on the right. The major change from conventional design was the provision of only two elevation settings, 45° and 75°. Range was varied by turning a rotating sleeve at the base that opened a variable number of gas ports. The design worked well, but was overly complex to build for such a small weapon. It was replaced in production by a new version, the M1940, with pressed-steel bipod legs. An even lighter version, the M1941, dispensed with the bipod completely, replacing it with a yoke fixed to the small baseplate. Both later models retained the feature of two fixed elevation settings pioneered by the M1938. Even with this simplified design, however, the Soviets discovered what other nations had; that such a small weapon could not justify the manufacturing costs. Production was terminated in early 1943 and phased out of service starting with TO&E reductions in December 1942 and elimination two years later.

For medium mortars the Soviets purchased a few samples of the Brandt 81mm Mle27/31

mortar and copied it, with a slightly increased bore, as the 82mm PM-36. Improvements were quickly made, including replacing the rectangular baseplate with a circular one and the addition of recoil units between the bipod and the barrel, and this was accepted as the 82mm PM-37. A major redesign was accomplished immediately before the war. This replaced the conventional bipod with one with a long monopod elevation rod fitted with two short legs at the bottom. The legs had stub axles on their outsides to which small steel wheels could be fitted for hand-towing of the mortar. This weapon was designated the 82mm PM-41. A final version, in which the steel wheels were permanently fitted, was designated the 82mm PM-43.

Two varieties of heavy mortars were developed. The 107mm GVPM-38 was intended for mountain troops and was optimized for pack transport, although a wheel limber was produced for use where appropriate. HE, smoke, incendiary and chemical rounds could be fired, either by impacting a fixed firing pin, or by trigger. The standard heavy mortar for the infantry was the 120mm regimental mortar, originally the 120mm PM-38. This weapon was usually carried on the same metal-frame 2-wheel limber as the 107mm and was towed behind a 20-round caisson. One of the best mortars of the war, it was even placed in production by the Germans in 1942 for their own use. Detail changes yielded the 120mm PM-41.

Production of mortars was as follows:

	1937	1938	1939	1940	1941	1942	1943	1944	1945
50mm	0	0	1,720	23,105	28,056	104,403	17,584	0	0
82mm	1,587	1,188	1,678	6,700	18,026	100,181	35,032	2,889	1,000
107mm	0	0	0	950	624	0	0	0	0
120mm	0	0	0	2,100	3,575	25,061	16,201	3,044	400

CHAPTER 8
WEAPONS OF THE RED ARMY: ARTILLERY

ANTI-TANK GUNS

The Red Army at the outset of the war in 1941 was armed primarily with a single type of anti-tank gun, the 45mm Model 1937. This was a derivative of the German Rheinmetall 37mm *PaK* 36, the standard German anti-tank gun of the period, which had been manufactured in the Soviet Union under licence since 1931 as the 37mm anti-tank Model 1930. The Red Army desired a larger calibre both to improve anti-armour performance and so as to have a gun which could fire a useful high-explosive projectile. The German 37mm projectile was too small for a good high-explosive round. It was modified to use the tube of the standard Soviet 45mm Model 1934 tank gun, with suitable strengthening of the trunnion and trails. The 45mm Model 1937 anti-tank gun proved to be a versatile weapon and quite potent for its day. With the advent of the T-34 and KV tanks in 1940–1, and the beginning of the armour race on the Eastern front, its utility in fighting tanks rapidly diminished as the Germans began to uparmour their vehicles. Nevertheless, the 45mm anti-tank gun remained in production through 1944. Although the Red Army recognized its shortcomings, it was cheap to produce and its light weight made it ideal for infantry units where motor traction, and often horses, were absent. By the middle of the war it was more often used in the pre-war infantry gun role, for direct-fire support using high-explosive ammunition rather than the anti-tank role.

The Red Army planned to replace the 45mm anti-tank gun with the new ZiS-2 57mm anti-tank gun in 1941. However, a controversy broke out among the Red Army's leaders over the purported thickness of German tank armour and its production was cancelled shortly after the outbreak of the war, with only 320 produced, in favour of producing new 85mm and 107mm anti-tank guns instead. As it turned out, German tank armour had been grossly exaggerated and the 85mm and 107mm anti-tank guns were much too large, heavy and expensive. Instead of the excellent 57mm ZiS-2, the Red Army had to make due with the increasingly obsolete 45mm anti-tank gun for the early years of the war.

By late 1942 it was evident that the usefulness of the 45mm Model 1937 anti-tank gun was rapidly diminishing. The capture of German 'arrowhead' hyper-velocity armour-piercing (HVAP) ammunition led to Soviet adaptation of the technology. Called 'subcalibre' rounds by the Red Army, a new round for the 45mm Model 1937 became available in April 1942. The ZiS-2 57mm anti-tank gun was resurrected and put back into series production in June 1943. However, the

The 82mm Model 1941 mortar was an attempt to improve the mobility of the weapon by providing it with small wheels for towing. These wheels attached to the base of the bipod but were removed before firing as is the case here. The later Model 1943 had the wheels permanently attached to the bipod. The 82mm mortar could hurl a 7.5lb mortar bomb about 3,400 yd.

ZiS-2 was too large and heavy for most rifle divisions which did not have adequate motor or horse transport; as a result, the 45mm gun was modernized by developing a new barrel to give the projectile higher velocity and better penetration. While not adequate to deal with the heavier German tanks such as the Panther or Tiger, it improved its lethality against the more common *PzKpfw* IV and *StuG* III. Production of the 45mm Model 1942 began in 1943, eventually replacing the 45mm Model 1937 anti-tank gun.

While not intended for anti-tank fighting, Soviet field artillery, especially the widely used ZiS-3 76.2mm divisional gun, was often called

upon to fight tanks. As a result, these units were issued with armour-piercing ammunition that was identical to the types used in contemporary tank guns. In August 1942 a sub-calibre round began to be issued as well. The Soviet Union also copied German-shaped charge (HEAT) ammunition. This was most commonly used with howitzers and low-velocity guns, such as the 76mm regimental gun and the M-30 122mm howitzer.

The battle at Kursk was a clear indication of the orientation in German armour development, and the growing numbers of Panther and Tiger tanks made it clear that a more potent weapon than the ZiS-2 57mm anti-tank gun would be needed. As a temporary expedient, some units were formed using 85mm anti-aircraft guns in the anti-tank role. As a long-term solution, work began on both 85mm and 100mm towed anti-tank guns in 1943. Ultimately, the BS-3 100mm anti-tank gun was selected for series production, which began on a limited scale in May 1944. Only 591 of these weapons were produced before the war ended, and only 185 were in troop service in January 1945 at the beginning of the final offensive operations against Germany.

There was considerable experimentation with other anti-tank guns during the war but the only other weapon to reach limited production was the 37mm ChK-M1 Model 1944 anti-tank gun. This was a special lightweight, low-recoil weapon intended for paratrooper operations. A total of only 472 were manufactured in 1944–5 and only 104 were issued to the troops. The Red Army received 63 37mm and 653 57mm anti-tank guns from the US, as well as 636 2pdr anti-tank and 96 6pdr guns from Britain, but none of the types were much appreciated or widely used.

The 120mm Model 1938 was the standard Red Army heavy mortar throughout the war. A slightly modified version, the Model 1943, used a single recuperator tube rather than the two on the earlier model. This weapon was so simple and dependable that the Germans simply copied the design for their own use. (S. Zaloga)

The 45mm Model 1937 anti-tank gun was derived from the German 37mm *PaK* 36 anti-tank gun but rechambered to fire both anti-tank and high-explosive ammunition. Although its effectiveness continued to diminish as the war dragged on, owing to the increasing thickness of German tank armour, its dual capability served it in good stead. In the later years of the war it was used to fire high-explosive more often than anti-tank ammunition.

As an expedient solution, the 45mm Model 1937 was redesigned with a new, longer barrel, resulting in the 45mm Model 1942. Although it could not penetrate the thicker frontal armour of the improved German tanks of 1943, it could still inflict damage against the lighter side armour. (S. Zaloga)

The Red Army introduced the excellent ZiS-2 57mm anti-tank gun into service in 1941 but its production was abruptly cancelled by Stalin's cronies owing to intelligence mistakes about German tank armour. Production was revived in 1943 to deal with the heavier German tank armour. The 57mm Model 1943, as seen here, used the same tubular trails as the related ZiS-3 76mm divisional gun, while the Model 1941 used rectangular trails. (S. Zaloga)

Type Model	45mm Model 37	45mm Model 42	57mm ZiS-2	100mm BS-3
Barrel length (calibres)	46	68.6	73	59.6
Combat weight (kg)	560	625	1,150	3,650
Rate of fire (rpm)	15–20	15–20	20–25	8–10
AP projectile weight (kg)	1.43	1.43	3.14	15.9
Sub-calibre weight (kg)	0.85	0.85	1.8	n/a
AP initial velocity (m/s)	760	870	990	890
Sub-calibre velocity (m/s)	985	1,070	1,270	n/a
Armour penetration @ 500m (mm)				
AP at 90°	43	61		200
HVAP at 90°		81	145	n/a
AP at 60°	35	50	84	150
HVAP at 60°		52	120	n/a
Armour penetration @ 1,000m (mm)				
AP at 90°	35	51		185
AP at 60°	28	41		140

Table 8.1 Anti-tank gun technical data.

REGIMENTAL GUNS

As in most contemporary armies, the Red Army used a short-barrelled howitzer for infantry support at the regimental level. The standard weapon was the 76mm Model 1927 regimental gun, a modification of the old Tsarist 3in Model 1913. It was modernized twice, in 1936 and 1939, to permit motorized towing, and the Model 1927/39 was the most common wartime version. This weapon was archaic and heavy compared to comparable German and American pack howitzers, and there were repeated attempts both before and during the war to replace it with a more modern weapon. As in the case of so many other Soviet weapons, it was adequate and so remained in production until 1944; the only concession was to mount it on a more modern carriage. In 1943 the weapon, the trails and frame of the 45mm Model 1942 anti-tank gun was used to create the 76mm regimental gun Model 1943. In 1944 a new lightweight howitzer was developed for mountain troops, the 76mm M-99 Model 1944 mountain gun. It was produced in small numbers during the war.

DIVISIONAL ARTILLERY

The Red Army retained the 3in gun calibre for its divisional guns during the war, even though other armies such as the US Army and the Wehrmacht began adopting a 105mm howitzer instead. The Red Army still had a significant number of the old Tsarist 76mm Model 1902 divisional gun in service, though most of these had been modernized with a longer tube after 1931 as the Model 1902/30. There were numerous attempts to field a new divisional gun, starting with the 76mm F-22 divisional gun in 1936, designed by Grabin's bureau. This gun was produced in significant numbers but was viewed by the artillery as too cumbersome due to its long barrel length.

The lack of reliable infantry anti-tank weapons forced the Red Army to rely on improvised means for defeating German tanks, including 'Molotov cocktails'. Although these were often nothing more than bottles of petrol with a flaming rag, there were factory produced versions which used small vials with chemicals strapped to the outside as a safer method to ignite them on contact with the enemy tank.

Close-range fire support for the infantry was provided by the stubby little 76mm Model 1927/39 regimental gun. This was based on the Tsarist 3in gun but updated to permit motorized towing. (S. Zaloga)

The carriage of the Model 1929/39 regimental gun was unnecessarily heavy and cumbersome. Therefore, in 1943 a 76mm tube was adapted to the same carriage as the 45mm Model 1942 anti-tank gun, resulting in the 76mm Model 1943 regimental gun. The weapon to the left is the 76mm ZiS-3 divisional gun. (S. Zaloga)

The Tsarist 3in divisional gun was modestly improved in 1930 by extending the barrel for longer range. The resulting 76mm Model 03/30 divisional gun was still in service in 1941 but most were lost in the summer fighting. (S. Zaloga)

The first modern divisional gun in Red Army service was the 76mm F-22 Model 1936. Although a fine weapon, it was expensive and quite heavy. The German Wehrmacht captured the F-22 in large numbers and used them in service as anti-tank guns until their own 75mm *PaK* 40 became available. Indeed the gun here is a former German weapon, captured by the US Army in North Africa. The German version was distinguished by a lower splinter shield and a muzzle brake. (S. Zaloga)

The F-22 was quickly followed into production by the F-22 USV Model 1939 which was an attempt to lighten and simplify it. It was the standard Red Army divisional gun at the outset of the war. (S. Zaloga)

Neither the F-22 nor the F-22 USV were sufficiently light and simple, and a third design, the ZiS-3, followed in 1941, based on the carriage of the short-lived ZiS-2 57mm anti-tank gun. This became the standard divisional gun of the Red Army after 1942 and was so successful that it was still being exported in the 1980s. (S. Zaloga)

The Red Army standardized on the 122mm M-30 howitzer before the war and it became its regular divisional howitzer. A simple and robust design, it is still in service around the globe. (S. Zaloga)

One of the more archaic pieces in service with the Red Army in 1941 was the 152mm Model 1910 field howitzer, an imported French Schneider design from Tsarist days. It is seen here with its standard horse-drawn limber. (S. Zaloga)

In addition, the small ground clearance made cross-country travel difficult and the crew duties were poorly laid out. In 1937 specifications were issued for a new divisional gun and the chosen weapon came again from the Grabin Bureau, ostensibly a modified version of the F-22 christened the F-22 USV, but in fact a new gun. With a shorter barrel and new carriage the weapon was accepted for service in July 1939. Both these guns were in widespread service in 1941 at the time of the German invasion, both as rifle divisional artillery and in the anti-tank brigades, but disappeared quickly due to heavy losses. Ironically, they continued in service with the Wehrmacht, where the F-22 proved to be very popular as an anti-tank gun until the German's own *PaK* 40 75mm gun became available.

The F-22-USV was successful, but was complicated and difficult to produce and Grabin's team began work on a new divisional gun in May 1941 based on an earlier 76mm AT gun. It passed its trials in July but production was denied by Marshall Kulik. Grabin managed to circumvent this order so that by the time it was officially accepted for service in February 1942 as the ZIS-3, some 1,000 guns had already been delivered. The ZIS-3 proved a highly successful weapon and was produced in larger numbers than any other field artillery piece in the world. By Western standards its 6.5kg projectile was

light for the divisional support role, but the Red Army compensated by the creation of a vast pool of GHQ artillery units with heavier weapons, and valued its utility as an anti-tank gun, both in separate anti-tank units and as a secondary role for the divisional artillery.

The divisional guns were supplemented with divisional howitzers in 122mm and, initially, 152mm calibres. The most common weapon at the outbreak of the war was the 122mm M1910 howitzer modernized as the M1910/30. An elderly design with wooden spoke wheels, box trail and a short L/13 barrel, the weapon was serviceable but well past its prime. The replacement was the 122mm M-30 Model 1938 howitzer. This was a new and modern design developed immediately before the war and it is still used widely around the world in many armies. The rubber-tyred wheels permitted motor traction and the longer L/19 barrel increased the range to a respectable figure.

At the outbreak of the war the organization tables provided for a battalion of 152mm howitzers in each division, and these were the old Tsarist Schneider/Putilov 152mm M1909, modernized as the M1910/30 that added a muzzle brake and made other detail changes. Some were also fitted for motor traction. They retained, however, the outdated requirement to be broken into two parts for transport, which slowed their time in and out of firing position.

Designation Variant	BM-82 Model 1937	PM-120 Model 1938	Model 1927	Model 1942	ZiS-3 Model 1942	M-30 Model 1938	M-10 Model 1938	D-1 Model 1943
Calibre (mm)	82	120	76.2	76.2	76.2	122	152	152
Type	mortar	mortar	gun	gun	gun	howitzer	howitzer	howitzer
Weight (kg)	56	270	780	600	1,116	2,500	4,150	3,600
Rate of fire (rpm)	20–25	12–15	10–12	10–12	20	5–6	3–4	3–4
Maximum range (km)	3.04	5.6	4.2	4.2	13.3	11.8	12.4	12.4
Projectile weight (kg)	3.3	16.5	6.5	6.5	6.5	21.7	40.0	40.0

Table 8.2 Divisional artillery technical data.

MOUNTAIN ARTILLERY

The old Tsarist Schneider-designed 76mm M1909 remained the standard mountain piece through the 1930s and continued to serve to the end of the war. Although a handy weapon that broke down into seven pieces for pack transport, some archaic features, including limited elevation and the use of fixed ammunition, limited its usefulness. Rather than develop a new weapon, the Soviets purchased the drawings and rights to an experimental Skoda mountain gun and further developed it into the 76mm M1938 mountain gun. This weapon elevated to 65° and fired separately-loaded ammunition with three charges, giving good plunging-fire capabilities at all ranges. The use of modern propellants also increased the range from 8,500 to 10,000m.

MEDIUM & HEAVY ARTILLERY

A replacement for the 152mm M1909/30 howitzer had already entered production as the M1938 (M-10) howitzer but within a month of the start of the war these weapons had been removed from the divisional structure and moved to separate GHQ artillery units. It was complicated and expensive, however, and production was halted shortly thereafter. The M1938 was a good weapon nonetheless, combining moderate weight with reasonable

range and a lethal projectile. A new 152mm howitzer, the M1943 D-1 was developed that mated a new barrel with the chassis of the 122mm M1938 field howitzer. The resultant weapon was light and powerful and remained in service for decades after the war.

Heavier artillery pieces than the divisional howitzers were deployed at corps level. The Red Army retained the Russian Schneider 107mm corps gun Model M1910, modernized with a longer tube as the Model M1910/30 after 1931. It was to be replaced by the 107mm M-60 corps gun Model 1940 but this expensive weapon was not produced in significant numbers prior to 1941 and production ended abruptly when its factory was evacuated in the autumn of 1941. Already, the Red Army had begun to shift over to a 122mm gun, the 122mm A-19 corps gun Model 1931, starting in 1936. This weapon was part of a common family of weapons, the same carriage being used for the corps-level 152mm ML-20 gun-howitzer Model 1937. These two weapons formed the basis for most Red Army corps artillery during the war.

The Soviet army made limited use of very heavy mortars at corps level, introducing the MT-13 160mm breech-loading mortar in January 1944. A total of about 535 of these weapons were delivered to special corps artillery batteries in 1944–45.

Designation Variant	M-60 Model 1940	A-19 Model 1937	ML-20 Model 1937	BR-2 Model 1935	MT-13 Model 1943	B-4 Model 1931	BR-5 Model 1939
Calibre (mm)	107	122	152	152	160	203	280
Type	gun	gun	gun-howitzer	gun	mortar	howitzer	mortar
Weight (kg)	3,957	7,117	7,128	18,202	1,080	15,790	18,390
Rate of fire (rpm)	3–4	3–4	3–4	1	3	0.5	0.5
Range (km)	17.5	20.4	17.2	27.0	5.1	16.0	16.4
Projectile weight (kg)	17.1	25.0	43.5	48.6	41.1	98.7	200.1

Table 8.3 Heavy field artillery technical data.

The 152mm Model 1910 was modernized in the 1930s for motorized traction, resulting in the 152mm Model 1910/30. It was used mainly in second-line rifle divisions. (S. Zaloga)

The Red Army fielded a fine new 152mm field howitzer, the M-10 Model 1938, before the outbreak of the war. Although well regarded, it was complicated and expensive to manufacture and production ended after the outbreak of the war. (S. Zaloga)

To replace the expensive M-10 Model 1938 field howitzer, the D-1 Model 1943 was developed, using the carriage of the widely used M-30 122mm howitzer. Although similar in appearance, it can be distinguished by its prominent muzzle brake. (S. Zaloga)

A family of heavy field guns was introduced in the mid-1930s, starting with the A-19 Model 1931/37 122mm field gun. This weapon can be distinguished from the 152mm gun-howitzer version by its longer barrel. It replaced older Tsarist 107mm field guns. (S. Zaloga)

The success of the A-19 122mm field gun led to the decision to adapt it to mount a larger 152mm gun-howitzer barrel, resulting in the 152mm ML-20 Model 1937 gun-howitzer. This version can be easily distinguished by its unusual slatted muzzle brake. (S. Zaloga)

The legendary *Katyusha* multiple rocket launchers were one of the favourite Red Army artillery weapons of the Second World War. This was one of the early types, a *BM-8-36*, which consisted of a thirty-six rail launcher for the 82mm M-8 rocket, mounted on a modified ZiS-6 lorry. (Terry Gander)

The Red Army retained its heaviest artillery in units of the Supreme Command Reserve (RVGK). The most important pieces during the war were a family of three weapons mounted on a common tracked carriage. These were the 203mm B-4 howitzer Model 1931, the 152mm BR-2 gun Model 1935 and the 280mm BR-5 mortar Model 1939. The Red Army made some use of even heavier weapons, including railway artillery, during the war. However, railway artillery was used primarily by the Navy for coastal defence, and is largely outside the scope of this handbook.

ROCKET ARTILLERY

The Red Army began developing artillery multiple rocket launchers shortly before the war and considered them so secret that they were officially referred to by the codename 'Guards Mortars' through the war. However, their wailing sound on launch led to the more common nickname *Katyusha* ('Little Katy') after a popular song of the time. The first type in service was the BM-13-16, which consisted of a ZiS-6 truck with sixteen rail launchers for 132mm M-13 rockets. This was followed shortly afterwards by the BM-8-36, which had thirty-six rails for the smaller 82mm M-8 rockets. During the course of the war, a variety of chassis were used for the *Katyusha*, including unarmoured tractors, light tank chassis and various trucks. After 1943, they were standardized on Lend-Lease trucks, especially the American US-6 Studebaker.

Improved versions of the rockets were developed. The M-30 rocket used the M-13 rocket engine but mated to a new, enlarged warhead. This was too large to fire from the rail launchers and so was launched from a copy of the German *Nebelwerfer* wooden-frame transport/launch containers. An improved type was developed in 1943, the M-31, which could be launched from either frame launchers or from a new truck launcher, the BM-31-12 with twelve launch cells. The Red Army in the Leningrad area copied a German *Nebelwerfer* rocket design as the M-28, which was also fired from static frame launchers. *Katyusha* multiple rocket launchers were a popular artillery weapon in the Red Army during the war, as their heavy salvo firepower was particularly demoralizing to enemy troops. From the industrial perspective, they were cheap and easy to manufacture in small plants that did not have the expensive tooling to produce conventional artillery. On the debit side, they were far less accurate than conventional tube artillery, they were much slower to reload and their rocket engines consumed considerably more propellant than a comparable round of artillery ammunition; as a result, they were used to supplement rather than replace conventional artillery, especially in the opening salvoes of major artillery strikes.

Rocket type	M-8	M-13	M-13-DD	M-20	M-28	M-30	M-31
Calibre (mm)	82	132	132	132	280	300	300
Length (m)	0.66	1.41	2.12	2.09	1.19	1.2	1.76
Weight (kg)	8.0	42.5	62.5	57.9	83.7	72	91.5
Explosive content (kg)	0.5	4.9	4.9	18.4	60.0	28.9	28.9
Maximum range (km)	5.9	8.47	11.8	5.05	1.95	2.8	4.3

Table 8.4 *Katyusha* technical data.

The most common *Katyusha* during the war was the *BM*-13-12, consisting of a twelve-rail launcher for the 132mm M-13 rocket. This particular example is mounted on a Lend-Lease Studebaker truck.

ANTI-AIRCRAFT ARTILLERY

The Red Army was relatively poorly equipped with anti-aircraft guns through much of the war at regimental and battalion level, and was forced to use improvised means such as rifle and machine gun fire. One of the most effective anti-aircraft weapons of the war was the Tokarev 4M Model 1931, which was a quadruple mounting of the standard 7.62mm Maxim Model 1910 water-cooled machine gun on a special base. However, this was too heavy for easy transportion and so was used either on special mobile mountings, such as trucks, or for fixed site defence. Attempts were made to develop lighter mountings for more modern machine guns. Only 626 Tokarev quad mountings for the Degtaryev 7.62mm PV-1 aircraft machine gun were manufactured in Leningrad and they were used mainly for static defence.

After considerable experimentation in the 1930s, the Red Army finally acquired several Bofors anti-aircraft guns from Sweden, which heavily inspired wartime weapons. The first weapon developed for divisional air defence was the 37mm 61-K Model 1939 based on the 40mm Bofors. Production began on a small scale in 1939 and it became the most common divisional air defence automatic cannon during the war. In 1944 a twin version, the V-47, was developed, but none saw service during the war.

In 1945 production of a self-propelled version, on a modified SU-76 assault gun chassis, began as the ZSU-37, but few if any saw combat during the war. Aside from truck-mounted 4M Maxims, the only self-propelled anti-aircraft guns used for tactical air defence were Lend-Lease types, especially the US-supplied M17 half-track with quad .50in calibre machine guns.

Another weapon developed on the basis of Bofors technology was the 25mm 72-K Model 1940 anti-aircraft gun, which entered production in September 1941. However, this weapon was intended to arm dedicated *PVO* air defence force regiments, not regular Army formations. It was not commonly deployed in Army units, though on some occasions units were issued with this weapon instead of the larger 37mm gun – but it never appeared in the numbers of its 20mm German counterpart.

High-altitude air defence was handled by the 76mm Model 1931 anti-aircraft gun which was patterned on the German Rheinmetall 76mm *FlaK* R gun. This was modernized as the 76mm Model 1938 anti-aircraft gun by the adoption of a more effective twin-axle carriage. These 76mm weapons were issued to Army divisions on a scale of four per rifle division, but many were used by dedicated *PVO* air defence force units. The *PVO* began receiving the 85mm Model 1939 anti-aircraft gun shortly before the war. This was the closest equivalent of the legendary German 88mm gun. It was

Designation Model	Model 1940	72-K Model 1939	61-K Model 1931	Model 1938	KS-12 Model 1939	KS-12A Model 1944
Calibre (mm)	25	37	76	76	85	85
Weight (kg)	1,075	2,100	3,650	3,047	4,300	5,000
Practical rate of fire (rpm)	240	80	20	20	15–20	15–20
Maximum ceiling (m)	4,570	6,700	9,300	9,300	10,500	11,600
Projectile weight (kg)	0.28	0.78	6.61	6.61	9.2	9.2

Table 8.5 Anti-aircraft gun technical data.

One of the standard anti-aircraft weapons of the Red Army was the Tokarev 4M Model 1931 quadruple anti-aircraft machine gun mounting. This consisted of four Maxim Model 1910 machine guns on a heavy pedestal mount with associated ammunition and water-cooling tank. Due to its size and weight, it was usually mounted on a lorry, such as the *GAZ-AAA* seen here, or emplaced in a fixed site.

Soviet light anti-aircraft guns were heavily influenced by imported Swedish Bofors designs. The 25mm 72-K Model 1940 was a standard design which entered service in late 1941. It is not well known outside the Soviet Union as it was intended for use by national air defence forces, not for tactical Army air defence, and so was not often captured by the Germans. (S. Zaloga)

Probably the most familiar Soviet anti-aircraft gun of the Second World War was the 37mm 61-K Model 1939 based on the imported Swedish 40mm Bofors gun. It bears a strong family resemblance to its Swedish ancestor and was used throughout the war by Soviet Army air defence units. (S. Zaloga)

The 85mm Model 1939 anti-aircraft gun was intended primarily for national air defence but was sometimes seen in front-line service. In 1943 the Red Army formed a number of expedient anti-tank brigades armed with the weapon to deal with the new German heavy tanks until a more suitable towed anti-tank gun became available. Unlike the Wehrmacht and its legendary 88mm gun, the Red Army did not use this weapon widely for tank fighting. (S. Zaloga)

not generally issued to Army units and, unlike its German counterpart, it was seldom used in the anti-tank role except on an expedient basis – such as in the summer of 1943 when special Army anti-tank units were formed for a defensive battle at Kursk. It was modernized during the war as the KS-12A Model 1944.

The Soviet Union received a significant number of anti-aircraft guns from Britain and the US during the war, including 5,511 40mm Bofors guns as well as 251 90mm guns from the US. Even more important was the delivery of British and American gun-laying radars which were considerably more sophisticated than their Soviet counterparts and helped to establish Soviet radar technology in the post-war years. In addition, a large number of AA directors were provided, including 6,109 from the US alone.

	1937	1938	1939	1940	1941	1942	1943	1944	1945
AT Guns									
45mm M1937	1,780	3,522	4,536	2,480	1,329	20,129	17,225	200	-
45mm M1942	-	-	-	-	-	-	4,151	4,628	2,064
57mm ZIS-2	-	-	-	-	-	-	1,855	2,525	5,265
100mm BS-3	-	-	-	-	-	-	-	341	1,140
Mortars									
160mm MT-13	-	-	-		-		-	600	800
Mountain Artillery									
76mm M1909	40	305	250	-	-		-	-	-
76mm M1938	-	n/a	n/a	n/a	n/a	n/a	n/a	n/a	n/a
Light & Field Artillery									
76mm M1927 Regimental Gun	-	1,000	1,300	900	3,918	6,809	2,555	-	-
76mm M1943 Regimental Gun	-	-	-	-	-	-	-	3,194	1,928
76mm F-22 field gun	417	1,002	1,503	-	-	-	-	-	-
76mm F-22 USV field gun	-	-	140	1,010	2,616	6,049	-	-	-
76mm ZIS-3 field gun	-	-	-	-	-	10,139	13,924	16,114	7,825
122mm M-30 M1938 howitzer	-	-	-	639	2,762	4,240	3,770	3,485	2,630
Medium & Heavy Artillery									
107mm M-60 field gun		-	-	24	103				
122mm M1931 & M1931/37 Corps Gun	78	150	256	469	442	385	414	160	245
152mm M-10 M1938 howitzer	-	-	4	685	833	-	-	-	-
152mm D-1 M1943 howitzer	-	-	-	-	-	-	84	258	715
152mm ML-20 Gun-How	148	500	567	901	1,342	1,809	1,002	275	325
203mm B-4BM howitzer	42	124	229	168	326	-	-	-	-
203mm BR-17 gun	-	-	-	3	6	-	-	-	-
305mm BR-18 howitzer	-	-	-	3	-	-	-	-	-
Multiple Rocket Launchers									
BM-8	-	-	-	-	400	900	400	500	200
BM-13	-	-	-	-	600	2,400	2,900	900	-
BM-31-12	-	-	-	-	-	-	-	1,200	600
Anti-Aircraft Guns									
25mm 72-K	-	-	n/a	n/a	300	236	1,486	2,353	485
37mm M1939	-	-	n/a	n/a	n/a	3,896	5,477	5,998	1,545
76mm M1931			-		-		-		-
76mm M1938	-	750			-		-		-
85mm M1939	-	-	20	940	3,371	2,761	3,715	1,903	712

Table 8.6 Soviet artillery production, 1937–45.

BIBLIOGRAPHY

The combat record of the Red Army in the Second World War has been covered extensively in many campaign histories of the war in Russian, English and many other languages. It is beyond the scope of this bibliography to list them all. Instead the focus of this bibliography is on publications dealing with the subjects of this book: the organization and equipment of the Red Army. Even in this more limited field, there are hundreds available, and listed here are some of the most essential.

For those readers looking for campaign books on the Red Army, by far the best overviews of the combat record of the Red Army in the Second World War are David Glantz and Jonathan House's *When Titans Clashed* (1995) and the 2-volume set by John Erickson (1975 and 1983). One of the most useful sources on a wide range of subjects is Kozlov's superb encyclopedia (1985), which unfortunately has not yet been translated into English. A pair of wartime books on the Red Army in the Second World War have been republished, a British one by the Imperial War Museum/Battery Press and an American one on a limited scale by military historian John Sloan; both provide a wealth of information but some caution should be used in relying on the data, for it was often based on incomplete or inaccurate wartime intelligence sources. Special mention must also be made of a unique document entitled

Boevoy sostav sovetskoy armii, a comprehensive order of battle of the Red Army during the war, listing all major units on a month by month basis. This collection began publication in 1963 by the Military Archives of the Soviet General Staff and remained classified as secret until recently. In 1996 it was made available outside Russia by East View Publications in microfiche format.

There are also two major sources of contemporary information on the Soviet Army. German Army intelligence (*Fremde Heere Ost*) began collecting captured Soviet Army documents in early 1942 but the supply dried up in the autumn of that year as the Germans were forced on to the defensive. For this brief period there are a large number of German translations of Soviet documents, including TO&Es. These are available scattered about in the widely distributed US National Archives microfilm collection of captured German records, mainly in group T-78. The US Library of Congress also has a large collection of Soviet Army field manuals from the 1930s. Tactical doctrine, outside the scope of this handbook, is well represented, as are drill regulations (*Stoevoi ustov*), which are useful for defining lower level unit organization.

For additional sources on Soviet military history, there are two excellent bibliographic surveys by Michael Parrish (1981) and John and Ljubica Erickson (1996). An invaluable source for historians interested in the Red Army is the *Journal of Slavic Military Studies* (formerly *The Journal of Soviet Military Studies*) which contains many fine articles as well as important archival source material. For those readers familiar with Russian, *Voenno-istoricheskiy zhurnal* remains a vital source on Soviet military history.

Aganov, S.Kh. *Inzhenerye voyska sovetskoy armii 1918–1945* (The Engineer Forces of the Soviet Army 1918–1945), Moscow, Voenizdat, 1985

Ananev, I.M. *Tankovye armii v nastuplenii* (Tank Armies in the Offensive), Moscow, Voenizdat, 1988

Babich, Yu.P. and Bayer, A.G. *Razvitie vooruzheniya i organizatsiya sovetskikh voisk v gody VOV* (Development of Weapons and Organization of the Soviet Ground Forces in WW II), Moscow, Frunze Academy, 1990.

Barker, A.J. and Walter J. *Russian Infantry Weapons*, New York, Arco, 1971.

Batitskiy, P.F. *Voyska protivo-vozdushnoy oborony strany* (National Air Defence Forces), Moscow, Voenizdat, 1968

Beaumont, J. *Comrades in Arms: British Aid to Russia 1941–45*, London, Davies Poynter, 1980

Bellamy, C. *Red God of War: Soviet Artillery and Rocket Forces*, London, Brassey's, 1986.

Belov, A.I. *Voennye sviazisty v boyakh za rodinu* (Communications Troops in Combat for the Homeland), Moscow, Voenizdat, 1984

Bolotin, D.N. *Soviet Small Arms and Ammunition*, Hyvinkaa, Finland, Finnish Arms Museum Foundation, 1995.

British Army's 1940 *Russian Army Handbook*, London, Imperial War Museum/Nashville, Battery Press, 1997

Dunn, W.S. *Hitler's Nemesis: The Red Army 1930–45*, Westport, Connecticut, Praeger, 1994.

——. *The Soviet Economy and the Red Army 1930–1945*, Westport, Connecticut, Praeger, 1995

Finnish Army Intelligence Branch. *Tietoja N-L: N Armeijasta* (Information on the Soviet Army), Helsinki, Finnish Ministry of Defence, 22 June 1941

——. *Tietoja Puna-Armeijan Organisaation Kehityksestä vv. 1940–1942* (Information on the Evolution of Red Army Organization 1940–42), Helsinki, Finnish Ministry of Defence, 21 March 1942

Erickson, J. *The Road to Stalingrad*, London, Weidenfeld & Nicolson, 1975

——. *The Road to Berlin*, London, Weidenfeld & Nicolson, 1983

Erickson, J. and Erickson, L. *The Soviet Armed Forces 1918–1992: A Research Guide to Soviet Sources*, Westport, Greenwood, 1996

Glantz, D. *A History of Soviet Airborne Forces*, London, Frank Cass, 1994

Glantz, D. and House, J. *When Titans Clashed: How the Red Army Stopped Hitler*, Lawrence, Kansas, University of Kansas Press, 1995

Gogolev, L.D. *Avtomobili-soldaty: Ocherki ob istorii razvitiya i voennom primenenii avtomobili* (Soldier's Automobiles – Notes from the Developmental History and Combat Experiences of Automobiles), Moscow, Patriot, 1990.

Harrison, M. *Soviet Planning in Peace and War 1938–1945*, Cambridge, Cambridge University Press, 1985

——. *Accounting for War: Soviet production, employment, and the defence burden 1940–45*, Cambridge, Cambridge University Press, 1996

Kharitonov, O.V. *Soviet Military Uniform and Insignia 1918–1958*, St Petersburg, Alga Fund, 1993

Kozlov, M.M. *Velikaya otechestvennaya voyna 1941–1945*, Moscow, Sovetskaya Entsiklopediya, 1985

Krivosheyev, General Colonel G.F. *Soviet Casualties and Combat Losses in the Twentieth Century* (trans. of *Grif sekretnosti i snyat* –

With the Secret Stamp Removed), London, Greenhill, 1997

Krupchenko, I.Ye. *Sovetski tankovye voyska 1941–1945* (Soviet Tank Forces 1941–1945), Moscow, Voenizdat, 1973

Losik, O.A. *Stroitelstvo i boyevoye primenenie sovetskikh tankovikh voysk v gody VOV* (The Development and Combat Employment of the Soviet Tank Forces in the Years of the Great Patriotic War), Moscow, Voenizdat, 1979

Nedelin, Gen Col. *Nadichie I organizatsiya artillerii RGK pered nachalom i vo vremya otechesvennoi voyny* (Organization of the RGK artillery before and during WW II), Moscow, Frunze Academy, 1947, declassified

Parrish, Michael. *The USSR in World War II: An Annotated Bibliography of Books Published in the Soviet Union 1945–75*, New York, Garland, 1981

Peredelskiy, G.Ye. *Otechestvennaya artilleriya* (Our Homeland's Artillery), Moscow, Voenizdat, 1986

Prochorkov, I. and Trussov, V. 'Die Raketenartillerie im Großen Vaterländischen Kriege' in *Wehr-Wissenschaftliche Rundschau*, 1968, No. 9, pp519–35

Reznichenko, I.N. *Taktika v boyevykh primerakh: polk* (Tactics in Combat Examples: the Regiment), Moscow, Voenizdat, 1974

Rzhevskiy, O.A. *Kto byl kto v VOV 1941–1945* (Who Was Who in the Great Patriotic War 1941–45), Moscow, Respublika, 1995

Shalito, A. et al. *Red Army Uniforms of World War II*, London, Windrow & Greene, 1992

Sharp, Charles. C. *Soviet Order of Battle of World War II* (multiple volumes), West Chester, Ohio, George F. Nafziger, 1995–6

Somov, Z.A. *K 50-letniyu pobedy v VOV 1941–1945: staticheskiy sbornik* (Statistical Digest on the 50th Anniversary of the Great Patriotic War 1941–1945), Moscow, MSK-SNG, 1995

Soshnikov, A.Ya. (ed.) *Sovetskaya kavaleriya* (Soviet Cavalry), Moscow, Voenizdat, 1984

Tyushkevich, S.A. *The Soviet Armed Forces: A History of Their Organizational Development*, Moscow/Ottawa, Soviet Ministry of Defence/trans. by Secretary of State Department, Canada, 1978

US Army's Handbook on USSR Military Forces, Technical Manual 30–430 of November 1945, John Sloan, 1980

Yanchinskiy, A.N. *Boevoe ispolzovanie istrebitelno-protivotankovoy artillerii RVGK v VOV* (Combat use of the RVGK Anti-Tank Artillery, Moscow, Voroshilov Academy, 1951, declassified

Yefimev, A.V. et al. *Bronepoezda v VOV 1941–1945* (Armoured Trains in World War II 1941–45), Moscow, Transport, 1992

Zaloga, S.J. and Grandsen, J. *Soviet Tanks and Combat Vehicles of World War Two*, London, Arms & Armour Press, 1984

Zaloga, S.J. *The Red Army of the Great Patriotic War*, Men-at-Arms No. 216, London, Osprey, 1989

——. *Inside the Blue Berets: A Combat History of the Russian Airborne Forces 1930–1995*, Novato, California, Presidio, 1995

INDEX

Anti-tank weapons
    37mm ChK-M1 anti-tank gun 201
    45mm anti-tank gun 199, 201, 202
    57mm ZiS-2 anti-tank gun 199, 202
    100mm BS-3 anti-tank gun 201
    Anti-tank dogs 196
    Anti-tank gun technical characteristics 203
    Anti-tank rockets 197
    Lend-Lease anti-tank weapons 201
    Molotov cocktail 196, 204–5
    PTRD anti-tank rifle 196
    PTRS anti-tank rifle 196
    RPG-40 anti-tank grenade 196
Armoured and mechanized units
    Aerosan battalion 97, 167
    Armoured car brigade 65, 93, 97
    Assault gun regiment (1942) 92
    Assault gun regiment (Apr 1943) 93
    Flamethrower tank battalion 154
    Light tank brigade (Nov 39) 63
    Heavy tank brigade (Nov 39) 64
    Heavy tank brigade (1945) 92
    Mechanized brigade (Sep 1942) 85
    Mechanized brigade Feb/Sep 1943) 86
    Mechanized corps (1940) 65–9
    Mechanized corps (1942) 82–4
    Mechanized corps (authorized strength) 87
    Motorcycle battalion 97
    Motorcycle regiment (May 1942) 97
    Motorized division (1941) 67
    Separate tank battalion (1941) 90
    Separate tank regiment (1942) 91
    Tank army 90
    Tank brigade (Aug 1941) 71–5
    Tank brigade (Dec 1941) 75
    Tank brigade (Jul 1942) 78
    Tank brigade (Nov 1943) 81
    Tank corps (pre-war) 61–2

Tank corps (Mar 1942) 75–8
Tank corps (late 1942) 80
Tank corps (Jan 1945) 82
Tank corps (authorized strength) 84
Tank division (June 1941) 67
Tank division (July 1941) 71
Armoured cars
    BA-10 armoured car 167
    BA-20 armoured car 164
    BA-64 armoured car 173
Army organization
    Tank army 90
Artillery weapons
    25mm anti-aircraft gun 218–19
    37mm anti-aircraft gun 218, 220
    76mm anti-aircraft gun 218
    76mm regimental gun 203, 206
    76mm Model 03/30 divisional gun 207, 210
    76mm F-22 divisional gun 207, 210
    76mm F-22 USV divisional gun 208, 210
    76mm ZiS-3 divisional gun 208, 210
    85mm anti-aircraft gun 218, 220
    122mm M-30 howitzer 209
    122mm A-19 gun 211, 213
    152mm ML-20 gun/howitzer 211, 214
    152mm M-10 gun 212
    152mm Model 1910 howitzer 209, 211
    152mm D-1 howitzer 211, 213
    anti-aircraft gun technical characteristics 218
    artillery production 221
    artillery technical characteristics 210–11
    Lend-Lease anti-aircraft guns 221
    RVGK heavy artillery 211
Artillery units
    Anti-aircraft division (1942) 128
    Anti-aircraft division (1943) 128–30
    Anti-aircraft regiment (1941) 126-28
    Anti-aircraft regiment (1943) 129

Anti-aircraft battalion (1941) 126
Anti-tank brigade (1941) 119
Anti-tank regiment (1941–2) 119–21
Anti-tank regiment (1943) 125, 126
Anti-tank battalion (1942) 121
Artillery division (1942) 137
Breakthrough artillery division 138, 140
Corps artillery regiment 132
Divisional anti-tank battalion 31
Divisional artillery regiment 27
Guards mortar regiment 141
Guards mortar division 142
Heavy artillery regiment 136–7
Horse artillery battalion (pre-war) 104
Mortar brigade 130
Mortar regiment 131
Motorized artillery regiment (pre-war) 132
Separate mortar battalion 130
Tank destroyer artillery regiment (1942) 120
Assault guns
    Assault gun technical characteristics 186
    ISU-122 heavy assault gun 176–8, 186
    ISU-152 heavy assault gun 178, 186
    SU-76 light assault gun 173-4, 186
    SU-85 tank destroyer 178, 182, 186
    SU-100 tank destroyer 186
    SU-122 medium assault gun 171, 174, 186
    SU-152 heavy assault gun 171, 186
Battalion organization
    Anti-aircraft battalion (1941) 126
    Anti-tank battalion (1942) 121
    Aerosan battalion 97
    Chemical battalion 154
    Divisional anti-tank battalion 31
    Flamethrower battalion 154
    Flamethrower tank battalion 154
    Horse artillery battalion (pre-war) 104
    Machine gun artillery battalion 56
    Motorcycle battalion 97
    Motorized rifle battalion (Nov 1943) 82
    Separate tank battalion (1941) 90
    Separate mortar battalion 130
    Ski battalion 50–3
    Special purpose motorized battalion 98–9
Brigade organization
    Airborne brigade (1941-2) 143, 145–8
    Airborne brigade (1943) 150–1
    Anti-tank brigade (1941) 119
    Armoured car brigade 65, 93, 97
    Light tank brigade (Nov 39) 63
    Heavy tank brigade (Nov 39) 64
    Heavy tank brigade (1945) 92
    Mechanized brigade (Sep 1942) 85

    Mechanized brigade Feb/Sep 1943) 86
    Motor rifle brigade (Apr 42) 76
    Mortar brigade 130
    Rifle brigade 34–5
    Rifle brigade (Oct 1941) 36–8
    Rifle brigade (Apr 1942) 38–40
    Rifle brigade (Jul 1942) 41–2
    Tank brigade (Aug 1941) 71-5
    Tank brigade (Dec 1941) 75
    Tank brigade (Jul 1942) 78
    Tank brigade (Nov 1943) 81
Cavalry units
    Cavalry corps (Jan 1942) 112
    Cavalry corps (Jun 1942) 113
    Cavalry division (pre-war) 101
    Cavalry division (1939) 106
    Cavalry division (1941) 107–8
    Cavalry division (1943) 115
    Cavalry regiment (pre-war) 104
    Cavalry regiment (Jul 1941) 107
    Cavalry regiment (Jan 1942) 111
    Cavalry regiment (Feb 1943) 114
    Light cavalry division (1941) 109–11
    Mountain cavalry division (1941) 107
Chemical Units
    Flamethrower battalion 154
Flamethrower tank battalion 154
Corps organization
    Airborne corps 149
    Cavalry corps (Jan 1942) 112
    Cavalry corps (Jun 1942) 113
    Mechanized corps (1940) 65–9
    Mechanized corps (1942) 82–4
    Mechanized corps (authorized strength) 87
    Tank corps (pre-war) 61–2
    Tank corps (Mar 1942) 75–8
    Tank corps (late 1942) 80
    Tank corps (Jan 1945) 82
    Tank corps (authorized strength) 84
Divisional organization
    Anti-aircraft division (1942) 128
    Anti-aircraft division (1943) 129
    Artillery division (1942) 137
    Breakthrough artillery division 138, 140
    Cavalry division (pre-war) 101
    Cavalry division (1939) 106
    Cavalry division (1941) 107–8
    Cavalry division (1943) 115
    Guards mortar division 142
    Light cavalry division (1941) 109–11
    Motorized division (1941) 67
    Mountain cavalry division (1941) 107
    Mountain infantry division 42–8

Rifle division (1939) 1–3
Rifle division (Apr 1941) 6–11
Rifle division (Jul 1941) 11–14
Rifle division (Dec 1941) 15–19
Rifle division (Mar 1942) 19–22
Rifle division (Jul 1942) 20, 22–4
Rifle division (Dec 1942) 24–8
Rifle division (Dec 1944) 34
Rifle division (emergency TO&E) 32
Rifle division evolution 35
Tank division (June 1941) 67
Tank division (July 1941) 71
Finnish War 1939–40 5
Fortified regions 53–9
Infantry units
    Airborne brigade (1941–2) 143, 145–8
    Airborne brigade (1943) 150–1
    Airborne corps 149
    Fortified regions 53–9
    Infantry regiment (reduced) 28
    Machine gun artillery battalion 56
    Motorized infantry regiment (Apr 41) 68
    Motorized rifle battalion (Nov 1943) 82
    Motor rifle brigade (Apr 42) 76
    Mountain infantry division 42–8
    Mountain infantry regiment 45
    Rifle brigade 34–5
    Rifle brigade (Oct 1941) 36–8
    Rifle brigade (Apr 1942) 38–40
    Rifle brigade (Jul 1942) 41–2
    Rifle division (1939) 1–3
    Rifle division (Apr 1941) 6–11
    Rifle division (Jul 1941) 11–14
    Rifle division (Dec 1941) 15–19
    Rifle division (Mar 1942) 19–22
    Rifle division (Jul 1942) 20, 22–4
    Rifle division (Dec 1942) 24–8
    Rifle division (Dec 1944) 34
    Rifle division (emergency TO&E) 32
    Rifle division evolution 35
    Ski battalion 50–3
    Special purpose motorized battalion 98–9
Katyusha (see rocket artillery)
Machine guns
    DP machine gun 193
    DShK machine gun 193
    DT machine gun 193
    Maxim machine gun 193
Mortars
    50mm mortar 198
    82mm mortar 198
    107mm mortar 198
    120mm mortar 198

Pistols
    Nagant Model 1895 189
    Tokarev automatic 189
Polish campaign 1939 62
Regimental organization
    Anti-aircraft regiment (1941) 126
    Anti-aircraft regiment (1943) 129
    Anti-tank regiment (1941-2) 119–21
    Anti-tank regiment (1943) 125
    Assault gun regiment (1942) 92
    Assault gun regiment (Apr 1943) 93
    Cavalry regiment (pre-war) 104
    Cavalry regiment (Jul 1941) 107
    Cavalry regiment (Jan 1942) 111
    Cavalry regiment (Feb 1943) 114
    Corps artillery regiment 132
    Divisional artillery regiment 27
    Guards mortar regiment 141
    Heavy artillery regiment 136–7
    Infantry regiment (reduced) 28
    Mechanized regiment (cav)(pre-war) 104
    Mortar regiment 131
    Motorcycle regiment (May 1942) 97
    Motorized infantry regiment (Apr 41) 68
    Motorized artillery regiment (pre-war) 132
    Mountain infantry regiment 45
    Separate tank regiment (1942) 91
    Tank destroyer artillery regiment (1942) 120
Rifles
    Moisin Nagant rifle 191
    Moisin Nagant carbine 191
    Tokarev SVT 192
    Tokarev AVT 192
Rocket artillery
    BM-8 214-15
    BM-13 215-17
    BM-31 215
    rocket artillery technical data 215
Self-propelled artillery see assault guns
Spanish Civil War 162
Sub-machine guns
    PPD 189
    PPS 190
    PPSh 190
Tanks
    BT fast tank 157–8, 160
    IS (Stalin) heavy tank 175, 182–3
    KV heavy tank 162–6, 169–70, 182–3
    Lend Lease tanks 172, 174
    T-20 Komsomoleyts artillery tractor 161
    T-26 light tank 157–8, 161
    T-28 medium tank 158, 160
    T-34 medium tank 162–3, 165, 168–70, 182–3

T-34-85 medium tank 178–9, 182–3
T-35 heavy tank 128
T-37 scout tank 158–9
T-38 scout tank 158
T-40 amphibious tank 162
T-50 infantry tank 162, 167
T-60 light tank 162, 167, 182–3
T-70 light tank 182–3

Tank production 180–1
Tank strength 69, 181
Tank technical characteristics 182–3
Trucks
  GAZ-AA, GAZ-AAA 1 ton truck 186
  Lend-Lease trucks 184–5, 187
  ZiS-5/ZiS-6 2-ton truck 183
  Truck production 187